America and Enlightenment
Constitutionalism

STUDIES OF THE AMERICAS

Edited by James Dunkerley
Institute for the Study of the Americas
University of London
School of Advanced Study

Titles in this series are multidisciplinary studies of aspects of the societies of the hemisphere, particularly in the areas of politics, economics, history, anthropology, sociology and the environment. The series covers a comparative perspective across the Americas, including Canada and the Caribbean as well as the USA and Latin America.

Titles in this series published by Palgrave Macmillan:

Cuba's Military 1990–2005: Revolutionary Soldiers
during Counter-Revolutionary Times
By Hal Klepak

The Judicialization of Politics in Latin America
Edited by Rachel Sieder, Line Schjolden, and Alan Angell

Latin America: A New Interpretation
By Laurence Whitehead

Appropriation as Practice: Art and Identity in Argentina
By Arnd Schneider

America and Enlightenment Constitutionalism
Edited by Gary L. McDowell and Johnathan O'Neill

Vargas and Brazil: New Perspectives
Edited by Jens R. Hentschke

Caribbean Land and Development Revisited
Edited by Jean Besson and Janet Momsen

America and Enlightenment Constitutionalism

Edited by
Gary L. McDowell
and
Johnathan O'Neill

Charles County Public Library
www.ccplonline.org

AMERICA AND ENLIGHTENMENT CONSTITUTIONALISM

First published in 2006 by
PALGRAVE MACMILLAN™
175 Fifth Avenue, New York, N.Y. 10010 and
Houndmills, Basingstoke, Hampshire, England RG21 6XS
Companies and representatives throughout the world.

PALGRAVE MACMILLAN is the global academic imprint of the Palgrave Macmillan division of St. Martin's Press, LLC and of Palgrave Macmillan Ltd. Macmillan® is a registered trademark in the United States, United Kingdom and other countries. Palgrave is a registered trademark in the European Union and other countries.

ISBN-13: 978–1–4039–7236–1

Library of Congress Cataloging-in-Publication Data

America and Enlightenment constitutionalism / edited by Gary L. McDowell and Johnathan O'Neill.
    p.cm.
Includes bibliographical references and index.
ISBN 1–4039–7236–2 (alk. paper)
    1. Constitutional history—United States. 2. United States—Politics and government—1775–1783. 3. Constitutional law—United States—European influences. 4. Enlightenment. I. McDowell, Gary L., 1949– II. O'Neill, Johnathan G. (Johnathan George)

KF4520.A76 2006
342.7302′9—dc22   2006044757

A catalogue record for this book is available from the British Library.

Design by Newgen Imaging Systems (P) Ltd., Chennai, India.

First edition: September 2006

10 9 8 7 6 5 4 3 2 1

Printed in the United States of America.
Transferred to Digital Printing in 2011

But why is the experiment of an extended republic to be rejected merely because it may comprise what is new? Is it not the glory of the people of America, that whilst they have paid a decent regard to the opinions of former times and other nations, they have not suffered a blind veneration for antiquity, for custom, or for names, to overrule the suggestions of their own good sense, the knowledge of their own situation, and the lessons of their own experience? To this manly spirit, posterity will be indebted for the possession, and the world for the example of the numerous innovations displayed on the American theatre, in favor of private rights and public happiness.

—James Madison, *The Federalist*, No. 14

Contents

Introduction

Gary L. McDowell and *Johnathan O'Neill*

By some estimates the Enlightenment began in 1687 with the publication of Isaac Newton's *Mathematical Principles of Natural Philosophy.* Others would place the start earlier, perhaps in 1642 with the publication of Thomas Hobbes's *De Cive,* in many ways the precursor of his more famous work, *Leviathan,* which appeared in 1651. Still others would push the origins back to Descartes's publication of the *Discourse on Method* in 1637, or even further to Francis Bacon's *Advancement of Learning* of 1605. All these thinkers and those who followed in their paths undertook to open to the scrutiny of human reason the mysteries of the universe and of man's place in it. Through science, they believed, the gloom of superstition and the dim lights of dogma would be replaced; their goal was, in the strictest sense, enlightenment.[1]

Whatever date one might choose to mark the beginning of the Enlightenment, the fact is it stretched far into the future, dominating the intellectual life of the eighteenth century and influencing most of the nineteenth and twentieth centuries. That "remarkable efflorescence" of human thought has never been without its defenders and advocates. To them, the very foundation of Western modernity is the result of all that is good in the thought of those seemingly disparate thinkers who emerged from the medieval shadows and sought to train the light of human reason on the world. Thus it is to that tradition—to the likes of Bacon, Descartes, Hobbes, and Newton along with John Locke and Adam Smith, among many others—that thanks are owed for everything from constitutionalism and the rule of law to advances in the natural sciences to liberal capitalism. Never, say the friends of the Enlightenment, has a body of thought done more to ameliorate the pain, insecurity, inconvenience, and suffering of so many at every level of society over such a long period of time.

Yet neither has the Enlightenment been without its critics. To many, the essence of the Enlightenment project was an effort to supplant faith with reason; inevitably, these critics insist, mankind was left stranded in an amoral netherworld where all too often the results have been predictably disastrous. From the terror that came in the wake of the French Revolution to the purges in the aftermath of the Russian Revolution to the startling atrocities of Hitler, all were the result of the errors of Enlightenment thought being drawn out to their logical and sad conclusions. As the twentieth century drew to a close, the Enlightenment and its legacy were beset by a host of critics offering alternatives, from postmodernists broadly considered to communitarians who had grown weary of the moral hollowness of individual rights that were bereft of any sense of public responsibility.[2]

When it comes to thinking about the Enlightenment and its place in human history, there seems to be no middle ground between its friends and its foes.[3] A few years ago *The Economist* observed this striking dichotomy once it had again become fashionable to argue that the Enlightenment had been "a catastrophic error."[4] The world seems divided between those who "regard western modernity as a marvel (despite its failings)" and others who see the Enlightenment tradition as nothing less than "a disaster (despite its superficial attractions)."[5] All is black or white with no muted shades of grey to be found. And, given the stark opposition, it is a debate that promises to continue indefinitely.

Whether one loves or hates the Enlightenment and all it has engendered in the past several hundred years, there is one unmistakable fact about it. There is no nation more closely associated with its most basic premises than the United States, both in its very creation and in its role of perpetuating those premises as the essence of the principles of ordered liberty and republican justice. After all, the United States was the first nation that could boast, as Alexander Hamilton would put it, of having been created from "reflection and choice" and was not merely the result of "accident and force" as were all the other nations of the world.[6] America was not just created, but was created in light of truths deemed to be universal.

In understanding the relationship of the United States to the Enlightenment, it is necessary to look both backward and forward. On the one hand, America was built upon a foundation that was, if not exclusively at least primarily, the result of well-established Enlightenment principles.[7] On the other hand, the Americans' European inheritance encouraged them to make their own original contributions to the Enlightenment.[8] Especially when it came to politics, Americans such as Benjamin Franklin, John Adams, James Madison, and Thomas Jefferson were innovators in, and contributors to, the assimilation of Enlightenment thinking as part of modern Western values. Their great political accomplishment in creating the American republic—from the Declaration of Independence to the U.S. Constitution—was in many ways a monument to that peculiarly modern frame of mind.

Near the end of his life, Thomas Jefferson could look back on the moment of national creation and suggest that it would be remembered as "the signal of arousing men to burst the chains under which monkish ignorance and superstition had persuaded them to bind themselves, and to assume the blessings and security of self-government" in a political order characterized by "the free right to the unbounded exercise of reason and freedom of opinion." To ages yet unborn, America's lesson would be unmistakable:

> All eyes are opened, or opening, to the rights of man. The general spread of the light of science has already laid open to every view the palpable truth, that the mass of mankind has not been born with saddles on their backs, nor a favored few booted and spurred, ready to ride them legitimately, by the grace of God.[9]

Jefferson's enthusiasm was that of an unapologetic student of the Enlightenment.

To assess the state of Enlightenment thinking the School of Advanced Study in the University of London hosted a conference on the subject of "America and the Enlightenment: Constitutionalism in the 21st Century." The conference drew together some of the most distinguished thinkers in a variety of disciplines to consider the topic, and the following collection consists primarily of the papers presented at that conference, plus essays by Gordon S. Wood and C. Bradley Thompson.

The first two chapters in part 1, "Enlightenment Philosophy and Constitutionalism," relate major features of the Enlightenment to pressing contemporary debates in political and legal theory. Steven D. Smith first orients the volume with a survey of the Enlightenment, arguing that the American founding built on it by premising a providential and normative cosmic order in which reason discerned at least some moral and political truth. However, today most liberal political and constitutional theorists who claim to be heirs of the Enlightenment actually invert its basic principles. Above all, they attempt to eviscerate its claim about the truth that reason can find. And, frequently with the aid of the U.S. Supreme Court's First Amendment jurisprudence, these theorists seek to subject all political discourse to their own standards, which are secular, perspectival, instrumental, and conventional. The result, writes Smith, is the impoverished legal-political discourse of "public reason." It is increasingly incapable of addressing citizens' deepest concerns with anything more than suspicion, avoidance, manipulation, and sometimes censorship. This situation has upended the Enlightenment and endangered its achievements.

Martin Loughlin advances this general analysis by focusing on the displacement of the Enlightenment understanding of natural rights by the superficially legal but deeply politicized discourse of "human rights." He then considers how this shift has affected the relationship between law and politics. In the post–World War II era this shift proceeded on the American model of judicial review, which was originally intended to protect rights previously announced in a textual fundamental law. Loughlin notes, however, that the new discourse of human rights lacks just what had constrained American courts before the post–World War II "rights revolution"—a theory of human nature and limited government rooted in the Enlightenment. The new notion of human rights has worked a radical alteration in not only the understanding of the character of law itself but also the relationship between law and politics. Now rights rather than rules established by legislation are the architectonic principles of the legal order. Rights often command, direct, and trump legislation. But with the severing of any connection to nature as a limit, any political claim can be and is articulated in the language of rights. This in turn has yielded an ingeniously creative but fundamentally political jurisprudence where courts define the sphere of individual liberty instead of ensuring that it exists in a realm beyond legal regulation. Loughlin urges recognition of the political character of rights discourse so that the political judgments involved in its elaboration or limitation can be more squarely met.

From these examinations of the contemporary transformation or abandonment of Enlightenment philosophy, the next three chapters return to that philosophy as originally presented my some of its most notable advocates. Frederick Rosen argues that the rediscovery of ancient Epicureanism was a major reason that the Enlightenment undermined the corporatist and religious conceptions of nature and morality inherited from medieval scholasticism. Epicurean materialism, sensationalism, atomism, and emphasis on security and comfortable self-preservation influenced thinkers from the early Renaissance through Hobbes, Locke, and John Stuart Mill. Further, in welcoming the aspiration for happiness and security among the many and not just the few, modern Epicureanism helped define the conception of legitimate political authority underlying modern constitutionalism. No longer would political authority be based on natural or divine higher law, but instead it would be based on the common agreement of individuals as to the best means of preserving the life, liberty, and property indispensable to their security and happiness. Yet, Rosen concludes, inquiry into what kind of government institutions might achieve these goals was not pursued because the Epicurean tradition was disinclined to rationalist systematizing.

The remaining thinkers treated in part 1 offered more definite prescriptions for government institutions and more systematic arguments for their underlying political authority. Yet, like modern Epicureanism, they measured legitimacy by the standards of individual rights and consent, rather than by custom, virtue, or religion. While Hobbes famously advanced the focus on rights and consent by overtly demoting religion, Robert Faulkner argues that the "political-theological problem" was similarly but more surreptitiously handled in Locke's too often neglected *First Treatise*. Clearing the ground for the regime of equality, rights, and social contract in the *Second Treatise* required that the *First Treatise* refute Robert Filmer's justification of divine right monarchy. In doing so, claims Faulkner, Locke also sought to displace biblical authority in favor of a philosophic and rational individualism reminiscent of Hobbes. Although Locke easily refuted Filmer, Faulkner concludes that in holding the Bible to his own standards rather than grappling with those it announces—by offering an epistemology to explain away the possibility of revelation—Locke's new basis for politics rested more on determined insistence than rational refutation.

Not long after Hobbes and Locke called upon the English experience to lay the philosophical foundations of modern constitutionalism, Montesquieu also looked hopefully to England. Paul A. Rahe shows that after the English victory at Blenheim (1704) ended France's continental ambitions, the French, Montesquieu among them, found England to be a topic worthy of study. Rahe argues that upon considering the political future of Europe, Montesquieu, in the *Persian Letters*, regarded the ancien régime as doomed. Further, in *Considerations* and *Reflections* Montesquieu held that nothing like a pan-European empire was possible or desirable any longer. This left England, that republic concealed under the form of a monarchy, which *The Spirit of the Laws* praised as the modern government whose direct object was political liberty. In *The Spirit of the Laws*, Rahe holds, Montesquieu showed how passionate vigilance in defense of liberty, or inquietude, set the English polity in motion. Modern republics like England were activated more by this fear of losing their liberty than by the older conception of republican virtue. As a result, the various components of the polity restlessly guarded one another. This yielded a counter-balancing of forces institutionalized in the separation of powers, which ensured the checking partisanship and moderation necessary for the preservation of liberty.

Americans inherited such fundamental political lessons of the European Enlightenment and founded their own constitutional republic. The first three chapters in part 2, "The Enlightenment and the Constitution in America," consider how the political culture of the American founding regarded itself as Enlightened; how the Enlightenment shaped the Virginia Constitution of 1776; and how the federal Constitution of 1787 helped unite the nation by extending Enlightenment political principles. Gordon S. Wood's chapter argues that the deep desire to be a coherent nation drove Americans' impassioned insistence that they were especially Enlightened. In the founding period it seemed that building a new nation and loyalty to Enlightenment ideas were one and the same, as when the egalitarian tendency of modern republicanism pushed in the same direction as the Lockean argument for the accessibility to all of sense perception and reason. Wood shows that however much we can doubt the Americans' claim to have been the most Enlightened people on earth, the founding period did contain notable increases in several indicia of the Enlightenment: economic prosperity; education, publishing, and reading; humanitarian social reform; and universalist and cosmopolitan sensibilities. Indeed, Wood concludes, it was only the realization of the Enlightenment in America, albeit limited, that provided the incentive and moral capacity for condemnation of the brutal treatment that Africans and Indians received at the hands of whites.

Colin Bonwick uses Virginia as a case study to argue that the Enlightenment remains helpful for understanding the constitution-making of the founding period. While fair-mindedly accounting for the admixture of other influences and for inevitable limitations, Bonwick claims that distinctly Enlightenment concerns with nature, reason, and progress were central factors in Virginia. Moreover, they have for too long been subordinated to the liberalism versus republicanism debate. Virginia shows that the Enlightenment created a spirit of free enquiry and willingness to innovate that was manifested in the concrete political doctrines derived from the philosophers considered in part 1: natural equality and natural rights; popular sovereignty; the separation of powers; and the duty of government to promote public safety and happiness.

J. R. Pole argues that the founding did not complete the task of nation-making. In fact it was a historical process, with interpretation of the Constitution itself being the site for this ongoing development. America was wedded to the Enlightenment proposition that a true political community was a "community of principle," and constitutional interpretation, especially of the Fourteenth Amendment, gradually helped create a polity where consent was more fully represented and equal rights more fully respected. This process was not uniform, predetermined, or without instances of regression. However, Pole argues that as a result of this process the Supreme Court has assumed a legislative power inconsistent with its role in the original constitutional design, and he concludes with some suggestions about how Congress might reassert its own power in response to the Court's overstepping.

The next two chapters in part 2 focus on James Madison, especially on his understanding of the relation between constitutionalism and the modern Enlightenment doctrine that public opinion or consent is the basis of legitimate political authority. Jack N. Rakove approaches the issue by first considering the tension between Madison's confident openness to constitutional innovation as compared to his wary insistence on the need for constitutional stability. The key to understanding this issue, writes Rakove, was Madison's belief that it was quite rare to have had inevitably untutored public opinion on the side of the enlightened political wisdom and delicate compromise contained in the Constitution. Too frequently involving the public directly in constitutional disputes would be a "ticklish" experiment because, although public opinion was the strongest component of the polity, it was by no means the most reasonable. Madison aimed to prevent the unsteady impulses of public opinion from imperiling the hard-won constitutional arrangements that were so carefully designed to encourage a politics of reason and moderation.

Pursuing a related inquiry, C. Bradley Thompson argues that Madison saw the goal of constitution-making as reconciling the modern Enlightenment doctrine of consent with the ancient idea that political wisdom was the preserve of a few, and perhaps even a single founder. America had achieved such a reconciliation when the Constitution written at Philadelphia won the consent of the people and was ratified. Thompson emphasizes that Madison's profound understanding of political prudence led him to argue, especially in *The Federalist* no. 37, that a perfect reconciliation, and indeed a perfect constitution, was impossible. The inevitable limitations imposed by circumstance, prejudice, fallible reason—and politics itself—counseled moderation of expectations and prudent acceptance of this Constitution as the best that could be achieved. Madison, Thompson concludes, realized that preservation of the Constitution's reconciliation between wisdom and consent required that it be treated as fundamental law. This in turn required that the prejudices and even the reverence of the people be on the side of the Constitution, whose wisdom was to garner political stability by moderating and enlightening the passions and interests of the very people who had consented to it.

The unifying theme of these chapters is the importance of various aspects of the Enlightenment not only for understanding America as it was, but as it is, and as it likely will continue to be. Whatever criticism one may level at the ways the American republic has developed, whatever alternatives might be put forward to challenge the most fundamental premises of the constitutional order, the fact is that American greatness—indeed, its exceptionalism—among the nations of the world from the time of the founding to our own day stems from, and is guided by, those principles that shine still from the dawn of modernity. Such is the power of those ideas that we think of simply as "the Enlightenment."

* * *

Permission to use the following previously published material in this volume is gratefully acknowledged: Steven D. Smith, "Recovering (From) Enlightenment?" *San Diego Law Review* 41 (2004): 1263–1210, copyright 2004 *San Diego Law Review* is reprinted in a slightly shorter version with the permission of the San Diego Law Review; Martin Loughlin's chapter appeared as "Rights," and is reprinted from *The Idea of Public Law* (2003), 114–130, by permission of Oxford University Press; Robert Faulkner's "Preface to Liberalism: Locke's First Treatise and the Bible" appeared in the *Review of Politics* 67 (2005): 451–472 and is reprinted with permission. Additionally, we thank Rebecca O'Neill for her diligent help in the preparation of the manuscript.

Notes

1. "There . . . was only one Enlightenment," Peter Gay once noted: "A loose, informal, wholly unorganized coalition of cultural critics, religious skeptics, and political reformers from Edinburgh to Naples, Paris to Berlin, Boston to Philadelphia . . . [which] made up a clamorous chorus . . . The men of the Enlightenment united on a vastly ambitious program, a program of secularism, humanity, cosmopolitanism, and freedom, above all, freedom in its many forms—freedom from arbitrary

power, freedom of speech, freedom of trade, freedom to realize one's talents, freedom of aesthetic response, freedom, in a word, of moral man to make his own way in the world." Peter Gay, *The Rise of Modern Paganism*, vol. 1, *The Enlightenment: An Interpretation* (New York: Alfred A. Knopf, 1967), 3.

2. See, e.g., Karlis Racevskis, *Postmodernism and the Search for Enlightenment* (Charlottesville: University Press of Virginia, 1993); Max Horkheimer and Theodor W. Adorno, *Dialectic of Enlightenment* (New York: Herder and Herder, 1972); and Michael J. Sandel, *Democracy's Discontent: America in Search of a Public Philosophy* (Cambridge, MA: Harvard University Press, 1996).

3. For an effort to assess the Enlightenment, especially the British Enlightenment, in an evenhanded way, see Roy Porter, *The Creation of the Modern World: The Untold Story of the British Enlightenment* (New York: W. W. Norton, 2000).

4. "Crimes of Reason," *The Economist*, March 16, 1996, 113.

5. Ibid., 115.

6. Jacob Cooke, ed., *The Federalist* (Middletown, CT: Wesleyan University Press, 1961), 3.

7. See, e.g., Bernard Bailyn, *The Ideological Origins of the American Revolution* (Cambridge, MA: Harvard University Press, 1967); Gordon S. Wood, *The Creation of the American Republic, 1776–1787* (Chapel Hill: University of North Carolina Press, 1969); Michael Zuckert, *Natural Rights and the New Republicanism* (Princeton: Princeton University Press, 1994); and Joyce Appleby, *Liberalism and Republicanism in the Historical Imagination* (Cambridge, MA: Harvard University Press, 1992).

8. See, e.g., Adrienne Koch, ed., *The American Enlightenment: The Shaping of the American Experiment and a Free Society* (New York: George Braziller, 1965); Henry F. May, *The Enlightenment in America* (New York: Oxford University Press, 1976); Morton White, *The Philosophy of the American Revolution* (New York: Oxford University Press, 1978); and Bernard Bailyn, *To Begin the World Anew: The Genius and Ambiguities of the American Founders* (New York: Alfred A. Knopf, 2003).

9. Merrill Peterson, ed., *Jefferson: Writings* (New York: Library of America, 1984), 1517.

Part I

Enlightenment Philosophy and Constitutionalism

Chapter 1

Recovering (From) Enlightenment?

Steven D. Smith

When we speak of the "Enlightenment," those of us who are not Buddhists commonly refer to a complex movement of thought, culture, temperament, and politics represented in its early phases by thinkers like Descartes and Locke and in its later phases by figures like Kant or, in America, Jefferson and Paine. This self-styled "Age of Reason," or what we might call the "historical" or "classical" Enlightenment, is often said to have succumbed in the nineteenth century to the forces of reaction and romanticism. But "the Enlightenment" is also invoked, most often by or on behalf of modern liberal political and constitutional theorists, to designate a sort of political-moral ideal that ostensibly has guided and continues to guide American constitutionalism. This more modern iteration is supposed to be connected to the historical Enlightenment, it seems, mainly on the basis of a professed allegiance to governance by "reason."

An invitation to discuss "alternatives to Enlightenment constitutionalism" in the twenty-first century might be taken as accepting this claimed connection and then soliciting proposals for a constitutionalism that would depart from the Enlightenment ideal. Understood in this way, though, the invitation is fraught with risks. "Reason" and the Enlightenment are typically associated, after all, with political commitments—to liberty, equality, freedom of conscience, freedom of speech—that are widely cherished and that few of us would wish to oppose.

So in this chapter I want to take a different tack. More specifically, I will argue that although there are indeed continuities between the classical Enlightenment and "the spirit of the Enlightenment" that animates contemporary thinkers, these continuities are partly cosmetic and in any case are overwhelmed by the discrepancies.[1] The modern "Enlightenment" orientation reflected in liberal political and constitutional theorizing is more accurately understood as an inversion than an extension of the most essential historic commitments of the Enlightenment. So if there is an attractive alternative to Enlightenment constitutionalism as currently understood, it likely lies in a recovery of the commitments of the classical Enlightenment. And the formidable (and for the moment, I fear, insuperable) obstacle to any such recovery is the modern Enlightenment.

The Classical Enlightenment

The historical Enlightenment was, as Roy Porter notes, "necessarily rather amorphous and diverse,"[2] and any description of it will reflect a selective interpretation. With that caveat, I suggest that for present purposes the classical Enlightenment can be understood in terms of several components that seemed, in the seventeenth and eighteenth centuries, nicely harmonious.

The Commitment to Truth

In his *Discourse on Method*, Descartes reports that he had "always had an especially great desire to distinguish the true from the false." And he immediately explains the practical thrust of this desire: he wanted truth, he says, "in order to see my way clearly in my actions, and to go forward with confidence in this life."[3] Descartes's report captures an essential impulse that drove the Enlightenment: a compulsion both to *know* truth and to *live by* it. Vocabulary varied, to be sure. Terms like "reason" and the "life of reason" incorporated this imperative. And instead of the diction of living according to "truth," the classical Enlightenment often favored the vocabulary of living in accordance with "nature"—as in the Declaration of Independence's invocation of "nature and nature's God." The idea was not novel, of course— "You shall know the truth, and the truth shall make you free" had been said before—but it was nonetheless fundamental to the project of the classical Enlightenment.

Reason, nature, and truth were guiding precepts for the framers of the American Constitution, or so they declared; their intention was to build a new constitutional order on the basis of the truths of human nature and the best political science, which they saw as revealing truths about government that had previously been obscure.[4] Tocqueville noticed this aspect of the founding: in an encomium to the framers of the Constitution he emphasized that "[t]hey had the courage to say what they believed to be true."[5] Moreover, in this respect, the framers were following the example of the signatories of the Declaration of Independence, who in declaring their intention to engage in a bloody conflict to break political bonds established over centuries had insisted that they were acting not merely from self-interest, but rather on the basis of fundamental and self-evident "truths." In what was more than a dramatic gesture[6] they had staked their "lives," "fortunes," and "sacred honor" on those truths.

Almost a century later, John Courtney Murray eloquently made the point. What Murray called the "American Proposition"

> rests on the . . . conviction that there are truths; that they can be known; that they must be held; for, if they are not held, assented to, consented to, worked into the texture of institutions, there can be no hope of founding a true City, in which men may dwell in dignity, peace, unity, justice, well-being, freedom.[7]

A commitment to living in accordance with truth presupposes, of course, that there is in fact a truth of the sort that prescribes *how to live*, and how to live *together*—hence, a *moral* and *political* truth. Modern thinkers occasionally distinguish this sort of overarching truth from the mundane facts or merely pragmatic propositions that pervade everyday life by capitalizing the word (often with a derisive tone).[8] So we could say that at the heart of the classical Enlightenment was a belief in, and a resolve to live by, the Truth.

Reason Versus Culture

The commitment to living by the Truth entailed, for the Enlightenment, the exercise of "reason"; and "reason" in turn implied an effort to break free of the impediments and errors of culture and tradition.[9] Indeed, reliance on received opinions embodied in culture was taken to be the opposite of "reason"; the whole point of "reason" was to free us from the moral and epistemic corruption that pervades culture and received tradition. Thus, Kant famously answered the question "What is enlightenment?" by explaining that it means thinking for oneself, and that an "inability to make use of one's own understanding without the guidance of another" is a form of "immaturity" reflective of "[l]aziness and cowardice."[10] The modern rationalist stance, Ernest Gellner explains, is "a programme for man's liberation from culture."[11]

The seminal example, once again, was set by Descartes, for whom reasoning entailed a resolution to "get rid of [all received judgments and opinions] once and for all" in order to start from scratch in developing reliable knowledge. "[I]n truly rationalist spirit," Gellner observes, Descartes "decided to declare independence of the accidental assemblage of beliefs, of all cultural accretion, and to set out independently on a re-exploration of the world." Later Enlightenment thinkers drastically revised the details of the Cartesian program, but "the spirit of the inquiry and its implicit terms of reference remained much as Descartes had formulated them." Thus, modern Enlightenment reason amounts to a "culture-defying individualism, a Robinson Crusoe posture."[12]

From our perspective, to be sure, this setting of reason in opposition to culture might seem misguided. A theme running through twentieth-century philosophy and associated with diverse thinkers such as Wittgenstein, Gadamer, MacIntyre, and Rorty holds that reason is inevitably embedded in culture, or tradition, or "forms of life." We always and necessarily think and talk from *within* a language, a "paradigm," an intellectual tradition. So the effort to detach reason from culture may seem akin to an attempt to separate speech from language or music from sound.[13] Though a strong proponent of Enlightenment reason, Gellner admits as much: it was never possible, he says, to detach reason from culture, as Descartes and his successors aspired to do. So what actually resulted was simply *a different kind of culture*—a rationalist culture.[14]

The Enlightenment's apparent naivete on this point is accentuated, it may seem, by the embarrassing fact that Enlightenment thinkers came nowhere near agreement about exactly what "reason" is, or how it works. Empirically minded thinkers such as Locke criticized the epistemology of rationalists such as Descartes and were in turn criticized by more skeptical thinkers such as Hume. Gellner's study acknowledges the large differences in what modern thinkers have taken "reason" to be. Given this diversity, a cynic might be excused for concluding that the Enlightenment is defined by an exuberant common commitment to a *word*, nothing more.

So, was the Enlightenment the illegitimate offspring of a rash misconception? Perhaps. There is no use denying that the luminaries of the Age of Reason were, as James Whitman observes, "fallible, and often comically fallible, human beings."[15] They may have been guilty of massive self-deception, as Carl Becker's classic study wittily argued.[16] Still, I think that there is a more charitable interpretation that would depict the Enlightenment conception of reason in a more sympathetic way. We might understand the Cartesian distinction between reason and culture, that is, in less overtly philosophical and also less absolute terms. The determination to liberate reason from culture might be seen not as a misguided attempt to leave culture behind altogether, like a spaceship leaving the planet for the outer reaches of the cosmos, but rather as an effort to get beyond or behind *particular aspects of a particular culture* that are seen to be decadent, exhausted, or inauthentic.

Even this more modest sort of effort may still be misguided or unduly optimistic, of course, but it is one that we can surely sympathize with, at least in the abstract. The phenomenon appears repeatedly throughout history. A culture or tradition or body of conventions comes to seem (to a few, perhaps not to most participants) empty, pointless, dead—little more than a burly corpse made up of inherited behaviors and rote questions and responses that can no longer elicit genuine belief or commitment. In this mood, Socrates ponders the moral discourse being practiced by his fellow Greeks and concludes that even though his neighbors seem satisfied with their ways of talking, for anyone who pays close attention the discourse leads only to confusion, or aporia. His interlocutors are "playing with words but revealing nothing."[17] Or a loose group of self-styled "Legal Realists" considers the "formalist" arguments that their contemporaries are engaged in and finds it hard to fathom how anyone could suppose that this form of argumentation actually produces satisfactory answers to legal disputes. The standard law-talk, it seems to the Realists, "is in terms of words; it centers on words; it has the utmost difficulty in getting beyond words."[18]

In such situations, it is natural to try to escape the corrupt conventions or dissolute discourse and to discover or recover something more solid—to return to "first principles." Thus, Jesus urges his followers to forsake artificial traditions in favor of the more fundamental injunctions to love God and neighbor.[19] The Protestant reformers rebel against what they believe to be decadent Christian traditions in an effort to return to primitive Christianity; their own descendants repeatedly undertake the same quest. Emerson and Thoreau inveigh against tradition and convention and in favor of "Nature" and a romantically conceived "Reason." Legal Realists and their successors deconstruct formalist legal reasoning and advocate its replacement by something they suppose to be more real and solid—"policy science," perhaps. The basic phenomenon is familiar enough: the disaffected come to believe that a particular culture or discourse has become empty or inauthentic, and they determine to find or return to something more solid.

More solid or, we might better say, more *true*: it is imperative to remember that Enlightenment reason grows out of a commitment to live by the truth. At the core of the classical Enlightenment was a sense—whether it was correct we need not say—that the scholastic philosophy and religious culture inherited from the Middle Ages and the more unsettled intellectual culture of early modernity were not grounded in truth. So eighteenth-century thinkers "made a great point of having renounced the superstition and hocus-pocus of medieval Christian thought."[20] In the aftermath of the breakup of Christendom and in the midst of struggles over religion, early modern Europe was suffering from a "crisis of belief,"[21] Stephen Toulmin argues—a crisis with disastrous practical consequences. In this context, Descartes's "reflections opened up for people in his generation a real hope of reasoning their way out of political and theological crisis. . . ."[22]

Thus interpreted, the Enlightenment separation of reason from culture was not necessarily a childish misconception, but rather an effort in improvement and renewal of the sort that admired figures have undertaken at pivotal moments throughout history. Nor should the obvious diversity in conceptions of "reason" necessarily prove embarrassing. "Reason" meant, in essence, a human capacity for grasping truth. Just how that capacity functioned was, to be sure, a source of ongoing reflection and, sometimes, disagreement. So conceptions of reason differed. But it would be wrong to conclude that "reason" signified nothing more than a word, or a slogan: what held the diverse conceptions together was the shared understanding that reason is a capacity for knowing and living by truth—or by Truth.

The Consensus Criterion

In different ways, Enlightenment thinkers gravitated to the view that agreement or consensus should serve as a sort of working principle governing the operation of reason. The commitment to what we can call a "consensus criterion" was a natural if complex and sometimes compromised consequence of the component just discussed—the separation of reason from culture.

Indeed, the consensus criterion might seem to be a natural consequence of "reason" itself. Both before and since the Enlightenment, that is, "reason" has usually been taken as describing a common human faculty, or even a feature that defines *what it means* to be human: the human being is supposed to be the "rational animal." And if reason is a common human faculty, then it seems to follow—doesn't it?—that arguments based on reason ought to be able to gain the assent of anyone who will honestly consider them. Thus, Thomas Aquinas had explained that in debating with those who do not accept Christian scripture "[w]e must, therefore, have recourse to the natural reason, to which all men are forced to give their assent."[23]

In the Middle Ages, to be sure, "reason" stood as a sort of junior partner to a higher source of truth, "revelation," which operated to guide and correct it. And the exercise of reason depended on training in a large body of philosophical and theological writings that conveyed the truths that reason and revelation had accumulated over the centuries: Aquinas's *Summa*s were the consummate expression of this medieval enterprise of reason. So it would hardly be surprising if persons untrained and unversed in this corpus of learning might fail to grasp the truth of vital matters: even what is self-evident, Aquinas explained, may not be self-evident *to us*.[24]

But we should not be quick to see anything duplicitous or hypocritical in the medieval view that truths known through reason might nonetheless be accessible only to those who have been properly trained in a body of received learning. Some such qualification will attend any conception of reason. Thus, Coke made essentially the same point to James I in explaining why the common law, though the "perfection of reason," could be known not through the "natural reason" possessed in ample measure by the king but only through "artificial reason" and with the aid of "long Study and Experience [in the law] before a man can attain to cognizance of it."[25] No doubt students in any complex and developed field—science, math, law—are told the same. In a related vein, Enlightenment thinkers themselves were acutely conscious of the fact that reason cannot operate in people whose minds are befogged by prejudice or passion—or religious enthusiasm or fanaticism. Hence the chant of the aroused French masses—aroused by a comely young woman chosen to serve as the "Goddess of Reason"—outside the newly christened Temple of Reason (the erstwhile Cathedral of Notre Dame): "Long live reason! Down with fanaticism!"

Though Americans were a bit calmer, still, as Henry May explains, "[s]elf-evident truth, most of the framers believed, was much more self-evident to some than to others. On the whole government worked best if it remained in the hands of gentlemen of generous education and large views."[26] So Enlightenment reason, it seems, has always understood itself and its claims to be subject to some such "reasonable persons" qualification: "reason" for the "reasonable."

Still, by separating reason from culture, and by purporting to renounce reliance on tradition and authority, the Enlightenment conception necessarily undermined that sort of qualification, and thereby shifted greater emphasis to consensus as a criterion for measuring the successful exercise of reason. If reason is something that all competent persons are capable of, then the results of reasoning ought in principle to be recognizable by all competent persons—not only by people acculturated in a particular religious or political tradition. The plowman should be on a par with the professor.[27] In this way, Enlightenment reason has a sort of "common denominator" quality: it steers inquirers away from the particular,[28] the local, the "sectarian," toward what everyone can understand and accept.

In science, this consensus criterion is expressed in the requirements that observations be mutually verifiable and that experiments be repeatable. Although these requirements cannot be transferred intact to moral and political thought, a similar principle is reflected in the effort to derive conclusions not from authority but rather from reasons and premises whose truth should be apparent to all honest inquirers. Once again, the Declaration of Independence manifests this assumption. It begins by expressing "a decent respect to the opinions" not merely of people brought up in a particular political or religious tradition, but rather "of mankind." And the Declaration goes on to offer what are held out as "self-evident" truths—truths that should be recognizable as such by "a candid world."

As the Declaration's language reflects, the overall Enlightenment commitment is still to truth. We are to live by truth, . . . which is known by reason, . . . the successful operation of which should be reflected in the achievement of consensus among "reasonable" persons. The connection linking consensus, reason, and truth needs emphasizing because, as we will see, consensus can be sought for purposes other than discerning truth.

Freedom of Expression

The association of reason with a consensus criterion is nicely compatible with one more specific political commitment commonly associated with the Enlightenment: freedom of expression. No doubt Enlightenment thinkers varied in the strength of their commitment to free speech. But they tended to favor the idea, at least in principle and sometimes in practice[29]—witness Jefferson's and Madison's resistance to the Alien and Sedition acts—and on their own premises they should have. Freedom of speech is related to a consensus-oriented conception of reason in two ways. First, freedom is a necessary condition of measuring or discerning the existence of consensus. Allowing people to express their views, that is, seems the only way to ascertain whether a real consensus exists: how are we to tell whether people agree unless they are free to say what they think? Second, even where people do not initially agree, an interchange of views seems calculated to lead people in the direction of consensus.

Or does it? The statement admittedly reflects a grand leap of faith—and one that experience over the last two centuries might seem to belie. Open, candid discussion seems likely to lead in the direction of an agreed-upon truth in a given domain on two assumptions: first, that there is in fact a truth to be found in that domain and, second, that thinking and discussing are efficacious means of discerning that truth. Conversely, if there is no truth to be discovered in a given domain—the domain of morality, for example—then there is no a priori reason to suppose that open discussion would be likely to lead toward consensus. And if discourse is understood not so much as a means of exchanging ideas about truth but rather in other terms— as an instrument for achieving one's interests, or as a manifestation of personal or collective identity—then there would be little reason to expect free discussion to lead either to truth or to consensus. On the contrary.

So once again, the commitment of the classical Enlightenment to freedom of expression rests on the more fundamental premise that truth, or Truth, exists and that human beings can and should know it and live by it. But what gives plausibility to that sanguine premise? It might almost seem that such a happy state of affairs could exist only in a providentially designed universe—one in which, as Descartes had thought, a benevolent deity could serve as a sort of guarantor of human understanding. And that, as it happens, was precisely what most Enlightenment thinkers (at least in America) *did* believe.

A Common, Providential Worldview

The premise positing the existence of Truth and the commensurability of Truth with the human mind was nicely consonant with a worldview that was uniformly embraced by the Enlightened architects of the American constitutional order. "The Constitutional debates," Henry May explains, "reveal beneath fierce disagreements a deep, taken-for-granted unity among Federalists and Anti-Federalists, conservatives and liberals, the party of commerce and the party of virtue—even between Calvinists and Deists." This agreement extended across a surprisingly broad spectrum of topics: "religion, human nature, theory of knowledge, political theory, history, and the right kind of governing class."[30]

One aspect of this consensus deserves special emphasis, both because it may seem surprising to modern thinkers and because, as suggested above, it served as a sort of presupposition for reasoning about the other topics, including those central to American constitutionalism. For much of Western history, the universe had been conceived of as a divinely instituted normative order or, as Louis Dupre puts it, an "ontotheological synthesis"[31]; and morality (including political morality) had been understood as the art or practice of living in harmony with that order. Imposing labels anachronistically, we may today suppose that since the Enlightenment was supposed to have been a "secular" movement rebelling against a tradition that was "religious," Enlightenment thinkers must have repudiated this belief in a providential order. But this supposition turns history on its head. Not only did the classical Enlightenment retain a faith in the existence of a normative cosmic order; the accomplishment of thinkers like Locke, as Carl Becker noted, was precisely to subvert religious doctrines such as the Calvinist idea of depravity that had undermined confidence in the capacity of human beings to comprehend and conform to that overarching order.[32]

The assumption of a providential order pervaded Jeffersonian thinking and provided the premise for reasoning on questions of all kinds—moral, political, or scientific. Was the earth created much as it is now? Or did it evolve over a long period of time? Do mammoths still exist? Do human beings have natural rights beyond the positive legal rights conferred on them by particular legal systems? Jefferson's answers to these questions (respectively yes, no, yes, yes) all derived from his belief in an overarching providential order in the universe.[33] In particular, the providential framework provided the basis for specific commitments to natural or human rights. For Jefferson, as Daniel Boorstin puts it, "no claim [of rights] could be validated except by the Creator's plan. . . ."[34] The essential idea is succinctly expressed, once again, in the Declaration: "We hold these truths to be self-evident that all men *are created* equal; that they are endowed *by their Creator* with certain inalienable rights. . . ."

The unapologetically religious character of eighteenth-century Enlightenment discourse, and more specifically its persistent reliance on the premise of a providential order, may be disconcerting to modern heirs of the Enlightenment. Henry May observes that "neglect of religion or of theology is one common error among historians of the Enlightenment."[35] And indeed, the divergence in this respect between classical Enlightenment thought and more modern thinking of an Enlightenment bent reflects a crucial divide between the classical and modern Enlightenments.

In the eighteenth-century context, though, reasoning on the assumption of an overarching normative order seemed entirely compatible with the Enlightenment conception of reason. "Reason," as noted, entailed a search for the "common denominator"—for what seemed true to everyone, regardless of the particularities of culture or the idiosyncrasies of the individual believer. But in the America of the founders, nearly everyone adhered either to some species of Protestantism or to some Protestant offshoot—unitarianism, deism, rational or natural religion. These diverse faiths shared a belief in a divine Author or Architect who created the universe according to an intelligent and benevolent plan. The few Catholics and even fewer Jews who might have registered on the Americans' intellectual landscape would not have dissented from this general proposition. And there were, James Turner argues, literally no atheists detectable on the scene—or at least none other than perhaps Joel Barlow: "What the orthodox called 'atheism' usually amounted to nothing but a Deistic denial of revealed religion. . . . For disbelief in God remained scarcely more plausible than disbelief in gravity."[36]

So in this context, the belief in a divinely ordained normative order had a nonsectarian quality—or at least it could seem to have this quality to the responsible, disciplined mind that did not allow itself to rove too far beyond the immediate "live" intellectual options or to dwell on exotic possibilities. No doubt a person of learning, like Jefferson, was aware at least on a purely cognitive level that in the far reaches of the world (or even in places he had visited—France, for instance) there were, for example, genuine atheists. But this remote fact need not disturb the present working consensus any more than a brief occasional encounter with believers in reincarnation troubles a modern Western secularist.

If reason sought the common denominator, in short, the providential worldview *was* the common denominator. Indeed, in the eighteenth-century climate of opinion, it would have been against reason to *doubt* the providential worldview. "All believed in a universe that was presided over by a benevolent deity, a universe that made sense in human terms and was intelligible to human reason," Henry May observes. And "most if not all of the framers would have found it impossible to imagine any other kind of universe."[37]

The Eighteenth-Century Convergence

In sum, the classical Enlightenment reflected a happy convergence of elements. A universe designed and governed by a benevolent providence provided the Truth by which people might aspire to live—a Truth that transcended any particular culture, and that was knowable because it was providentially commensurate with the operations of the human mind. Through free and honest discussions people might hope to come ever closer to a full and shared understanding of this Truth.

The Modern Ideal: Inverting the Enlightenment

The historical Enlightenment, as noted, is often said to have dissolved in the nineteenth century. But many modern political and constitutional theorists continue to invoke it—or to have it invoked in their behalf—in support of a liberal vision of American constitutionalism. So how is the modern ideal related to the classical position just discussed?

A preliminary caution is in order. The modern Enlightenment, like the classical one, is "necessarily rather amorphous and diverse." So what I will be calling "the Enlightenment ideal" will again reflect a selective and contestable interpretation. Its contestability will be especially conspicuous because, unlike Descartes and Jefferson, the partisans of the modern Enlightenment are our friends and neighbors (and often ourselves); we know that their views—or *our* views—are complex, and that we differ among ourselves. Not everyone who might be classified as a partisan for present purposes will happily claim to descend from the Enlightenment. John Rawls—that "titan of our age"[38]—is an especially troublesome case. I think that he must be taken as the most influential contemporary American theorist of the Enlightenment ideal, and that any discussion of that ideal needs to refer to ideas associated with him. Yet not only did Rawls disclaim the label—or at least qualify it[39]—but his position was complicated and, it seems, ever developing. So let it be clear that my purpose in what follows is not to offer a definitive interpretation of Rawls—or any other particular thinker—but rather to try to extract a sort of ideal or orientation that, subject of course to variations and different degrees of commitment, animates a good deal of the thought of influential theorists such as Rawls, Stephen Macedo, Martha Nussbaum, Robert Audi, Amy Gutmann, Thomas Nagel, Ronald Dworkin, Bruce Ackerman, and Kent Greenawalt, and that has discernible if complicated effects on actual constitutional decisions and doctrines.

The Ongoing Commitment to "Reason"

The most obvious connection linking the modern ideal to the historical Enlightenment is a shared professed commitment to governance in accordance with "reason." Modern theorists enthusiastically embrace the vocabulary of "reason"—indeed, one sometimes wonders whether their word processors have been infected with a virus that spreads the word "reason" and its cognates through their writings like an epidemic[40]—and, moreover, their understanding of reason exhibits important resemblances to the Enlightenment conception. Most significantly, modern heirs to the Enlightenment legacy persist in emphasizing the distinction separating reason from culture and tradition. And they claim to embrace the consensus criterion at least as warmly as the historical figures did.

These aspects of Enlightenment reason are readily apparent in Rawls's influential writings. The ideal of a political community shaped by and committed to "public reason"[41] pervades Rawls's thought. The separation of reason from culture and tradition is reflected in Rawls's insistence that public reason must remain "freestanding" and independent of any and all "comprehensive views"—views which might well grow out of and reflect particular cultures or intellectual traditions. Instead, the content of reason is confined to "presently acceptable general beliefs and forms of reasoning found in common sense, and the methods and conclusions of science when these are not controversial."[42] By confining reason to these largely uncontested materials, Rawls hopes to build on and secure an "overlapping consensus" among "reasonable" views.[43]

Although theorists differ among themselves, Rawls's vision of "public reason" is in essential respects like the "democratic deliberation" favored by other theorists. In an essay advocating what he calls "liberal public reason," Stephen Macedo notices the common themes uniting the "public reason" of theorists like Rawls and the "deliberative democracy" of theorists like Amy Gutmann and Dennis Thompson.[44] These common themes, moreover, are precisely those that flow from the Enlightenment conception of reason, with its consensus criterion. The core demand is that public deliberation should "be carried on in terms that are mutually acceptable," not on the basis of "sectarian" views.[45]

In this particular, therefore, modern liberal theorists can plausibly claim to be faithful heirs of the Enlightenment. In other respects, though, they depart from the classical position. The departures are not minor; moreover, they have the effect of turning essential Enlightenment aspirations upside down.

The Disintegration of the Classical Position

In the eighteenth century, the components discussed above seemed nicely harmonious. But two centuries later this happy congruity has been decisively shattered. The breakdown of the eighteenth-century convergence has been in large measure a result of several currents, ironically, that are often associated with the Enlightenment itself. We can briefly notice three such developments: democracy, pluralism, and secularism.

Though modern partisans of Enlightenment (such as, outstandingly, Dewey) may claim "democracy" for their cause, the thinkers of the historical Enlightenment were typically not great friends of democracy.[46] Henry May argues that both in Europe and in America, the partisans of Enlightenment were generally suspicious of "the people," and that the major democratizing force was in fact radical Protestantism.[47] Nonetheless, the Enlightenment commitment to "equality" (expressed in the Declaration of Independence) together with the acceptance of consensus as the criterion of reason contained a democratizing impulse—one that played itself out over the next two centuries through a great enlargement of the franchise, expansion of educational opportunities, and in other ways. One result of this development was that the number of people who presumptively "counted" for purposes of determining the existence of a consensus increased exponentially. This expansion, we might surmise, would almost necessarily make the achievement of a genuine consensus on momentous issues more difficult. The difficulty would be compounded by the increasing pluralism—religious, political, cultural—that, as theorists like Rawls stress, now appears to be a corollary of Enlightened political commitments to freedom of religion and freedom of expression.

If democracy and pluralism hindered the achievement of consensus by multiplying viewpoints, an evolving secularism undermined the particular basis for consensus that the eighteenth century had enjoyed. As discussed, the so-called "secularism" of the classical Enlightenment had seemed compatible with a providential worldview, but this partnership dissolved as, among other things, modern science offered a new vision of how the universe is constituted. Though it now appears that secularization is neither as uniform nor as inexorable as it once seemed,[48] it still dominates some sectors of the culture, especially the academy (which of course imagines itself to be the main bastion of Enlightenment)[49]; and one consequence of that change has been that in those sectors the belief in a divinely established normative order, widely shared in the eighteenth century, has by now come to seem at best highly sectarian.

As these developments have subverted the comfortable alliance among the components of the eighteenth-century Enlightenment, the meaning of the slogan of "reason," or of a collective life governed by "reason," has changed as well, becoming in important ways just the opposite of the classical meaning.

Reason or Truth?

Most fundamentally, the classical belief that "reason" is valuable as an adjunct to the commitment to living in accordance with Truth has given way to a radically altered understanding in which reason—or at least the kind of "public reason" that is supposed to govern the political community—is carefully and deliberately *insulated against* questions and claims of Truth.

The first step in the divorce of reason from Truth comes with the conclusion that reason should be independent of "religious" premises or values, or of a religious worldview. Religious beliefs, after all, cannot satisfy the consensus criterion that is the working principle of "reason." Purged of religion, public discourse becomes "secular" (or so the modern proponents of Enlightenment suppose).[50] In this spirit, Kathleen Sullivan asserts that the U.S. Constitution brought about "the establishment of the secular public order."[51] And the modern Supreme Court has stumbled in the general direction of this conclusion. Thus, modern establishment doctrine, though notoriously capricious in its operations, at least purports to limit government to acting for secular *purposes* and in ways that have primarily secular *effects*.[52]

These secularity requirements limit what government can *do* (as well as *why* government can do what it does); they also regulate what government can *say*. This kind of regulation is evident in the "no endorsement" construction that has been added to establishment doctrine over the last couple of decades. Though implementation has been erratic, current doctrine holds that government cannot do or say anything that sends a message endorsing or disapproving of any religion.[53] This prohibition has the effect of discouraging the inclusion of religion in public decision-making, because religious statements offered in support of a measure may condemn it by causing the measure to be perceived as an endorsement of religion.[54]

Notice that the exclusion of religion from public decision-making is not based—not officially, at least—on any assumption that religion is *false*. Indeed, defenders of current doctrine insist on the point: the secularity imperative is supposed to be simply "neutral" toward religion. And Rawls maintains—though many critics and even supporters remain unpersuaded—that his own version of political liberalism does not pass judgment on the truth of religious or other comprehensive views—even of those declared to be "unreasonable."[55] Hence, both the secularity requirement of constitutional doctrine and the Rawlsian notion of public reason purport to be compatible with the possibility that religion is a source or manifestation of important truths. But it is simply not the role of *government*—and of the "reason" that is supposed to guide government—to concern itself with such truths.

Though religion is the most conspicuous of the belief systems to be excluded from the domain of public reason, it is not the only one. After all, if there is no consensus supporting religion, or any particular religion, there is probably no consensus in favor of any other general view or philosophy of life, human nature, or morality. Thus, theorists like Rawls and Macedo are clear that *no* "comprehensive view of truth and the human good as a whole,"[56] religious *or* secular, can properly be invoked in the exercise of "public reason." And though actual constitutional doctrine is much less explicit on this point, a similar constraint is arguably implicit, as we will see, in the instrumental rationality ostensibly mandated by a wide variety of doctrines.

By excluding any "comprehensive view of truth" from the domain of public reason, theorists like Rawls and Macedo deflect the suspicion that they are simply hostile to religion. But they also make it clear that "reason," for all of its prominence in their positions, is no longer serving the function of guiding people to live in accordance with Truth.[57] That sort of Truth, rather, is beyond the purview of reason, or at least of "public reason"; it is something for people to pursue individually or in private associations. Public reason is now seen as serving other, more political and social values such as "cooperativeness," "reciprocity," and "a common citizenship."[58]

Indeed, it would be at most a slight exaggeration to say that whereas in the classical Enlightenment the purpose of reason was to orient discourse toward Truth, under the modern ideal the purpose of "public reason" is precisely to *prevent* claims about Truth from entering into public discourse. The commitment to "reason" gradually evolves—or deteriorates—into a commitment to "reasonableness," which consists precisely of a willingness (in the interests of fairness and "getting along") to *refrain* from pushing "reason" too deep or too far. In a humorous mood, Michael Zuckert captures the change by imagining a comment of Calvin on the modern posture (though the comment might as well come from the signatories of the Declaration of Independence who, as noted, pledged all they had in the defense of what they took to be self-evident truths):

> For shame, Professor Rawls. Is a bit of threat to your comfort and safety all it takes to scare you off your "convictions"? . . . Do you men of Harvard know nothing of truth? Martin Luther said, "Here I stand, I can do no other." He knew the princes of church and state would give

him no peace, no rest, yet he stood. And you Harvard philosophers, what do you say? "Here I sit. I dare do no more."[59]

By separating reason from truth in a large sense, or from the "whole truth," the modern ideal inverts the classical position. And that inversion manifests itself in other aspects of the modern ideal as well.

The Instrumentalization of Discourse

The rejection of a providential worldview—and the exclusion of "comprehensive views" generally from public reason—means that reason cannot operate in the same way it did in the classical scheme of things. So how *is* reason to work in public decision-making without violating the consensus criterion?

The most tempting prospect, it seems, is to view reason in instrumental or means-end terms—that is, as a method for figuring out how to achieve shared goals in the most efficient way. Not surprisingly, instrumentalism dominated much of twentieth-century legal thought.[60] And the Supreme Court has often imported an instrumental conception of reason into its doctrines.[61]

Instrumental reasoning is apt enough when shared goals or values in fact exist and the question is how best to realize them. With respect to other kinds of questions, however, instrumental reasoning seems less efficacious. It has little to say, for example, on vital questions of distributive justice.[62] In addition, instrumental rationality, though it may provide valuable clarification of alternatives, stands mostly mute before controversies primarily reflecting deep-seated differences in values or moral commitments—such as abortion or affirmative action. Perhaps most fundamentally, means-end reasoning is largely powerless to provide justifications for the most fundamental commitments of the American constitutional order, such as the "truths" of equality and natural rights asserted in the Declaration of Independence. The problem deserves closer attention.

The Problem of Justification

The possibility of devising satisfying justifications for central commitments to things such as equality and human rights is of course a controversial matter about which volumes have been written; here we can only notice the difficulties. But it is no secret that the problem of providing a persuasive philosophical justification for rights is a daunting one.[63] Arguments about equality are similarly voluminous and complex, but it may be worth considering one analysis directly relevant to the issue here.

In an essay called "On Equal Human Worth: A Critique of Contemporary Egalitarianism," Louis Pojman notes that an assumption that all humans are of equal worth is central to virtually all modern political theorizing. But what is the justification for this assumption? The notion of equal worth is hard to square with the empirical evidence: "Take any capacity or ability you like: reason, a good will, the capacity to suffer, the ability to deliberate and choose freely, the ability to make moral decisions and carry them out, self-control, sense of humor, health, athletic and artistic ability, and it seems that humans . . . differ in the degree to which they have those capacities and abilities."[64] Pojman reinforces the point with almost gruesome vividness. Referring to an essay in which Gregory Vlastos imagines humans explaining to a Martian visitor that "the human worth of all persons is equal," Pojman proceeds to imagine the Martian's response:

> He invites Vlastos to consider Smith, a man of low morals and lower intelligence, who abuses his wife and children, who hates exercising or work, for whom novels are dull and art a waste of time, and whose joy it is to spend his days as a couch potato, drinking beer, while watching mud wrestling, violent sports, and soap operas on TV. He is an avid voyeur, devoted to child pornography. He is devoid of intellectual curiosity, eschews science, politics, and religion, and eats and drinks in a manner more befitting a pig than a person. Smith lacks wit, grace, humor, technical skill, ambition, courage, self-control, and wisdom. He is anti-social, morose, lazy, a freeloader who feels no guilt about living on welfare, when he is perfectly able to work, has no social conscience, and barely avoids getting caught for his petty thievery. He has no talents, makes no social contribution, lacks a moral sense. . . . But Smith is proud of one thing: that he is "sacred," of "infinite worth," of equal intrinsic value as Abraham Lincoln, Mother Teresa, Albert Schweitzer, the Dalai Lama, Jesus Christ, Gandhi, and Einstein. . . . From the egalitarian perspective, . . . Smith is of equal intrinsic worth as the best citizen in his community. We could excuse the Martian if he exhibited amazement at this incredible doctrine.[65]

So then what is the justification for saying that all persons are in some important sense of equal worth? Pojman argues that as a historical matter, the idea of human equality descends from a religious tradition. Often the justification takes the form of a claim that all humans are made by God in his image. The justification is also expressed in the imagery of family: "The language of human dignity and worth implies a great family in which a benevolent and sovereign Father binds together all his children in love and justice."[66] And that rationale can be given more analytical form: Pojman identifies two principal justifications in the religious tradition, which he calls "the Essentialist Argument" and "the Argument from Grace."[67]

But these are precisely the sorts of rationales that an Enlightened "public reason" seeks to filter out of public discourse and public justification. "What distinguishes most contemporary egalitarianism from earlier natural law modes is its self-conscious secularism," Pojman observes. "There is no appeal to a God or a transcendent realm."[68] So Pojman examines ten leading secular arguments advanced by theorists such as Dworkin, Rawls, Kai Nielsen, Joel Feinberg, Thomas Nagel, and Alan Gewirth; and he finds all of these arguments wanting.[69] Sometimes the arguments turn on demonstrable fallacies or on flagrant and unsupported discursive leaps; more often they do not actually offer any justification for equality at all but instead simply assert or assume it, or else posit that in the absence of any persuasive justification one way or the other we should adopt a "presumption" of equal worth.

Pojman concludes that egalitarian commitments are "simply a left-over from a religious world view now rejected by all of the philosophers discussed in this essay."[70] Secular egalitarians are free riders, living off an inheritance they are embarrassed to acknowledge. And he wonders whether "perhaps we should abandon egalitarianism and devise political philosophies that reflect naturalistic assumptions, theories which are forthright in viewing humans as differentially talented animals who must get on together."[71]

In sum, divorcing reason from any comprehensive views—and in particular from the providential worldview widely held during the American founding—pushes reason in a secular and instrumentalist direction. But mere instrumental and secular rationality, for all their uses, seem impotent to justify the most basic commitments of the American constitutional order.

Manufacturing—and Manipulating—Consensus

Responses to this challenge vary, of course, but it seems that the characteristic stance of modern liberal theorists of an Enlightenment bent, following the example of the architects of international human rights, is simply to spurn the demand for "justifications" and to base the central commitments to equality and rights on an ostensible consensus within the relevant constituency. George Fletcher observes in this vein that "[m]odern philosophical approaches toward equality . . . are strongly committed, vaguely, to some position on the spectrum, but they offer no reason why they are so intensely committed to this value. . . . In the contemporary liberal culture, equality is one of those values that has become so deeply held that it is neither questioned nor justified."[72]

This stance might seem to be a blatant abdication of the Enlightenment demand that all practices and beliefs be justified by reason. Still, there is a nice logic to the position. After all, the demand for "justifications" may plausibly be understood as asking that partisans of liberal constitutionalism show how their commitments are derived from a persuasive comprehensive view—or from Truth. Eighteenth-century justifications took that form, as we have seen. But of course this sort of argument from Truth is precisely what modern "public reason" seeks to discourage, at least as part of *public* discourse. So any attempt at justification in this sense arguably would betray the modern Enlightenment ideal.[73] Conversely, modern reason still embraces the consensus criterion. And the happy fact is, Stephen Macedo argues, that "America does enjoy a widespread consensus on basic guarantees that constitute the core of a political morality" including commitments to "fair cooperation, civility among citizens who disagree reasonably, a belief in basic liberties, and due process and the rule of law . . ."[74]

Though it is nicely congruent with the modern Enlightenment orientation, however, this philosophically demure, consensus-oriented approach remains vulnerable to potent objections. In the first place, the core political ideals are *not* supported by any universal consensus. Even the broad ideals of the Declaration of Independence—human equality, natural or human rights—do not enjoy any consensus across the spectrum of world cultures.[75] So the consensus on which modern partisans of Enlightenment rely seems limited to the people of liberal democracies or perhaps even, as Macedo says, of America.

But this limitation negates the Enlightenment resolution to make reason independent of culture; it effectively turns "reason" into a complacent endorsement of the ideals and values of the culture that in our self-satisfaction we happen to inhabit. Indeed, proponents of the modern Enlightenment ideal may be quite frank in acknowledging that they simply have nothing to say—or no arguments to make— to people who do not already share their basic premises and commitments.[76] For old-style partisans of a more hard-edged reason like Ernest Gellner, this acceptance of culture as providing the grounds for judgment is simply disguised nihilism[77]—hardly what the Enlightenment aspired to. In the modern tendency to present liberal commitments as simply those of a particular culture Vittorio Hosle perceives a "Nietzschean self-dissolution of enlightenment."[78]

Moreover, even if we are content to ground central political commitments in a merely local consensus, that consensus exists, if at all, only at the most abstract level—at the level of generalities like "equality," "reciprocity," "fairness," and "dignity." Modern partisans of Enlightenment depend on these concepts to do a great deal of work in justifying more specific decisions involving distributive justice or rights. But the concepts are at best very abstract; in some instances, such as "equality" and "reciprocity," they are largely formal, and thus innocent of substantive content.[79] Meanwhile the actual argumentative work and the particular conclusions in specific controversies demand more specific and substantive—and contested—premises. So how does a theorist—or a court—get from a very general and perhaps purely formal premise to a specific substantive conclusion without offending the consensus criterion that modern reason uses as a working principle?

The crude answer would be, as the old farmer told the lost tourist, "You cain't get there from here." But the practical questions of life demand answers, so answers will somehow be forthcoming; and the standard rhetorical moves that serve to deliver those answers have become familiar. One tactic is to invoke a generic concept such as "equality" while tacitly importing a more specific substantive conception that would be controversial if openly stated.[80] Criticizing Rawls's position, for example, Michael Zuckert argues that although there may be a cultural consensus favoring the *concept* of equality, "there is also a wide range of disagreement over what about persons makes them equal, and over what the claim of equality entitles them to." But "when Rawls brings the agreement on the *concept* of equality into his system he treats it as if it were an agreement on a *conception*." No such agreement exists, however, so the "shift from concept to conception is simply arbitrary and illegitimate within the terms of Rawls's own thought."[81]

A different but equally familiar strategy is to gerrymander the constituency so as to eliminate dissenters who might disturb the necessary consensus. Reason, as noted, speaks only to "reasonable" people, so those who inconveniently disagree with a necessary proposition can easily be placed outside the boundaries by being declared "unreasonable." In this vein, the writings of theorists like Rawls, Macedo, and

Gutmann and Thompson teem with pronouncements declaring what "reasonable" people believe, and disfellowshipping dissenters from the congregation of the "reasonable."

For those who inhabit the cultural neighborhood of Rawls, Macedo, and Gutmann, the exclusionary implications of "public reason" or "democratic deliberation" may be easy to overlook, or at least to excuse. The claims of public reason will seem almost truistic; and Rawls, Macedo, Dworkin, and associated representatives of the modern Enlightenment will appear to be the personification of sweet reasonableness. Conversely, to those who dwell in other neighborhoods—even within the broad community called "America"—the confident claims of these Enlightened thinkers will seem smug, incredible, and almost inexplicable. Thus, perplexed at the spectacle of "[l]iberal ideologues, who celebrate tolerance and pluralism while at the same time condemning any meaningful dissent from their own thin idea of the good as not merely wrong but contrary to the dictates of reason itself," Paul Campos is reduced to speculating that Rawlsian claims about "reasonableness" and the "overlapping consensus" can enjoy plausibility only among a select group of academicians whose world is effectively limited to those who "work at the same institutions, attend the same conferences, read the same newspapers, live in the same suburbs, and send their children to the same schools."[82]

In a similar vein, Stanley Fish painstakingly shows how a variety of prominent liberal thinkers, always respectful of "Enlightenment decorums," effectively "elevat[e] the decorum of academic dinner parties to the status of discourse universals."[83] Fish argues that when theorists like Gutmann and Thompson talk about "reason" and "reasonableness," "all they are doing is negotiating a very small circle that begins and ends with their own prior conviction and a vocabulary made in its image. The key word in that vocabulary is 'reasonable.' But all that is meant by the word is what my friends and I take to be so."[84]

Proponents of "public reason" will answer, of course, that Fish's characterization is unfair: citizens are classified as "unreasonable" not because the theorists disagree with their substantive opinions but rather because these citizens misunderstand or disrespect something like the principle of "reciprocity" on which a pluralistic community must depend.[85] But this criterion of "reciprocity," upon closer inspection, turns out to add nothing to the judgment that a person or view is unreasonable. After all, "reciprocity," like "equality," is in itself a formal principle; it gets "bite" only when filled with particular substantive content. Reciprocity can be extended or denied, that is, on the basis of all sorts of substantive terms: it is as much a manifestation of *reciprocity* to let everyone participate in the discussion so long as they accept a generally theistic framework—basically the eighteenth-century view—as it is to let everyone participate in the discussion so long as they *do not* employ a theistic framework, which is roughly the view taken by many secular liberals today. Thus, no one need have any quarrel with the idea of "reciprocity" in itself. In reality, disputes are always about what substance to pour into that congenial vessel, and the accusation that some person or group is unwilling to accept the criterion of *reciprocity* amounts to a veiled way of saying that the accused is unwilling to accept the *substantive terms* that the accuser would want to be (reciprocally) respected.

More specifically, the modern partisans of Enlightenment want reciprocity on what they deem "reasonable" terms. But in this way we end up with a circularity: a person is said to be "unreasonable" because he disrespects the requirement of "reciprocity," but to say that he disrespects the requirement of reciprocity turns out to be just a way of saying that he is not being "reasonable." Hence, "reciprocity" adds nothing (except beguiling packaging) to the partisan and conclusory judgment of "reasonableness."

To be sure, partisans of the modern Enlightenment may argue that in excluding "unreasonable" persons and views from disturbing the "overlapping consensus," they are merely invoking a legitimate and necessary qualification—and one that Enlightenment thinkers have always invoked. It is true—isn't it?—that the process and products of "reason" will be recognizable only to "reasonable" people? Moreover, even during the historical Enlightenment, ostensible appeals to consensus—or to the judgment of all "mankind" (as in the Declaration of Independence)—were tacitly understood to be much more limited in their intended audience: reason was, as noted, mostly a pastime for "gentlemen of generous education and large views."[86] Nonetheless, two important differences separate the modern invocation of seemingly spurious consensuses from the eighteenth-century practice.

First, the exclusion of persons from the "reasonableness" category seems more conspicuous today—and more conspicuously arbitrary. In the eighteenth century, the class of "gentlemen of generous education" might well have been at least roughly coextensive with the class of people who exercised the franchise and enjoyed a significant degree of literacy. Today, by contrast, the masses of people excluded for various purposes from the category of the "reasonable" would encompass thousands or even millions of citizens who function successfully in life (often in professions requiring intelligence and training), who have some or perhaps considerable education, and who are eligible to vote and hold public office.[87] In this context, it is hard to understand the label "unreasonable" to mean anything other than "in unacceptable disagreement with me."

Second, the function of consensus in modern thinking is in fact quite different than it was for the classical Enlightenment—and thus not amenable to the same sorts of restrictions. In the seventeenth and eighteenth centuries, as discussed, consensus was a criterion of and a means to *truth*—much as the requirement of mutual verifiability continues to be in science. If a proposition is true, then through reason all competent and honest people should in principle be able to apprehend its truth. And a moral or political proposition could be true, or false, because there was thought to be a Truth, or a "Nature," that the proposition could correctly or incorrectly represent—in the same way that a proposition in physics or chemistry (about the movements of particles, or about cold fusion) can be true or false because there is a material reality that the proposition may or may not represent correctly. Thus, if for Jefferson "[t]he word 'right' was always a signpost pointing back to the divine plan of the Creation,"[88] a proposition about rights would be true if it correctly represented that plan—false if it did not. On this understanding, it made sense—in principle, anyway—to count the opinions of those who might have some presumptive competence to grasp the objective Truth or Nature that was at issue, and to disregard the opinions of anyone who lacked such an ability.

By contrast, contemporary theorists describe the value of consensus not in terms of a test of truth, but rather in terms of political and social values such as fairness, civility, and cooperation. Consensus is prized for its political not its philosophical or epistemic value. In this context, to say that a person, or moral or philosophical view, will not be counted because she or it is "unreasonable" is tantamount to saying *not* that the person lacks some epistemic capacity or that the view is *false*—False relative to *what*? What would that judgment even mean?—but rather that the person or view is offensive to the group that is running the discussion. In this way, the modern Enlightenment lapses into a sort of high-toned neo-tribalism.

The Inversion of Freedom of Expression

The classical Enlightenment, as we noticed earlier, was inclined to be friendly to the idea of freedom of expression. The modern Enlightenment is more ambiguous on this point. On the one hand, modern partisans of Enlightenment maintain the legacy of opposition to familiar or conventional forms of censorship.[89] Not only is such opposition a prominent part of the Enlightenment legacy; the modern heirs of that legacy may sense that traditional censorship is based on moralistic or religious rationales that should be relegated to the private sphere in any case. So it is natural for proponents of the modern ideal to favor freedom of expression in these familiar contexts.[90]

In a less overt but arguably more important way, however, the modern Enlightenment has a strongly censorial cast. We have already noticed how the modern ideal of "public reason" attempts in varying degrees to cleanse public discourse of the explicit invocation of religion or other "comprehensive views." Critics of such restrictions plausibly see them as an effort to suppress expression—and in the area that has typically been regarded as the core First Amendment concern (that is, political speech). The "public reason" of the modern Enlightenment thus stands as a censor looming over public discussion.

Consider, for example, Rawls's analysis of the vexed issues of sexual conduct and same-sex marriage. In popular, public, and academic debate, these issues generate wide-ranging discussion addressing a broad spectrum of legal, moral, psychological, sociological, and even theological concerns. But in a debate governed by the constraints of "public reason," much of this discussion would be ruled out of bounds. "[T]he government would appear to have no interest in the particular form of family life, or of relations among the sexes," Rawls peremptorily declares, "except insofar as that form or those relations in some way affect the orderly reproduction of society over time." Much of what people currently argue about and, it seems, care about is accordingly decreed to be irrelevant to legal and political concerns. In particular, many of the familiar arguments that appeal to moral values or religious convictions would be deemed inadmissible, not because the arguments are *false*—as to that public reason has nothing to say—but because they "reflect religious or comprehensive moral doctrines."[91] The discussion thus becomes much simpler and the proper conclusions far easier to reach: that is because much of the current debate has been censored to meet the standards of "public reason."

To be sure, liberal theorists usually do not extend the constraints of public reason to *all* public discussion (though if public reason could actually work as advertised it is puzzling *why* its beneficent jurisdiction should be confined). Rawls, for instance, insists that decisions be made on the basis of "public reason" only with regard to "constitutional essentials" and "questions of basic justice"; he is ambivalent about extending similar constraints to less vital political issues.[92] Not surprisingly (but perhaps ironically), Rawls's supporters tend to emphasize the very limited coverage of the idea of public reason.[93] Even where the constraints are in force, moreover, Rawls would not necessarily *forbid* the expression of views that do not meet the demands of public reason: citizens would be permitted (and sometimes even encouraged) to air their nonconforming views so long as—Rawls calls this "the proviso"—"in due course proper political reasons . . . are presented that are sufficient to support whatever the comprehensive doctrines introduced are said to support."[94] These indulgences do little to moderate the censorial force of public reason: they amount to telling citizens that on the most important public issues it is permissible to express views about religion, or Truth—only on the condition that the final decision does not depend on those views. This seems tantamount to saying that people can express their nonconforming views so long as those views make no difference to the actual outcome of the debate.[95]

Indeed, Rawls himself concedes that if the constraints of public reason were legally enforced they would be "incompatible with freedom of speech." He attempts to deflect concern by explaining that the constraints will be backed only by a "moral duty."[96] As John Stuart Mill emphasized, however, social or cultural constraints can be as inhibiting to freedom of expression as legal restrictions are[97]; and the modern partisans of Enlightenment ardently cultivate *those kinds* of constraints. Thus, Jeffrie Murphy points out that in the Rawlsian scheme, citizens who resist the constraints of public reason "are not to be coerced, but they are legitimately to be criticized—perhaps even made to feel bad or shunned—in short to be made the object of social but not legal pressure."[98] Moreover, it is misleading to suggest that the censorship promoted by the modern Enlightenment ideal is not legally enforced. The legal sanction typically consists not of criminal punishment, but rather of judicial invalidation of measures thought to have been adopted on the basis of nonconforming grounds. As we have seen, this sort of sanction is very much (if very haphazardly) in force—especially in the establishment clause context, but in other areas of law as well. Citizens who would introduce disfavored rationales into public debate are put on notice, in effect, that by doing so they risk invalidation of the measures they favor.

In this sense, the modern institution of judicial review based on the assumption that laws and government actions are valid only if based on, and defensible in terms of, secular and instrumental justifications is itself a sort of overweening censor over public deliberation. Robert Nagel has explored this aspect of modern constitutionalism. The rationalism of modern constitutional law "tends to denigrate important values and to stunt political discourse," Nagel argues.[99] In particular, "courts often operate under the assumption that beliefs that originate in tradition . . . are impermissible bases for public policy, unless they can be justified by some rational standard extrinsic to the tradition." Consequently, "the felt interests of those who hold affection for tradition are systematically (although, of course, not always) slighted."[100] And the prevailing rationalism tends to discount and filter out the views of these constituencies, arguably comprising much of society, that are not given to formulating rationalist or theoretical articulations of their beliefs.[101]

More specifically, Nagel painstakingly explains how the Supreme Court has directly either acted as censor or supported other government censors in areas such as sex-specific advertising, abortion, and racial integration.[102] And in a subtle but pervasive way, he argues, the very proclivity of Americans to look to courts for the resolution of so many difficult controversies—and the willingness of courts to provide and impose such resolutions—reflects a sort of self-censorial impulse.

> [T]he Court not only occasionally exemplifies our inclinations toward mind control but also in a larger sense embodies our need to escape ourselves. The degree to which in modern times we increasingly and unshakably are dependent on this institution is a sign of how much we want to censor ourselves.[103]

In sum, the modern Enlightenment for the most part retains the specific inherited commitments to freedom of expression; but its more vital impulse, most clearly reflected in its descriptions of the "ideal" of "public reason" in terms of large bodies of belief that should be discouraged or excluded from public discourse, has a strongly censorial character. And this censorial bent is entirely consonant with the central logic of the modern Enlightenment. The classical Enlightenment, as we have seen, was motivated by a desire to live in accordance with Truth and by a confidence (perhaps reflecting the prevailing providential worldview) that discussion would naturally lead human beings in the direction of Truth. Having effectively abandoned those premises and reoriented the political task toward civility and cooperation, the modern Enlightenment has little reason to be enthused about the specific practical commitment to free expression.

There is nothing surprising about this conclusion. Children have long been taught that it is bad manners to talk about religion or other potentially controversial subjects in certain kinds of society. Where the goal is cooperation and civil peace, potentially inflammatory subjects are best left alone: people who breach this etiquette are silenced by being ignored, frowned at, and not invited back. The modern Enlightenment ideal of "public reason" represents the political elaboration of this conventional—and censorial—wisdom.

The Exhaustion of Enlightenment Culture?

Starting out as an effort to break free of culture and tradition, the Enlightenment has itself become a sort of tradition: thus, scholars talk easily of "Enlightenment culture" or "the Enlightenment tradition." Though this development might be thought to constitute a sort of self-contradiction, the development was also unavoidable; and it would be harsh to take the modern Enlightenment too much to task for succumbing to the inevitable. As noted earlier, it seems more charitable in any case to interpret the classic distinction between reason and culture not as asserting a strong and philosophical (but also untenable) dichotomy, but rather as expressing a sense that *the particular culture* within which Descartes and his successors lived had become exhausted and inauthentic—unable to support genuine, meaningful discourse or to command sincere assent.

Does the culture in which lawyers and scholars—and citizens—live today display similar characteristics of exhaustion? I believe we can see in the public discourse advocated by modern partisans of Enlightenment a sort of degenerative dynamic that seems constituted to render that discourse incapable of speaking to us on any deep level or in any convincing way.

Start with John Coleman's observation that "[s]ecular Enlightenment language remains exceedingly 'thin' as a symbol system."[104] It is a symptom of this "thinness," I think, that even secular theorists sometimes resort to a religious vocabulary in order to convey their most profound commitments. For instance, Ronald Dworkin makes pervasive use of the language of the "sacred" in trying to explain the value of human life.[105] But, as Michael Perry argues, Dworkin cannot give any satisfying secular account vindicating this usage; rather, it seems that Dworkin is "trading on the greater strength of the objective sense in which the word is ordinarily used" in order to underscore a commitment that a secular vocabulary is too weak to convey.[106]

The "thin" quality of secular public discourse is not accidental, moreover, but rather deliberate; it would be only a slight exaggeration to say that Enlightenment discourse *aspires to* thinness. As discussed above, Enlightenment reason adopts consensus as a working or operational principle: only premises, beliefs, and modes of argument and inference generally accepted by "reasonable" persons independent of personal idiosyncrasies or cultural particularities can qualify for the label of "reason." As a community becomes increasingly pluralistic, the Enlightenment conception of reason necessarily excludes more and more, and the material available for reasoning accordingly becomes increasingly meager.

As the material available for argument and justification becomes scantier, however, a worrisome prospect appears: What if the discursive resources available within the domain of secular "public reason" are insufficient to resolve a difficult issue, or to provide a satisfying justification for a decision on such an issue? This worry is hardly academic. On the contrary, it seems almost inevitable that at least for highly controversial issues—abortion is only the most obvious—the limited resources of public reason in a radically pluralistic society will be incapable of providing a persuasive basis for decision and justification.[107]

In this predicament, the community would seem to face an unappealing set of alternatives. Lacking any adequate basis in "reason" to make a decision, the community might simply be paralyzed—unable to decide or act. Or, more realistically, the community might make a decision anyway—by smuggling in considerations that do not enjoy the support of any consensus and that cannot plausibly be presented as part of a justification limited to "public reason."[108] We can readily imagine the consequences of choosing this alternative. As such smuggling becomes a common practice, it will be hard to conceal from active participants in the discourse. They will come to understand that public debate often does not explicitly set forth the "real reasons" that in fact motivate the parties to the debate, and that public justifications often fail to present the considerations that in reality determined the decisions for which the justifications are being offered. Everyone is keeping his or her cards hidden, so to speak. Thus, a climate of suspicion will come to pervade the discourse. Moreover, the more generic reasons given for a decision will often be so palpably unpersuasive that it will be natural for those who oppose a particular decision to regard the justification as spurious and disingenuous—as virtually no justification at all. The decision will thus come to have a "Because I said so" quality. (Think of *Roe v. Wade.*) In this way, what began as (and what may still advertise itself as) an enterprise in governance on the basis of reasoning from and toward mutually acceptable commitments will become—or at least will appear to many of those affected to be—the disingenuous exercise of raw power. The prospect brings to mind Alasdair MacIntyre's description of modern moral discourse as "a rhetoric which serves to conceal behind the masks of morality what are in fact the preferences of arbitrary will and desire."[109]

We can appreciate this dynamic, I think, by reference to one of the most thoughtful and balanced treatments of public discourse in contemporary normative theory. Kent Greenawalt's work on the subject is characterized both by the familiar commitment to public reason and liberal constitutional values but also, less typically, by a sincere appreciation of the importance of religion in the lives of many citizens. In an early book on the subject, he astutely pointed out that the complacent assumption that all citizens ought to be able to bracket their religious convictions in public decision-making misconceives the way religion works in the lives of many citizens. And he showed that at least some important issues *cannot* be settled purely on the basis of rational or "publicly accessible" grounds.[110] Greenawalt has consistently sought a moderate or compromise position which would not exclude religious citizens from participation in public life but which would nonetheless adhere to the ideal of a nonsectarian and generally accessible "public reason."

In his effort to find such a "middle ground," Greenawalt has argued that in many contexts it is appropriate for participants to *rely on* their religious convictions in making political decisions but that these convictions should not be openly *expressed* in public discussion or justification. Instead, the arguments or justifications should be presented in more generic terms: not "*God commands . . .,*" but rather "*The public good is best served* by. . . ." (emphasis added). This translation of religious beliefs into the secular language of public reason will be less offensive to nonbelievers, and Greenawalt argues—persuasively, I believe—that the translation need not be *dishonest*; it is only *less revealing* of the full reasons for the position taken. Incomplete disclosure is not equivalent to misrepresentation.[111]

There are surely contexts in which the strategy recommended by Greenawalt is appropriate, perhaps even ethically required.[112] Notice, though, that incomplete disclosure has its own costs, which may be debilitating over the course of time. Suppose that on difficult issues and for the laudable purposes that influence Greenawalt, I routinely provide you with generic justifications for my positions—justifications that, though honest as far as they go, deliberately decline to reveal the deeper reasons for my views and actions. And suppose you do the same with me. Over time we will surely come to understand that we are both engaged in this common practice. What will this understanding do to the quality of our mutual conversation?

Well, in the first place, our discussion can hardly be a very profound or satisfactory exercise of "reason." How could it be, when the decisive grounds for our views and actions are not exposed for examination? We will be engaged more in trading conclusions—or at best "mid-level" and largely conclusory premises—than in examining our deepest convictions and commitments. Further, while our generic strategy may help us to "just get along" in the short run, it is unlikely to lead to any deep rapport or mutual understanding. So long as we stick to this strategy, we will not really get to know and understand each other.

Worse than that, our strategy is likely to breed mutual suspicion. You tell me that you favor political decision X for (generic) reason Y, but I understand that you are not disclosing what is actually the decisive consideration—and that if you did, I would almost surely not accept it. (You understand that I would not accept it, and I understand that you understand this; otherwise you would have incentive to disclose it, and no reason *not* to disclose it.) For all I know, your generic reason may be concealing—from me, and perhaps from yourself as well—what is actually a self-serving motive. It may well be that in purporting to give me "reasons," you are in reality merely trying to manipulate me—to exercise power over me. The pretense of "reason" may be merely an exercise of the "will to power."

I have been speaking speculatively and hypothetically of a dynamic whereby the Enlightenment conception of reason and the kind of discussion it prescribes might deteriorate into a thin discourse of suspicion, manipulation, and willfulness. Does this hypothetical description have any application to the public discourse, and in particular the constitutional discourse, that prevails in the United States today? I think the evidence is overwhelming that it does: Ronald Dworkin is surely not wholly idiosyncratic in perceiving American public discourse today as "the most degraded and negative political discourse in the political world."[113]

The indictment seems peculiarly applicable to contemporary constitutional discourse. Consider the judgments of two respected constitutional scholars. H. Jefferson Powell contends that American constitutional discourse is "incoherent rationally" and hence is not so much an expression of reason as a manifestation of "violence [that] is increasingly wayward, increasingly brutal." "[C]onstitutionalism," Powell asserts, "is one of the most seductive masks worn by state violence."[114] Anthony Amsterdam (along with many other critics, of course) caustically condemns the Supreme Court's decision in *Bush v. Gore*, calling it an instance of "sickening hypocrisy and insincere constitutional posturing"; but the decision, Amsterdam goes on, is not distinctive but merely especially brazen in these respects. "[T]he court finally has revealed unmistakably what it does all the time and usually gets away with: masking result-driven, political, unprincipled decisions in the guise of obedience to rules of law which the justices feel completely free to twist and retwist to suit their purposes."[115]

These pronouncements may seem hyperbolic or even, in Amsterdam's case, almost hysterical. But if the analysis given earlier is correct, the suspicion these statements exude is precisely the attitude that the degenerative dynamic of Enlightenment discourse—of "public reason"—seems constituted to produce.

The problem was diagnosed almost half a century ago by John Courtney Murray. "As we discourse on public affairs," Murray argued, "on the affairs of the commonwealth, we inevitably have to move upward, as it were, into realms of some theoretical generality—into metaphysics, ethics, theology."[116] But of course these are precisely the realms that the modern Enlightenment, as exemplified by thinkers like Rawls, *excludes* from the jurisdiction of "public reason"—because no "overlapping consensus" is likely to obtain there. The result, however, is not a genuine consensus, but simply an impoverishment of the public domain. In the sort of public conversation fostered by the modern Enlightenment Murray perceived "a climate of doubt and bewilderment in which clarity about the larger aims of life is dimmed and the self-confidence of the people is destroyed, so that finally what you have is . . . impotent nihilism."[117] The irony is that this loss of content is not in fact compensated for by any gain in genuine consensus or civility.

> The fact is that among us civility—or civic unity or civic amity, as you will—is a thing of the surface. It is quite easy to see through it. . . . There is not simply an exchange of arguments but of verbal blows. You do not have to probe deeply beneath the surface of civic amity to uncover the structure of passion and war.[118]

Renewing the Enlightenment?

The preceding discussion has suggested that although the modern Enlightenment retains—rhetorically, at least—a commitment to governance in accordance with "reason," this commitment has been transformed into almost the opposite of what it meant in the period leading up to and including the American founding. The eighteenth-century providential worldview which furnished the framework for reasoning has been abandoned, at least for purposes of public and academic discourse. The imperative to live according to Truth has been radically amended to become an admonition *against* bringing Truth into public discourse. And the predictable result has been the development of a public discourse that seems increasingly exhausted and inauthentic—unable to address our real questions and concerns or to generate genuine conviction. Thus, Morton Horwitz observes a "crisis of legitimacy in constitutional thought in which the generally accepted paradigms and modes of thought are no longer felt capable of yielding convincing solutions to constitutional questions."[119]

So the question arises: Might we not be in need of a new Enlightenment—one that would challenge the current intellectual culture in the same way that the classical Enlightenment challenged the culture it inherited from the Middle Ages and early modernity? Is the modern Enlightenment ideal—an ideal promoted in various forms by so many mainstream thinkers and scholars—ripe to be enlightened by a renewed commitment to finding and living by truth, or by Truth?

Perhaps—but there are difficulties. Most obviously, it is difficult to know where the course of trying to live by Truth would lead us today. Would we end up with "natural law," or with the naked nihilism of a brutally honest Social Darwinism? With Plato, or with Thrasymachus? Fear of something like the latter alternative is perhaps the principal bulwark sustaining the modern Enlightenment ideal even though it is no longer the carrier of belief and hope that it reflected two centuries ago.

In addition, the parallel to the origins of the historical Enlightenment is inexact. To be sure, the culture of modern liberal democracy bears many resemblances to the complacent, moderately skeptical intellectual culture of the late sixteenth century against which, at least in Stephen Toulmin's interpretation, the historical Enlightenment was a reaction. But that reaction, Toulmin says, grew out of more than intellectual dissatisfaction with a prevailing nonchalant attitude towards truth: the prevalent attitude was associated as well with social breakdown, and in particular with an inability to curb the destruction being wrought by religious warfare. Today, by contrast, America enjoys relatively high levels of material prosperity and an absence of conspicuous religious or social strife. There is, to be sure, a "culture war" that implicates the passionate concerns of many Americans[120]; still, that struggle is not at this point a source of massive violence and destruction in the way the wars over religion were in the sixteenth and seventeenth centuries.

In short, conditions in America (and in particular for the academic elite, at least in their *material* circumstances) are relatively comfortable at the moment, and comfort is compatible with complacency—toward, among other things, concerns such as "truth." Mill notwithstanding, it is usually easier, if less heroic, to be a pig satisfied than Socrates dissatisfied.

To be sure, the present comfortableness may be thin and also transitory. Some observers see in our current situation signs of moral and cultural decay.[121] Robert Nagel senses just below the cheerful surface of American culture "a brooding fear of potential disaster," and he sees the modern dependence on judicial review as a "recurring manifestation of . . . self-doubt."[122] He may be right. But as Nagel himself argues, this anxiety has in recent decades prompted not honest self-scrutiny or an effort to rethink or return to fundamental truths, but rather a pattern of denial: more energetic "self-deception in a culture already afraid that it is too dependent on euphemism and evasion."[123]

There is a second and perhaps even more important gap in the historical parallel. The intellectual culture of the late Middle Ages and early modernity was strikingly unlike modern Enlightenment culture in at least one crucial respect: it never renounced a concern for truth. On the contrary, the intellectual achievements of the Middle Ages grew out of a massive effort to articulate, and to build a society upon, an overarching truth. The very first chapter of Aquinas's *Summa Contra Gentiles* asserts that "[t]ruth must consequently be the ultimate end of the whole universe, and the consideration of the wise man aims principally at truth." Later thinkers such as Montaigne may have harbored greater doubts about the scope of human understanding, as Toulmin argues, but they did not disavow the commitment to finding and living by as much truth as was attainable. So in trying to redirect life toward a greater conformity with truth, the classical Enlightenment was building on a commitment that was already in place.

By contrast, modern Enlightenment culture, as discussed above, is characterized by a self-conscious effort to distance at least public discourse from the larger questions of truth, or from the "whole truth"; and this effort is reinforced by post-modern squeamishness about the vocabulary and the very possibility of truth, and especially of Truth. In this setting, one can imagine a confrontation in which a revivified but disconcerted Descartes asserts that the prevailing modern discourse in the public realm has lost its commitment to truth. A Rawls might respond, "Excellent! That's what we've been working for," while a yawning Rorty might remark, "This sort of talk about 'truth' bores me. Can't we *please* discuss something else?"[124]

Prognosis is always hazardous, to be sure, but a renewed commitment to truth—in constitutional discourse, in public deliberation generally—does not seem imminent. We can speculate about "Alternatives to

Enlightenment Constitutionalism," but it appears that for the time being, we may have no alternative except to hunker down for what looks to be a long, dark night of Enlightenment.

Notes

1. Bruce Ackerman, *We the People: Foundations* (Cambridge: Belknap Press of Harvard University Press, 1991), 59–60.
2. Roy Porter, *The Enlightenment*, 2nd ed. (London: Palgrave Macmillan, 2001), 9.
3. Rene Descartes, "Discourse on Method," in *Discourse on Method and Meditations on First Philosophy*, trans. Donald A. Cress, 4th ed. (Indianapolis: Hacknett Publishing Company, 1998), 6.
4. See, e.g., Jacob Cooke, ed., *The Federalist* (Middletown, CT: Wesleyan University Press, 1961), no. 9. For a more extensive discussion of how the framers saw the Constitution as an unprecedented manifestation of reason, see Steven D. Smith, *The Constitution and the Pride of Reason* (New York: Oxford University Press, 1998), 3–4, 31–47.
5. Quoted in Henry F. May, *The Divided Heart: Essays on Protestantism and the Enlightenment in America* (New York: Oxford University Press, 1991), 159.
6. Cf. Joseph Ellis, *Founding Brothers* (New York: Alfred A. Knopf, 2001), 5:

   > "Based on what we now know about the military history of the American Revolution, if the British commanders had prosecuted the war more vigorously in its earliest stages, the Continental Army might very well have been destroyed at the start and the movement for American independence nipped in the bud. The signers of the Declaration would then have been hunted down, tried, and executed for treason."

7. John Courtney Murray, S. J. (Society of Jesus), *We Hold These Truths* (New York: Sheed and Ward, 1960), xi.
8. Richard Rorty explains that "[u]ncapitalized, 'truth' and 'goodness' name properties of sentences, or of actions and situations. Capitalized, they are the proper names of objects—goals or standards that can be loved with all one's heart and soul, and mind, objects of ultimate concern." Richard Rorty, *Consequences of Pragmatism* (Minneapolis: University of Minnesota Press, 1982), xiv.
9. Cf. Donald W. Livingston, "The Founding and the Enlightenment: Two Theories of Sovereignty," in *Vital Remnants: America's Founding and the Western Tradition* ed. Gary L. Gregg, rev. ed. (Wilmington, DE: ISI Books, 1999), 242, 244: "[R]eason is conceived as being independent of tradition. Tradition is the great horror of the Enlightenment."

10. See generally Immanuel Kant, *An Answer to the Question: What is Enlightenment?*, reprinted in *What is Enlightenment? Eighteenth-Century Answers and Twentieth-Century Questions*, ed. James Schmidt (Berkeley: University of California Press, 1996), 58.

11. Ernest Gellner, *Reason and Culture* (Oxford: Blackwell, 1992), 13.

12. Ibid., 18, 13, 14. See also Stephen Toulmin, *Cosmopolis: The Hidden Agenda of Modernity* (Chicago: University of Chicago Press, 1990), 175: "[T]he idea of 'starting again with a clean slate' has been as recurrent a preoccupation of modern European thinkers as the quest for certainty itself. The belief [is] that any new construction is truly rational only if it demolishes all that was before it and starts from scratch."

13. Cf. Toulmin, *Cosmopolis*, 178: "The belief that, by cutting ourselves off from the inherited ideas of our cultures, we can 'clean the slate' and make a fresh start, is as illusory as the hope for a comprehensive system of theory that is capable of giving us timeless certainty and coherence."

14. Gellner, *Reason and Culture*, 159.

15. James Q. Whitman, "Reason or Hermeticism: A Comment," *Southern California Interdisciplinary Law Journal* 5 (1997): 193–204, 193, 195.

16. See Carl Becker, *The Heavenly City of the Eighteenth-Century Philosophers* (New Haven: Yale University Press, 1932).

17. Plato, *Gorgias*, 489e, in *The Collected Dialogues of Plato*, ed. Edith Hamilton and Huntington Cairns (New York: Pantheon Books, 1961).

18. Karl N. Llewellyn, "A Realistic Jurisprudence—The Next Step," *Columbia Law Review* 30 (1930): 431–465, 431, 443.

19. Mark 7:1–16, 12:28–34.

20. Becker, *Heavenly City*, 29–30.

21. Toulmin, *Cosmopolis*, 45.

22. Ibid., 71.

23. Saint Thomas Aquinas, *Summa Contra Gentiles*, I, chap. 2.

24. Saint Thomas Aquinas, *Summa Theologica*, II.II., Q. 94, A. 1.

25. For a summary of the incident, see William Searle Holdsworth, *A History of English Law*, 12 vols. (London: Methuen and Co., 1937), 5: 429–431.

26. May, *Divided Heart*, 155.

27. Cf. Jefferson to Peter Carr, August 10, 1787, in *The Portable Thomas Jefferson*, ed. Merrill D. Peterson (New York: Penguin Books, 1975), 423, 425: "State a moral case to a ploughman and a professor. The former will decide it as well, and often better than the latter, because he has not been led astray by artificial rules."

28. Donald Livingston explains that Enlightenment thinkers saw "reason" as the opposite of "tradition" precisely because tradition was an embodiment of "scandalous particularities." Livingston, "Founding and Enlightenment," 244.

29. Cf. Christopher T. Wonnell, "Truth and the Marketplace of Ideas," *University of California at Davis Law Review* 19 (1986): 669–728, 669, 670: "The linkage between free speech and truth seemed particularly persuasive in Enlightenment thinkers convinced of the power of human reason."

30. May, *Divided Heart*, 147–148; emphasis deleted, 150.

31. Louis Dupre, *Passage to Modernity: An Essay in the Hermeneutics of Nature and Culture* (New Haven: Yale University Press, 1993), 3, 11, 18.

32. Becker, *Heavenly City*, 65.

33. Overwhelming evidence for this assertion is marshaled in Daniel Boorstin, *The Lost World of Thomas Jefferson* (1948; repr., Chicago: University of Chicago Press, 1993). See also generally Henry F. May, *The Enlightenment in America* (Oxford: Oxford University Press, 1976).

34. Boorstin, *Lost World*, 196. See also page 194: "The word 'right' was always a signpost pointing back to the divine plan of the Creation."

35. Henry F. May, *Ideas, Faiths, and Feelings* (New York: Oxford University Press, 1983), 131, 135.

36. See James Turner, *Without God, Without Creed: The Origins of Unbelief in America* (Baltimore: Johns Hopkins University Press, 1985), 44.

37. May, *Divided Heart*, 151.

38. Michael P. Zuckert, "Is Modern Liberalism Compatible with Limited Government? The Case of Rawls," in *Natural Law, Liberalism, and Morality*, ed. Robert P. George (Oxford: Clarendon Press, 1996), 49, 80.

39. Rawls asserts that his position is unlike "Enlightenment liberalism" in that it does not present liberalism as a comprehensive doctrine and does not attack orthodox Christianity. John Rawls, *Political Liberalism* (New York: Columbia University Press, 1993; paper ed., 1996), xl (reference is to the 1996 edition); John Rawls, "The Idea of Public Reason Revisited," in *The Law of Peoples* (Cambridge, MA: Harvard University Press, 1999), 131, 176.

40. See, e.g., Rawls, *Political Liberalism*, li: "[W]e must give them reasons they can not only understand . . . but reasons we might reasonably expect that they as free and equal might reasonably also accept."

41. See ibid., 212–254.

42. Ibid., 224.

43. Ibid., 134.

44. Stephen Macedo, "In Defense of Liberal Public Reason: Are Slavery and Abortion Hard Cases?" in *Natural Law and Public Reason*, ed. Robert P. George and Christopher Wolfe (Washington, DC: Georgetown University Press, 2000), 11, 13, 25–26.

45. Ibid., 25.

46. Cf. Robert K. Faulkner, "Jefferson and the Enlightened Science of Liberty," in *Reason and Republicanism: Thomas Jefferson's Legacy of*

Liberty, ed. Gary L. McDowell and Sharon L. Noble (Lanham: Rowman and Littlefield Publishers, 1997), 31, 34: "While Jefferson celebrated a self-governing people, he despised and feared city mobs and, in general, the unenlightened."

47. May, *Divided Heart,* 163–166.
48. See Peter L. Berger, "The Desecularization of the World: A Global Overview," in *The Desecularization of the World,* ed. Peter L. Berger (Grand Rapids, MI: William B. Eerdmans Publishing Company, 1999), 1.
49. See ibid., 10: "There exists an international subculture composed of people with Western-type higher education, especially in the humanities and social sciences, that is indeed secularized. This subculture is the principal 'carrier' of progressive, Enlightened beliefs and values."
50. This supposition glosses over major difficulties. From the fact that Enlightenment reason no longer supports the providential worldview within which the founding generation operated, does it logically follow, one might ask, that this conception *does* impel us to adopt a "secular" worldview or discourse? Isn't that worldview also controversial— and hence ruled out by the consensus criterion? The modern partisan of Enlightenment is likely to respond, I think, that a secular worldview *is* uncontroversial (among properly educated and "reasonable" people, at least), or that a secular worldview is "neutral" among the controversial alternatives, or that a secular worldview is what we are left with by default from the inability of "reason" to support any more theologically or metaphysically ambitious worldviews. All of these responses are deeply problematic, but for immediate, mainly descriptive purposes we need not be too scrupulous on this point.
51. Kathleen M. Sullivan, "Religion and Liberal Democracy," *University of Chicago Law Review* 59 (1992): 195–223, 195, 201.
52. *Lemon v. Kurtzman,* 403 U.S. 602, 612–613 (1971).
53. See, e.g., *Capitol Square Review Bd. v. Pinette,* 515 U.S. 753 (1995).
54. See, e.g., *Wallace v. Jaffree,* 472 U.S. 38 (1985) (striking down a "moment of silence" law under the particular circumstances of the case in part because of statements by the sponsor that the Court interpreted as expressing a religious purpose).
55. For a careful exposition and critical analysis of Rawls's position on this point, see J. Judd Owen, *Religion and the Demise of Liberal Rationalism* (Chicago: University of Chicago Press, 2001), 100–121.
56. Macedo, "In Defense of Liberal Public Reason," 18.
57. The theorists are perfectly candid on this point. Macedo explains, e.g., that "philosophical and religious views . . . proceed from the point of view of a *comprehensive conception of truth* and the human good as a whole." But "in the modern world, . . . people disagree about the views of truth as a whole," and consequently such views are not appropriate bases for public discourse. Ibid., 18 (emphasis added).
58. Ibid., 23–24.

59. Zuckert, "Is Modern Liberalism Compatible with Limited Government?" 72. Cf. Owen, *Religion and the Demise of Liberal Rationalism*, 127: "The 'virtue' of getting along, of not insisting on anything (too) controversial, is elevated by Rawls to the highest possible plane . . . Nothing, Rawls tells us, can be so important that it is worth disrupting the peaceful scheme of social cooperation."

60. See generally Robert Samuel Summers, *Instrumentalism and American Legal Theory* (Ithaca: Cornell University Press, 1982).

61. See Robert F. Nagel, *Constitutional Cultures* (Berkeley: University of California Press, 1989), 106–107.

62. Cf. Richard A. Posner, *Economic Analysis of Law*, 5th ed. (New York: Aspen, 1998), 287: "But the efficiency ethic takes the existing distribution of income and wealth, and the underlying human qualities that generate that distribution, as given, and within very broad limits (what limits?) is uncritical of the changes in that distribution that are brought about by efficient transactions between persons unequally endowed with the world's tangible and intangible goods."

63. See, e.g., Mary Ann Glendon, "Foundations of Human Rights: The Unfinished Business," *American Journal of Jurisprudence* 44 (1999): 1–14, 1, 1–2, 12–13. Michael Perry, a long-standing proponent of human rights, concedes that the justification for human rights is perhaps the only essential matter of public concern for which no secular justification is available: human rights, Perry concludes, are "ineliminably religious." Michael J. Perry, *The Idea of Human Rights: Four Inquiries* (New York: Oxford University Press, 1998), 11–41.

64. Louis P. Pojman, "On Equal Human Worth: A Critique of Contemporary Egalitarianism," in *Equality: Selected Readings*, ed. Louis P. Pojman and Robert Westmoreland (New York: Oxford University Press, 1996), 294.

65. Ibid., 287.

66. Ibid., 295.

67. The first argument holds that "God created all humans with an equal amount of some property P, which constitutes high value." The second argument suggests that "actual value may be different in different people but grace compensates the difference." Ibid.

68. Ibid., 282.

69. Ibid., 283–294.

70. Ibid., 283.

71. Ibid., 296. For an analysis closely paralleling Pojman's in important respects, see George P. Fletcher, *Our Secret Constitution* (Oxford: Oxford University Press, 2001), 91–105.

72. Ibid., 95–96.

73. In this vein, J. Judd Owen explains that "Rawlsian liberalism's desire to refrain from touching upon the truth of any comprehensive doctrine whatever entails a silence about its own truth." Owen, *Religion and the Demise of Liberal Rationalism*, 109. For the same

reason, Owen claims, " 'public reason' cannot itself be justified or even argued for with public reasons. It can only be asserted." Ibid., 120.

74. Macedo, "In Defense of Liberal Public Reason," 27.
75. Ernest Gellner explains that "[i]ndividualism, egalitarianism, freedom, sustained innovation—these traits are, in the comparative context of world history, unusual, not to say eccentric." "No wonder that Americans tend to treat these principles as universal and inherent in the human condition. The preamble to the American Declaration of Independence informs them that its truths are self-evident, and Americans tend to assume it to be so. But they are nothing of the kind: these assumptions are in fact heretical or unintelligible in most other cultures." Ernest Gellner, *Postmodernism, Reason, and Religion* (London: Routledge, 1992), 52.
76. See, e.g., Rawls, *Law of Peoples*, 132 (noting, with respect to those with a "zeal to embody the whole truth in politics," that "[p]olitical liberalism does not engage those who think in this way"), at 178 ("They assert that the religiously true, or the philosophically true, overrides the politically reasonable. We simply say that such a doctrine is politically unreasonable. Within political liberalism nothing more need be said.")
77. See Gellner, *Postmodernism, Reason, and Religion*, 49.
78. Vittorio Hosle, *Objective Idealism, Ethics, and Politics* (Notre Dame, IN: University of Notre Dame Press, 1998), 44.
79. The classic modern exposition is Peter Westen, "The Empty Idea of Equality," *Harvard Law Review* 95 (1982): 537–596, 537.
80. I discuss this rhetorical strategy in the religion clause context at greater length in Steven D. Smith, *Getting Over Equality* (New York: NYU Press, 2001), 13–20.
81. Zuckert, *Modern Liberalism*, 77–78 (emphasis added).
82. Paul F. Campos, "Secular Fundamentalism," in *Against the Law*, ed. Paul F. Campos, Pierre Schlag, and Steven D. Smith (Durham, NC: Duke University Press, 1996), 181, 201–202.
83. Stanley Fish, *The Trouble with Principle* (Cambridge, MA: Harvard University Press, 1999), 194, 68.
84. Ibid., 195.
85. See, e.g., Rawls, *Political Liberalism*, 49–50.
86. May, *Divided Heart*, 155.
87. For example, Rawls's famous abortion footnote, in which he peremptorily pronounces "to that extent unreasonable" any doctrine (and presumably any person embracing such a doctrine) that would restrict abortion beyond approximately the trimester framework of *Roe v. Wade*, would surely exclude millions of Americans for purposes of that issue. See Rawls, *Political Liberalism*, 243, n. 42. For some less than lucid (to me, at least) backtracking, see Rawls, *Law of Peoples*, 169, n. 80.

88. Boorstin, *Lost World*, 194.
89. Rawls, e.g., rehearses and reaffirms the standard received doctrines and decisions protecting freedom of speech and press. Rawls, *Political Liberalism*, 340–356.
90. In newer, less familiar contexts, the inheritance may speak less clearly, and may also pose conflicts between expression and other Enlightened values such as equality. Hence, issues involving, for instance, "hate speech" or pornography that arguably promotes the subordination of women may leave the partisans of Enlightenment uncertain and divided. See Owen M. Fiss, *The Irony of Free Speech* (Cambridge: Harvard University Press, 1996), 5–15.
91. Rawls, *Law of Peoples*, 147. Rawls allows, though, that other values beyond the reproduction of society might be admissible for consideration, including "the equality of women" and the needs of children.
92. Compare ibid., 134 ("The idea of public reason does not apply to the background culture with its many forms of non-public reason nor to media of any kind.") with Rawls, *Political Liberalism*, 215: "My aim is to consider first the strongest case where the political questions concern the most fundamental matters . . . Should [the limits of public reason] hold there, we can then proceed to other cases. Still, I grant that it is usually highly desirable to settle political questions by invoking the values of public reason."
93. See, e.g., Philip Quinn, "Religious Citizens Within the Limits of Public Reason," *The Modern Schoolman* 78 (2001): 105–124, 105, 107, 117.
94. Rawls, *Law of Peoples*, 152.
95. I acknowledge, however, that Rawls's explanation on this point seems less than clear, and hence might be interpreted more leniently. For example, the requirement that a nonconforming argument be supported by "public reasons" that are "sufficient" conceivably might be understood to impose only something like constitutional law's traditional, very minimal "rational basis" requirement; in that case, both the restrictiveness and the significance of the public reason ideal would be drastically diluted. Absent further illumination, there seems no way to know. Cf. Rawls, *Law of Peoples*, 153 ("Yet the details about how to satisfy this proviso must be worked out in practice and cannot feasibly be governed by a clear family of rules given in advance.")
96. Ibid., 136. Once again, supporters emphasize this limit. See Quinn, "Religious Citizens," 120.
97. John Stuart Mill, *On Liberty*, ed. Currin V. Shields (Indianapolis: Bobbs-Merrill Co., 1956), 7.
98. Jeffrie G. Murphy, "Religious Conviction and Political Advocacy (A Commentary on Quinn)," *The Modern Schoolman* 78 (2001): 125–134, 125, 127.
99. Nagel, *Constitutional Cultures*, 111–112.

100. Nagel, *Constitutional Cultures* 116–117.
101. Robert F. Nagel, *Judicial Power and American Character* (New York: Oxford University Press, 1994), 151–154.
102. Ibid., 110. See generally ibid., 103–121.
103. Ibid., 143–144.
104. John A. Coleman, *An American Strategic Theology* (New York: Paulist Press, 1982), 193.
105. Ronald Dworkin, *Life's Dominion* (New York: Vintage Books, 1994), 68–101.
106. Perry, *Idea of Human Rights*, 25–29.
107. Rawls attempts to avoid this problem by stipulating that an "essential feature of public reason is that its political conceptions should be complete," meaning that it is adequate to "give a reasonable answer to all, or to nearly all, questions involving constitutional essentials and matters of basic justice." Rawls, *Law of Peoples*, 144–145. A discourse lacking such completeness, it seems, would not qualify as a form of "public reason." This stipulation does nothing to address the problem, however, but merely prompts a reformulation of the objection: *not* "[p]ublic reason will leave many questions unanswered," but rather "[p]ublic reason (so defined) does not exist."
108. Rawls purports to forbid this course but instead suggests that "when there seems to be a stand-off, that is, when . . . arguments seem evenly balanced on both sides, . . . citizens must vote for the ordering of political values they sincerely think *the most reasonable.*" Ibid., 168 (emphasis added). So put, this imperative seems akin to a recommendation that says that if you have to choose between what look to be two equally sized pieces of pie, pick the piece that looks bigger. In any case, it is misleading to describe the problem under consideration here as a situation in which the "arguments seem evenly balanced on both sides"; the real problem is that the circumscribed resources of public reason are inadequate to convincingly justify *any* answer to a question.
109. Alasdair MacIntyre, *After Virtue*, 2nd. ed. (Notre Dame, IN: University of Notre Dame Press, 1984), 71.
110. See generally Kent Greenawalt, *Religious Convictions and Political Choice* (New York: Oxford University Press, 1988).
111. See, e.g., Kent Greenawalt, *Private Consciences and Public Reasons* (New York: Oxford University Press, 1995), 137–140, 163–164.
112. I have discussed this point (and Greenawalt's effort to find a moderate position) at greater length, and favorably, in Steven D. Smith, "Augustinian Liberal," *Notre Dame Law Review* 74 (1999): 1673–1690.
113. Ronald Dworkin, *Sovereign Virtue* (Cambridge, MA: Harvard University Press, 2000), 369.
114. H. Jefferson Powell, *The Moral Tradition of American Constitutionalism* (Durham: Duke University Press, 1993), 262, 47.

115. Anthony G. Amsterdam, "The Law Is Left Slowly Twisting in the Wind," *L.A. Times*, December 17, 2000, M5.

116. See, e.g., Murray, *We Hold These Truths*, 15.

117. Ibid., 12.

118. Ibid., 18–19.

119. Morton J. Horwitz, "Foreword: The Constitution of Change: Legal Fundamentality without Fundamentalism," *Harvard Law Review* 107 (1995): 30–117, 30, 40.

120. See James Davison Hunter, *Culture Wars* (New York: Basic Books, 1991).

121. See, e.g., Gertrude Himmelfarb, *The De-Moralization of Society* (New York: Alfred A. Knopf, 1994), 221–257; Hosle, *Objective Idealism*, 41 (asserting that "we are manifestly living in a time of moral, political, artistic, and intellectual decay").

122. Nagel, *Judicial Power*, 142, 156.

123. Ibid., 155.

124. Asserting that "truth is not the sort of thing one should expect to have a philosophically interesting theory about," Rorty explains that when pragmatists like himself "suggest that we not ask questions about the nature of Truth and Goodness, they do not . . . have a 'relativistic' or 'subjectivist' theory of Truth or Goodness. They would simply like to change the subject." Rorty, *Consequences of Pragmatism*, xiii–xiv.

Chapter 2

The Positivization of Natural Rights

Martin Loughlin

Although the idea of rights constitutes an important strand of modern political thought, for most of the modern era it has generally remained subservient to other claims of sovereignty, nationalism, and democracy. It is only since the Second World War that rights discourse has been able to establish itself as a common currency of both politics and law. Contemporary public discourse, especially that which appeals to such core values as liberty, equality, and justice, is now invariably cast in the language of rights. We live today in an "age of rights."[1]

This contemporary "rights revolution"[2] is linked to the triumph of social power over political power, to the emergence of a more individualistic conception of society, and, at least in an ideological sense, to the formation of a political order built on the foundation of the rights-bearing individual. Rights discourse has therefore acquired its thrust from a radical shift in our understanding of the political relationship between state and citizen. The traditional focus of political thought—on the rights of sovereigns and the duties of subjects[3]—has been inverted, the emphasis now being placed on the rights of citizens and the obligations of government. Since rights and duties are twin aspects of a reciprocal relationship,[4] this looks like a distinction without a difference. But in practice, this inversion has had an important effect on the way governmental authority is constituted. It is only when rights are given positive institutional effect that this effect is disclosed. This positivization of the basic rights of citizens has the potential to reconfigure the architecture of constitutional law.

To assess this potential, it is necessary to trace the intellectual source of the modern rights movement and chart its influence on contemporary legal and political practice. Although the rights revolution is a recent phenomenon, its intellectual origins go back quite a way.

Most roads lead back to the Enlightenment, and this particular one charts the reconstitution of governmental authority after the American and French revolutions. At its center runs a belief in some notion of natural rights.[5]

Writing in 1767, Rousseau commented that: "The great problem of politics, which I compare to the problem of squaring the circle in geometry . . . [is]: How to find a form of government which puts the law above man."[6] The need for a transcendent principle was acutely felt in the late eighteenth century, when the Americans and the French overthrew their established orders and were obliged to devise new frameworks of government. These revolutions, paradoxically, "drove the very 'enlightened' men of the eighteenth century to plead for some religious sanction at the very moment when they were about to emancipate the secular realm fully from the influences of the churches and to separate politics and religion once and for all."[7] While this led some, such as Robespierre, to promote a cult of the Supreme Being,[8] many of the most influential figures of the period appealed to "nature." This was a conception of nature occupying a key location between man and God. For the American colonists in particular, the only route to knowledge of God's will was through the discovery of the laws of nature, and these, as Jefferson said, would doubtless be "the laws of 'nature's God'. "[9]

Although this belief in the existence of inalienable natural rights has had a contentious history, natural rights discourse has certainly had a significant impact on modern constitutional thought. Our concern, however, is less with the history than with a pattern of juristic thought. The objective will be to investigate how a political discourse of natural rights has permeated legal discourse and then, through positivization—that is, through the institutionalization of a conception of law as an expression of basic rights—has reconfigured the relationship between law and government.

Natural Rights and Political Order

The source of natural rights doctrines can be tracked back beyond the Revolutionary documents of the late-eighteenth century to the early modern period, when the foundations of political authority, rooted in classical natural law, were first questioned.[10]

In classical natural law, law was conceived as a catalogue of duties. On the premise that all beings have a natural end, natural law derived a basic duty of humans to realize their destiny. Humans were thus placed under a duty to pursue the virtuous life. In this classical image, law did not establish general norms of conduct: "the law is . . . merely society's medicine which re-establishes order, putting each person in his place when this cosmic order, like a diseased organ, is disturbed."[11] With an image of law as that which is right, classical natural law did not recognize the idea of subjective rights, of rights vested in the individual and enforceable against the collectivity.

The altered worldview which made possible the emergence of the idea of subjective rights happened during the early modern period, when the classical structure of duties was challenged by a conception of political order based on individual rights. This shift was recorded most dramatically in the work of Hobbes. Since Hobbes is best known, to lawyers at least, as a theorist who promoted a conception of law as the command of the sovereign authority, thereby becoming one of the most influential authors of legal positivism, this claim might seem surprising. However, it is not his solution to the question of political order that is relevant, but his method of characterizing the problem.

Hobbes began with the individual as a bearer of natural rights within a state of nature, a depiction of the natural state of existence that was innovative.[12] His sense of the natural was distilled from his understanding of how people actually live. Arguing that people are mainly driven by passion rather than reason, Hobbes derived natural law from the most powerful of all passions—that of self-preservation. He argued that the one fundamental natural right that people possess is the right to preserve themselves. It is this need to maintain their personal security that makes people entering civil society give up their natural rights in favor of an all-powerful sovereign.

Hobbes argued that in the compact which marks the transition from the state of nature to the establishment of civil society, this natural right is extinguished.[13] His analysis therefore suggests that obligation to others arises from contract: justice basically requires individuals to fulfill their contractual commitments. It was this aspect of Hobbes's theory of natural right that Locke modified and extended. Presenting a more benign account of the natural state, in which people acquire ownership of commodities through the expenditure of their labor, Locke argues that the main reason people contract with one another to place themselves under a governing authority is the preservation of their property.[14] When a system of government is established, natural rights are not alienated but are exchanged for state-sanctioned civil rights. For Locke, private autonomy is secured through property and contract and the function of government is to preserve and protect this right. Government fulfills a defined and limited set of tasks, and if it fails properly to discharge these responsibilities power devolves back to the people. For the purpose of preserving their natural rights, the people retain a right of rebellion.[15]

The early modern political theorists thus devised schemes of government based not on an objective natural order which humans have a duty to preserve, but on the centrality of the individual as a rights-bearing subject. But if individuals are liberated from the frame of a natural ordering, where are they to obtain instruction on the good? If a political theory rests on subjective right, especially in a Lockean scheme where natural rights are retained in the commonwealth, this surely will lead to mere license, as each individual pursues what he or she most desires.

Recognizing this problem, natural rights theorists have argued that once the link with a preordained natural order is broken, guidance is supplied by our power of reason. Rousseau's attempt to supply a solution has been especially influential. He argued that the limits of liberty are not determined vertically, by appealing to some transcendental standard, but horizontally.[16] In Leo Strauss's concise formulation of Rousseau's position: "I am just if I grant to every other man the same rights which I claim for myself, regardless of what these rights may be."[17] Rousseau's insight reaches its apogee in Kant's objective principle of morality, the categorical imperative: act according to that maxim which we can will should become a universal law.[18]

For natural rights theorists, political order is justified by some form of social contract entered into by rights-bearing individuals: individuals give up a portion of their natural rights to secure civil order. Government does not reflect a natural order imposing duties on subjects; it is a juridical order established for the protection of subjective rights. And once the foundation of political order is conceived as a Kantian imperative, the affinity between morality and politics is readily identified.

Natural Rights and Modern Constitutions

Natural rights theories have flourished in European political thought for only short periods. Richard Tuck has indicated that rights theories have prospered only in two significant historical periods: from 1350 to 1450 and from 1590 to 1670.[19] Placed in the context of European thought, Tuck suggests not only that these periods "are freakish and fitful," but that "their dismantling has been a matter of high priority for succeeding generations."[20] Nonetheless, Lockean rights theory, formulated at the tail end of the latter period, has had a real impact on the modern political world.

Locke's influence on political practice was certainly not due to the rigor and lucidity of his philosophical analysis. In Carl Becker's assessment, Locke's work "is not particularly cogent unless you accept his assumptions as proved, nor lucid until you restate it to suit yourself." Rather, continued Becker, "it is lumbering, involved, obscured by innumerable and conflicting qualifications—a dreary devil of an argument staggering from assumption posited as premise to conclusion implicit in that assumption."[21] Locke's influence was essentially fortuitous. For various circumstantial reasons, his theories exerted a powerful hold on the leaders of the two great revolutions of the late eighteenth century. This can be gauged by the form and phrasing of Thomas Jefferson's draft of the American Declaration of Independence, which closely followed Locke's *Second Treatise*.[22] But Locke's conclusions needed little argument, since to the colonists they were simply an expression of common sense.[23]

Although the language of rights constituted the American colonists' "native tongue," such rights claims "came in many forms— and anyone who set out to catalogue them faced an exhausting task."[24] Can, then, a differentiation be made between inalienable natural rights and bundles of conventional rights whose exercise were subject to regulation by the state? During the Revolutionary era, such a division was both impractical and unnecessary. This political work was, after all, undertaken by practical reformers, not professional philosophers. It is sufficient to recognize that the appeal to nature provided the most powerful rhetorical justification in defense of these higher-order claims. The language of natural rights was deployed regularly in debate and explicitly invoked in the early declarations.[25]

The discourse of natural rights was often blended with historical arguments, both through appeals to traditional common law rights and to the principles of the British Constitution. But the influence of these claims should not to be taken too seriously.[26] The colonists invoked a highly rationalistic conception of the common law. This was the common law refracted through the prism of Coke, Locke, and Blackstone, that is, the common law permeated with the doctrine of natural rights.[27] Roger Sherman, one of the most influential of the American founders, summed up the way in which this historical argument was used: "the colonies adopt the common law not as common law, but as the highest reason."[28] Similarly, the precepts of the British Constitution, the founders claimed, were rooted "in the law of God and nature."[29]

What the founders could not avoid, however, was the fact that traditional English liberties—the liberties expressed in the great charters of Magna Carta, the Petition of Right, and the Bill of Rights—were universally recognized to be concessions yielded by the sovereign. These liberties were "civil privileges, provided by society, in lieu of the natural liberties given up by individuals."[30] On this vital point, the Hobbesian approach had to be contrasted with American (i.e., Lockean) ideas of individuals as the carriers of inalienable natural rights. Thus, the function of civil society and its government in the American conception, Wilson argued, was "to secure and to enlarge the exercise of the natural rights of its members."[31] This appeal to natural rights was nothing less than a call for deliverance from the shackles of history.[32] In American political discourse, natural rights provided the foundation for constructing a formal constitution of political society. And their consequent actions led to a revolution in constitutional understanding.

Although the term "constitution" has been in use over many centuries, its meaning has changed in the modern period. In the fifteenth century, Sir John Fortescue, echoing Roman law usage, used the term as a synonym for formally enacted law. "The customs and the judgements of the law of nature," Fortescue observed, "after they have been reduced to writing, and promulgated by the sufficient authority of the prince, and commanded to be kept, are changed into a constitution or something in the nature of statutes."[33] While the idea of limitations on government existed within the structure of medieval government, the terminology of constitutional government did not. Although a broader formulation gradually entered into common usage, constitution generally referred to the entire body of laws, institutions, and customs that comprised the commonwealth.[34] This sense of constitution is one which the British have retained within the technical vocabulary of the law.

The modern alteration in meaning of the term "constitution" is directly traceable to the American act of founding. It is highlighted most clearly in the work of Thomas Paine. In *Rights of Man*, Paine argued that governments derive their authority from one of three sources: superstition (i.e., priestcraft), force (especially of conquerors), and reason (especially concerning "the common rights of man").[35] The general type to which particular regimes conform can be identified, he suggested, by asking whether governments have arisen *out* of the people or *over* the people. The answer lies in the constitution of a country. This requires a clear definition of that term. A constitution, Paine suggested, "has not an ideal, but a real existence; and whenever it cannot be produced in a visible form, there is none."[36] Elaborating, Paine declared that a constitution "is a thing *antecedent* to a government, and a government is only the creature of a constitution. The constitution is not the act of its government, but of the people constituting a government."[37]

Using the analogy of the relation of court to legislature, Paine argued that a constitution "is to a government, what the laws made afterwards by that government are to a court of judicature. The court of judicature does not make the laws, neither can it alter them; it only acts in conformity to the laws made: and the government is in like manner governed by the constitution."[38] From Paine's perspective, English government, having arisen from conquest rather than society, arose over the people. Despite modifications, "the country has never regenerated itself" and "is therefore without a constitution."[39]

Although the American Revolution brought about a shift in the idea of the constitution, its new, modern sense carries a twofold meaning. For Paine the expression referred primarily to the constituting act—the constitution as antecedent to government—whereby a people constitutes itself as a state. But the term was also used to refer to the product of the constituting act, that is, to the formal document establishing the framework of government.[40]

The colonists were familiar with the idea of having the framework of government written in documentary form from the company charters that provided them with their institutions of government, so this latter sense of a constitution came readily to them.[41] But the use of a formal constitutional document was new in that it was intended to establish a body of fundamental law. The makers of the Constitution wanted not only to establish the formal separation of governmental powers, in which "ambition must be made to counteract ambition,"[42] but also to ensure that the Constitution took effect as higher-status law.[43] Alexander Hamilton recognized that it was for the judges to ascertain the meaning of the Constitution just as they determined "the meaning of any particular act proceeding from the legislative body" and that "if there should happen to be an irreconcilable variance between the two, that which has the superior obligation and validity ought, of course, to be preferred; or, in other words, the Constitution ought to be preferred to the statute."[44]

The American Constitution thus instituted the idea of fundamental law embodied in a text, but also the sense that a constitution formed a hierarchy of laws. The integrity of this framework would be policed by the judiciary. This type of institutional protection must therefore rank as a further innovation flowing from the Revolution.[45] The American Constitution takes its place as the first modern constitution.

The American Revolution was shortly followed by the French Revolution, an action which Finer calls "the most important single event in the entire history of government."[46] While the American Revolution imposed a new constitutional superstructure on an existing set of representative institutions, thereby formalizing a change in the governing regime, in France an entire system was destroyed and a new order recast. The French Revolution "razed and effaced all the ancient institutions of France, undermined the foundations of all other European states, and is still sending its shock-waves throughout the rest of the world."[47]

The great significance of the American and French revolutions lies not so much in the fact that the established order had been overthrown in the name of the rights of the people, but that "the people" had acted to vindicate their natural rights. On this point, the French were directly following the American revolutionaries.[48] In furtherance of their natural rights, the state was reconstituted and the functions of government delimited. By establishing a modern constitution that laid down this formal framework of government, the people no longer needed to rely on Locke's residual right of rebellion; citizens could now expect an independent judiciary to protect their basic rights.

Natural Rights and Positive Law

Utilizing a discourse of natural rights, the American and French revolutionaries reconstituted political order and formally adopted new model constitutions. The primary instrument through which these changes were instituted was the formal declaration of fundamental rights. These declarations set in train the positivization of natural rights.

The essence of positivization has been captured by Jürgen Habermas, who referred to the process as "the autonomous creation, by contract, of legal compulsion springing solely from the compulsion of philosophical reason."[49] But this shift of supreme juristic significance was not effected immediately and was not without its ambiguities. It was not until 1803 that the Supreme Court asserted its power to refuse to enforce congressional legislation that conflicted with the Court's interpretation of the Constitution.[50] And notwithstanding Paine's commendation that "in America the law is King,"[51] it was only in the latter-half of the twentieth century that the Supreme Court initiated a rights revolution.

These charters of rights were ambivalent. There is little evidence to suggest that they were ever intended to be of central importance.

Significantly, they were presented either in the form of a preamble (in the case of the French and some earlier American state declarations) or as amendments (in the American case) to these new constitutions.[52] While these charters did reflect the spirit of the new arrangements, it was not obvious that they would give rise to justiciable rights. In part, this was because of the novelty of the exercise, which generated a degree of ambiguity concerning the role of the charters. But there is plenty of evidence to indicate that a distinction was maintained between a political discourse of rights and a legal discourse of rules.

While many constitutions and declarations of rights were drafted during the course of the American Revolution,[53] it is instructive to compare the language adopted in the first, the Virginia Declaration of Rights in 1776, with that deployed in the federal Amendments of 1789. The Virginia Declaration uses normative language (e.g., "That elections of members to serve as representatives of the people, in assembly, ought to be free"), suggesting that the Declaration will merely provide a guide to the form government should take.[54] By contrast, the federal Bill of Rights uses imperative language (e.g., "Congress shall make no law respecting the establishment of religion . . ."), indicating that it was intended to have legal effect. Clearly, the Revolutionary period was one in which the effects of rights institutionalization were actively being considered, and lessons were gradually being learned.

On this issue, the contrast between the American Bill of Rights and the French Declaration is interesting. Although the latter was intended to be modeled on the former, Arendt argues that the French Declaration laid down "primary positive rights, inherent in man's nature, as distinguished from his political status, and as such [the rights] tried indeed to reduce politics to nature."[55] Drawing directly on man's natural rights, the Declaration was meant to provide the source of all political power. Functioning purely in the political realm, the Declaration therefore maintained a clear distinction between the political and the legal. Consider, for example, the terms of Article 4, which states,

> Political liberty consists in the power of doing whatever does not injure another. The exercise of the natural rights of every man has no other limits than those which are necessary to secure to every other man the free exercise of the same rights; and these limits are determinable only by the law.

Article 4 provides a good illustration of Rousseau's idea of the horizontalization of rights, of natural rights being restricted by what is necessary to secure the equality of such rights for all.[56] But in indicating that the limitations of such rights are to be determined by law, it reasserts law as a regime of sovereign commands.

The conception of law reflected in Article 4 thus maintains the Hobbesian distinction between law and right. And since this issue is central to the positivization of natural rights, it needs to be explicated. Hobbes argued that many people have become confused about the distinction between right and law. Right, he explained, "consisteth in liberty to do, or to forbeare" whereas law "determineth, and bindeth." Law and Right, he continued, "differ as much, as Obligation, and Liberty; which in one and the same matter are inconsistent."[57] In *De Cive*, Hobbes elaborated on this position:

> But since all the movements and actions of the citizens have never been brought within the scope of the law, and cannot be because of their infinite variety, the things that are neither commanded nor forbidden must be almost infinite; and each man can do them or not at his discretion. In these man is said to enjoy his own liberty, and liberty here is to be understood in this sense, viz. as that part of natural right which is allowed and left to the citizens by the civil laws. Water stagnates and corrupts when it is closed in by banks on all sides; when it is open on all sides it spreads, and the more outlets it finds the freer it is. So with the citizens: they would be without initiative if they did nothing except at the law's command; they would be dissipated if there were no legal restrictions, and the more things left unregulated by the laws, the more liberty they enjoy. Both extremes are faulty; for laws were invented not to extinguish human actions but to direct them; just as nature ordained banks not to stop the flow of the river but to direct it. The extent of this liberty is measured by the good of the citizens and of the commonwealth. Hence it is, in the first place, contrary to the duty of those who rule and have authority to make laws that there be more laws than the good of the citizens and the commonwealth do essentially require.[58]

Within the British tradition, this Hobbesian conception is relatively straightforward. Natural rights are essentially forms of political claim. Law, by contrast, presents itself as a body of rules authorized by the sovereign authority; legal rights are the consequence of positive law.[59] So the British have a political tradition of civil liberty to protect themselves from the restrictive effects of the law.

This clear distinction between positive law (the body of rules) and politics (the discourse through which notions of the right and the good are deliberated and disputed) is complicated by the positivization of natural rights. In this respect, the American approach marked an advance over the French. Unlike the French Declaration, the American Bills of Rights were not intended to provide the foundation stone of the state. The American Bills assumed both the existence of the state and the realities of political power and instituted a set of restraining controls on the exercise of that power. In doing so, however, the distinction between the political (the sphere of natural rights) and the legal (the sphere of command) became blurred.[60]

So long as a traditional understanding of the role of judges and courts in the system of government was maintained, the implications of this innovation were suppressed. As Jellinek has noted, "[T]he theory of natural rights for a long time had no hesitation in setting forth the contradiction between natural law and positive law without demanding the realization of the former through the latter."[61] During the twentieth century, as the rights movement acquired momentum the extent of the juristic and political challenge was revealed. The rights revolution pioneered in the United States during the latter-half of the twentieth century was the unfolding of Alexander Hamilton's claim that "the majesty of the national authority must be manifested through the medium of the courts of justice."[62] The rights revolution— the second great American revolution—is essentially the consequence of working through the institutional implications of the first.

The Rights Revolution

The rights revolution, the juristic consequences of a political revolution, is a postwar phenomenon. American constitutional scholars have presented cogent arguments for treating both the period of Reconstruction in the 1860s[63] and the New Deal in the 1930s[64] as critical moments in the constitutional transformation of rights discourse. Nevertheless, as Richard Primus has argued, the rights explosion stems from the postwar period.[65] Only in the latter half of the twentieth century do we see "the resurgence of normative foundationalism in the form of 'human rights' and other universal, non-positivist ideas, the thickening of rights against racial discrimination, against invasions in personal privacy, in favor of free expression."[66] The rights phenomenon has recently become the subject of contentious debate in the United States.[67] But although rights talk has penetrated further and deeper in the United States, there is no doubt that its influence is rapidly extending.[68] Rights discourse now transcends the boundaries of nation-states, has entered the international arena, and is even claimed by Hardt and Negri to form a central plank in the new global form of sovereignty that they call "Empire."[69]

In the course of being positivized, the language of natural rights has altered; most people now refer not to "natural" rights but instead to "human" rights. The phenomenon, nevertheless, remains the same:[70] it is essentially an appeal to some fundamental set of rights that inhere in the individual and demand recognition whether or not they have been enacted in the law of particular states. This rights explosion is a political response to twentieth-century threats. This is explicit in Arendt's observation that anti-Semitism, imperialism, and totalitarianism, "one after the other, one more brutally than the other, have demonstrated that human dignity needs a new guarantee which can be found only in a new political principle, in a new law on earth, whose validity this time must comprehend the whole of humanity."[71] The character of this modernized version of natural right has been identified by Michael Ignatieff:

> Constitutions do not create our rights; they recognize and codify the ones we already have, and provide means for their protection. We already possess our rights in two senses: either because our ancestors secured them or because they are inherent in the very idea of being human. Such inherent rights would include the right not to be tortured, abused, beaten, or starved. These inherent rights we now call human rights, and they have force whether or not they are explicitly recognized in the laws of nation-states. Thus human rights may be violated even when no state law is being infringed.[72]

This emerging human rights discourse is a political response to pressing political issues, especially about the treatment of minorities in an era of democratization.[73] Our concern, however, is not with this political discourse, but with its juristic consequences. Through the modern process of constitutionalization, the doctrine of natural rights has insinuated itself into the fabric of positive law, engendering a radical shift in our understanding of the character of law.

Natural rights have generally taken the form of negative liberties, serving mainly to define a zone of individual autonomy which government must not invade. As a consequence of rights institutionalization, however, there has been a growing tendency to treat rights rather than rules as the basic items of legal order. Once this rights-based conception of law becomes fixed in juristic thought, rights that once operated to place statute law in bounds are conceived as forming the architectonic principles of legal order. Basic rights are thus transmuted from the sphere of subjective right into fundamental norms that penetrate and give shape to objective law.[74]

By assuming this architectonic status, rights revolutionize our understanding of positive law. Since rights acquire their weight from ethical considerations, the traditional attempt to separate law from matters of politics or morality no longer is convincing. This fuels a tremendous expansion in the creativity of legal argument, as basic values of dignity, autonomy, and equality are explicated into ever more ingenious forms of rights claims. With the appearance of the rights-bearing citizen, individuals begin to present themselves as subjects of international law.[75] Rights discourse in effect elevates itself above the arena of state law and into the realm of universal right. Law, once a form of coercive order, now presents itself as a means of maintaining freedom. Once founded on sovereign authority and authorized by representative democracy, law is now based on rights and legitimated by an appeal to moral autonomy. Law, in short, is no longer fundamentally a matter of will, but an aspect of reason.

This expansion in law's empire has particularly important consequences for constitutional law. Most obviously, constitutional law, which once was conceived to incorporate not only the formal rules regulating governmental institutions but also more fundamentally the prudential practices of political right,[76] becomes susceptible to total institutionalization. Once positive law presents itself as a universal phenomenon, such political precepts become liable to be given precise and authoritative meaning by a revitalized judiciary. Contrary to Hobbes's claim, "all the movements and actions of the citizens" are now—potentially—"brought within the scope of the law."[77] What is commanded or forbidden now more than ever depends on the circumstances in which the power of command is exercised, determined not by rules laid down by legislatures but through adjudicative processes concerned with resolving competing claims of rights. Liberty is no longer the sphere of individual autonomy beyond the constraints of the law; liberty must now be defined by the operations of the law. These shifts mark a boundary change between the political and the legal, with law being elevated to a transcendental realm that frames the conduct of politics. The consequence is that the political critique of law can no longer come mainly from the outside; the moralization of law means that political critique must also come from within.

Conclusions

In seeking to understand the impact of the contemporary rights revolution on juristic thought, our starting point should be that although the rights revolution has been fuelled by the rhetoric of natural or human rights, the idea of nature no longer offers any fixed, objective point against which conduct can be evaluated. Although more sophisticated human rights advocates acknowledge this, the point is not always accepted. "Human rights activism," Ignatieff notes, "likes to portray itself as an anti-politics, in defense of universal moral claims designed to delegitimize 'political' (i.e., ideological or sectarian) justifications for the abuse of human beings."[78] But such activism, he concedes, "is bound to be partial and political" and, in practice, "impartiality and neutrality are just as impossible as universal equal concern for everyone's human rights."[79] If the first American Revolution was an emancipation from history, this second revolution is an emancipation from nature.[80]

Individuals may have good reasons for embracing a political discourse of human rights. From the perspective of institutionalization, however, this is beside the point. Recognizing the political character of rights discourse leads us directly to the challenge of the positivization of basic rights. Even if it is the case that "human rights politics is disciplined or constrained by moral universals"[81] (whatever these may be[82]), handing over the responsibility for identifying, ranking, and enforcing basic rights to the processes of adjudication is a contentious and risky political maneuver. Every important social and political conflict can be reinterpreted in the form of a competing rights claim. Sometimes these involve rival conceptions of equality (e.g., equality of opportunity against equality of distribution), but more often they take the form of a conflict between right-as-freedom and right-as-security, between autonomy and the prevention of harm to others.[83] Despite the Herculean judge's claimed ability to reach the "right answer,"[84] the fact is that such disputes cannot be resolved through the deployment of the language of the law. Rights adjudication is intrinsically political; it requires judges to reach a determination on the relative importance of conflicting social, political, and cultural interests in circumstances in which there is no objective—or even consensual—answer.[85]

There may be sound practical reasons for vesting such political responsibilities in lawyers and judges. No one has articulated these reasons more eloquently than Tocqueville, who suggested that in the modern era lawyers provide "the most powerful existing security against the excesses of democracy."[86] Lawyers acquire "certain habits of order, a taste for formalities, and a kind of instinctive regard for the regular connection of ideas, which naturally render them very hostile to the revolutionary spirit and the unreflecting passions of the multitude."[87]

In a democratic age, lawyers form the true aristocracy, and they "secretly oppose their aristocratic propensities to the nation's democratic instincts, their superstitious attachment to what is old to its love of novelty, their narrow views to its immense designs, and their habitual procrastination to its ardent impatience."[88] In short, they provide the invaluable service of "neutraliz[ing] the vices inherent in popular government."[89] At a time when the executive dominates the legislature, the judiciary is able to offer a useful check on the exercise of governmental power.

As the institution which "will always be the least dangerous to the political rights of the Constitution"[90], a judiciary which controls neither the purse nor the sword can still impose beneficial discipline and rationality over the processes of political reasoning. But such gains come at a price. Basing political order on individual rights, and therefore paradoxically basing the legitimacy of society on a thoroughly asocial principle, is in itself controversial.[91] But handing the task of explicating these rights to an institution whose entire modus operandi is rooted in a conviction that there are right answers to all disputes in law and that such answers are revealed through the deployment of some unique legal logic, must be doubly contentious. For many, Tocqueville's bulwark—the secretive and aristocratic propensities of lawyers—has become what Koskenniemi labels "a culture of bad faith," and this may be simply too high a price to pay.[92]

Ultimately, any stance on the positivization of natural rights involves an uncertain exercise in political judgment. This form of constitutional rights discourse appeals to canons of legal reason, but actually involves an exercise in prudential political reasoning. Our judgments turn on two basic questions. First, do we believe that this expanding culture of rights—which may soon extend to social and economic issues[93]—gives sound expression to our aspirations to autonomy, equality, dignity, and justice, or is its formalism and adversarialism more likely to generate a destructive stridency in political engagement?[94] Secondly, do we trust the judiciary to sustain a sound tradition of prudential reasoning through rights? *Sapere aude!*, have courage to use your own understanding, may have been the motto of the Enlightenment,[95] but it is not clear today whether or how it might assist us in dealing with this situation.

Notes

This paper was delivered at the conference on *America and the Enlightenment: Constitutionalism in the 21st Century* and was subsequently published in Martin Loughlin, *The Idea of Public Law* (Oxford: Oxford University Press, 2003), chap. 7. It appears here, by permission, in modified form.

1. See Norberto Bobbio, *The Age of Rights*, trans. Allan Cameron (Cambridge: Polity Press, 1996); Louis Henkin, *The Age of Rights* (New York: Columbia University Press, 1990).
2. Charles R. Epp, *The Rights Revolution: Lawyers, Activists, and Supreme Courts in Comparative Perspective* (Chicago: University of Chicago Press, 1998); Michael Ignatieff, *The Rights Revolution* (Toronto: Anansi, 2000).
3. See, e.g., Thomas Hobbes, *On the Citizen* (1647), ed. and trans. Richard Tuck and Michael Silverthorne (Cambridge: Cambridge University Press, 1998), 7, 10: "This book sets out men's duties, first as men, then as citizens and lastly as Christians" and is intended to investigate "the right of a commonwealth and the duties of its citizens."
4. See, e.g., Max Radin, "Natural Law and Natural Rights," *Yale Law Journal* 59 (1950): 214–237.
5. See, e.g., Bernard Bailyn, *The Ideological Origins of the American Revolution* (Cambridge, MA: Belknap Press of Harvard University Press, 1967), 27: "In pamphlet after pamphlet the American writers cited Locke on natural rights and on the social and governmental contract."
6. Jean-Jacques Rousseau's letter to the Marquis de Mirabeau, July 26, 1767, cited in Hannah Arendt, *On Revolution* (Harmondsworth: Penguin, 1973), 183.
7. Ibid., 185–186. Cf. Peter Gay, *The Enlightenment: An Interpretation* (New York: Knopf, 1966), 322: "The philosophes' claim to distance themselves from their Christian world has rarely been fully honored. Instead, the philosophes have been sarcastically commended for 'merely' secularizing religious ideas and caricatured as medieval clerks in modern dress, ungrateful and forgetful heirs of the Christian tradition who combated the pious wish for salvation in the name of a secular salvation disguised as progress . . . who laughed at religious idolatry but had their own saints—Bacon, Newton and Locke."
8. See Arendt, *On Revolution*, 184–185; François Furet, *The French Revolution, 1770–1814*, trans. Antonia Neill (Oxford: Blackwell, 1996), 147–149.
9. See Carl Becker, *The Declaration of Independence: A Study in the History of Political Ideas* (New York: Harcourt, Brace, 1922), 37.
10. Richard Tuck, *Natural Rights Theories: Their Origins and Development* (Cambridge: Cambridge University Press, 1979). Cf. Brian Tierney, *The Idea of Natural Rights: Studies on Natural Rights, Natural Law and Church Law, 1150–1625* (Atlanta: Scholars Press, 1997), chaps. 1 and 2.
11. Luc Ferry, *Rights—The New Quarrel between the Ancients and the Moderns. Political Philosophy*, trans. Franklin Philip (Chicago: University of Chicago Press, 1990), 1: 21.
12. See Thomas Hobbes, *Leviathan* (1651), ed. Richard Tuck (Cambridge: Cambridge University Press, 1996), chap. 13.

13. But see ibid., chap. 14, 93 where Hobbes indicated that "not all rights are alienable." Since the covenant establishing political order is designed to promote security, the entire surrender of all natural rights (e.g., by pledging not to resist force) would, he argued, be absurd.

14. John Locke, *Two Treatises of Government* (1680), ed. Peter Laslett (Cambridge: Cambridge University Press, 1988), ii.124.

15. Ibid., ii.149.

16. Jean-Jacques Rousseau, *The Social Contract* (1762), trans. Maurice Cranston (Harmondsworth: Penguin, 1968), ii.4: "The commitments which bind us to the social body are obligatory only because they are mutual; and their nature is such that in fulfilling them a man cannot work for others without at the same time working for himself."

17. Leo Strauss, *What is Political Philosophy? And other Studies* (New York: Free Press, 1959), 51.

18. In his *Groundwork of the Metaphysics of Morals* Kant also reformulated the categorical imperative thus: "Act always so that you treat humanity whether in your person or in that of another always as an end, but never as a means only." See Immanuel Kant, *Political Writings*, trans. H. B. Nisbet and ed. Hans Reiss (Cambridge: Cambridge University Press, 1970), 22–23.

19. Tuck, *Natural Rights Theories*. For criticism of this periodization see Brian Tierney, "Tuck on Rights: Some Medieval Problems," *History of Political Thought* 4 (1983): 429–441.

20. Ibid., 177.

21. Becker, *Declaration of Independence*, 72.

22. "We hold these truths to be self-evident," Jefferson declared, "that all men are created equal; that they are endowed by their Creator with certain inalienable rights; that among these are life, liberty and the pursuit of happiness. That, to secure these rights, governments are instituted among men, deriving their just powers from the consent of the governed."

23. See Bailyn, *Ideological Origins*, chap. 2; Morton White, *The Philosophy of the American Revolution* (New York: Oxford University Press, 1978).

24. Jack N. Rakove, *Original Meanings: Politics and Ideas in the Making of the Constitution* (New York: Vintage Books, 1997), 290–292. See also Forrest McDonald, *Novus Ordo Seclorum: The Intellectual Origins of the Constitution* (Lawrence, KA: University Press of Kansas, 1985).

25. See, e.g., *Resolutions of the House of Representatives of Massachusetts*, October 29, 1765: "1. *Resolved*, That there are certain essential Rights of the *British* Constitution of government which are founded in the Law of God and Nature, and are the common Rights of Mankind—Therefore 2. *Resolved*, That the Inhabitants of this Province are *inalienably* entitled to those essential rights in common with all Men: and that no Law of Society can, consistent with the Law

of God and Nature, divest them of those Rights"; Virginia
Declaration of Rights, 1776: "1. That all men are by nature equally
free and independent, and have certain inherent rights, of which,
when they enter into a state of society, they cannot by an compact
deprive or divest their posterity."; Pennsylvania Declaration of Rights,
1776: "1. That all men are born equally free and independent, and
have certain natural inherent and inalienable rights, amongst which
are the enjoying and defending life and liberty, acquiring, possessing
and protecting property, and pursuing and obtaining happiness and
safety." See Jack N. Rakove, *Declaring Rights: A Brief History with
Documents* (Boston: Bedford Books, 1998), 48, 81, 85.

26. Bailyn, *Ideological Origins*, 30–31: "Just as the colonists cited with
    enthusiasm the theorists of universal reason, so too did they associate
    themselves, with offhand familiarity, with the tradition of the English
    common law . . . The common law was manifestly influential in shap-
    ing the awareness of the Revolutionary generation. But, again, it did
    not in itself determine the kinds of conclusions men would draw in the
    crisis of the time."

27. Cf. Michael Oakeshott, "Contemporary British Politics," *Cambridge
    Journal* 1 (1947–1948): 474–490, 490: "The common law rights and
    duties of Englishmen were transplanted throughout the civilised
    world. . . . In this process some of their flexibility was lost; the rights
    and duties were exported; the genius that made them remained at
    home. Peoples, desirous of freedom, but dissatisfied with anything less
    than the imagination of an eternal and immutable law, gave to these
    rights the false title of Nature. Because they were not the fruit of their
    own experience, it was forgotten that they were the fruit of the
    experience of the British people. . . . What went abroad as the
    concrete rights of an Englishman have returned home as the abstract
    Rights of Man, and they have returned to confound our politics and
    corrupt our minds."

28. Cited in Becker, *Declaration of Independence*, 116.

29. Ibid., 99. Cf. John Phillip Reid, "The Irrelevance of the Declaration,"
    in *Law in the American Revolution and the Revolution in the Law*, ed.
    Hendrik Hartog (New York: New York University Press, 1981), 46–89.

30. James Wilson, "Lectures on Law" in *The Works of James Wilson,
    Associate Justice of The Supreme Court of The United States*, ed. J. De
    Witt Andrews (Chicago: Callaghan and Company., 1898), i.296–309,
    302; cited in Knud Haakonssen, "From Natural Law to The Rights of
    Man: A European Perspective on American Debates," in *A Culture of
    Rights: The Bill of Rights in Philosophy, Politics And Law—1791 and
    1991*, ed. Michael J. Lacey and Knud Haakonssen (Cambridge:
    Cambridge University Press, 1991), 19–61, 20.

31. Ibid., 303. See also William S. Carpenter, *The Development of
    American Political Thought* (Princeton: Princeton University Press,

1930), 29: "James Otis envisaged the transformation within the British Constitution of the common-law rights of Englishmen into the natural rights of man, but he also saw these natural rights as limitations upon the authority of government."

32. In this respect, the religious aspects of the Revolutionary movement are vitally important: on which see Georg Jellinek, *The Declaration of the Rights of Man and of Citizens: A Contribution to Modern Constitutional History*, trans. Max Farrand (New York: Henry Holt and Company, 1901), chap. 7; Barry Alan Shain, *The Myth of American Individualism: The Protestant Origins of American Political Thought* (Princeton, NJ: Princeton University Press, 1994).

33. Sir John Fortescue, *De Laudibus Legum Anglie*, ed. and trans. S. B. Chrimes (Cambridge: Cambridge University Press, 1942), 37. Cf. Justinian, *Institutes*, I.2.6: "[W]hatever the emperor has determined (*constituit*) be rescript or decided as a judge or directed by edict is established to be law: it is these that are called constitutions."

34. In 1738, e.g., Viscount Bolingbroke defined the constitution as "that Assemblage of Laws, Institutions and Customs derived from certain fix'd principles of Reason, that compose the general System, according to which the Community hath agreed to be governed." Cited in Graham Maddox, "Constitution," in *Political Innovation and Conceptual Change*, ed. Terence Ball, James Farr, and Russell L. Hanson (Cambridge: Cambridge University Press, 1989), 50–67, 59.

35. Thomas Paine, *Rights of Man* in *Rights of Man, Common Sense and other Political Writings*, ed. Mark Philp (Oxford: Oxford University Press, 1995), 83–331, 120.

36. Ibid., 122.

37. Ibid.

38. Ibid., 123.

39. Ibid.

40. Cf. Arthur Young's comment on the French Constitution in 1792, which he says "is a new term they have adopted; and which they use as if a constitution was a pudding to be made by a receipt." Cited in Charles Howard McIlwain, *Constitutionalism: Ancient and Modern* (Ithaca, NY: Cornell University Press, 1947), 1–2.

41. See S. E. Finer, *The History of Government* (Oxford: Oxford University Press, 1997), iii.1395–1405.

42. James Madison, Alexander Hamilton, and John Jay, *The Federalist Papers* (1788), ed. Isaac Kramnick (Harmondsworth: Penguin, 1987), no. 51 (Madison).

43. See Edward S. Corwin, "The 'Higher Law' Background to American Constitutional Law," *Harvard Law Review* 42 (1928): 149–185 (pt. I), 365–409 (pt. II).

44. *Federalist Papers*, no. 78 (Hamilton).

45. See Gordon S. Wood, *The Creation of the American Republic, 1776–1787*, rev. ed. (Chapel Hill: University of North Carolina Press, 1998), 273–282.

46. Finer, *History of Government*, 1517. For Hegel, as Habermas notes, "the French Revolution becomes the very key to the philosophic concept of World History": see Jürgen Habermas, "Natural Law and Revolution," in *Theory and Practice*, trans. John Viertel (Boston: Beacon Press, 1973), 82–120, 86.

47. Finer, *History of Government*, 1517.

48. See Jellinek, *Declaration*, 20: "The French Declaration of Rights is for the most part copied from the American declarations or 'bills of rights.' "

49. Habermas, "Natural Law and Revolution," 86.

50. *Marbury v. Madison*, 5 US (1 Cranch) 137 (1803).

51. Thomas Paine, "Common Sense," in *Rights of Man, Common Sense and other Political Writings*, 5–59, 34.

52. That a Bill of Rights did not form part of the Constitution approved by the Federal Convention in 1787 and then subsequently was added at the First Federal Congress in 1789 owes much, in both instances, to the influence of James Madison. See Lance Banning, *The Sacred Fire of Liberty: James Madison and the Founding of the American Republic* (Ithaca, NY: Cornell University Press, 1995), chap. 9. For a summary of Madison's position see Rakove, *Declaring Rights*, 100: "Madison's ideas about the protection of human rights departed in significant ways from the beliefs that Americans held at the outset of the Revolution. Where traditional theory located the principal dangers to rights in the arbitrary acts of the executive, Madison realized that in a republic, the legislature could prove more oppressive. Where traditional theory held that the problem of rights was to protect the people *against* government, Madison realized that in a republic the pressing necessity was to find ways to protect one segment of the community—individuals and minorities—against the self-interested desires of popular majorities acting *through* government. And where traditional theory sought to protect the customary rights of local communities against the centralizing organs of the nation-state, Madison hoped to empower the national government to intervene *within* the states to defend rights against the threats that individuals faced within the very communities where they lived" (emphasis is in the original).

53. During the Revolution, eleven of the thirteen states drafted new constitutions of government, and eight of the eleven attached some declaration of rights to these documents: see Rakove, *Declaring Rights*, 36.

54. Ibid., 36–37, also notes that the Virginia Declaration was approved more than two weeks before the Constitution was adopted. Neither document referred to the other and it remained unclear whether the Declaration was to form part of the Constitution.

55. Arendt, *On Revolution*, 108.

56. See above text accompanying note 16.
57. Hobbes, *Leviathan*, 91.
58. Hobbes, *On the Citizen*, 150–151.
59. See, e.g., William Blackstone, *Commentaries on the Laws of England* (Oxford: Clarendon Press, 1765–1769), i.121: "This natural liberty consists properly in a power of acting as one thinks fit, without any restraint or control, unless by the law of nature . . . Political . . . or civil liberty . . . is no other than natural liberty so far restrained by human laws (and no farther) as is necessary and expedient for the general advantage of the publick."
60. Furet, *French Revolution*, 74 expresses this point differently: "In the American example, those rights were perceived as having preceded society and also being in harmony with its development; moreover, they had been inscribed in its past by the jurisprudential tradition of the English common law. In the France of 1789, however, emphasis was placed on a certain political voluntarism: the law, produced by the sovereign nation, was established as the supreme guarantee of rights. . . . So it was society's responsibility, through the intermediary of the law, to ensure the rights of individuals; that law which was constantly referred to in the articles of the declaration as the 'expression of the general will'."
61. Jellinek, *Declaration*, 56–57.
62. *Federalist Papers*, no. 16 (Hamilton).
63. See Akhil Amar, *The Bill of Rights: Creation and Reconstruction* (New Haven: Yale University Press, 1998).
64. See Bruce Ackerman, *We the People: Foundations* (Cambridge: Belknap Press, 1991).
65. Richard A. Primus, *The American Language of Rights* (Cambridge: Cambridge University Press, 1999), esp.ch.5. This thesis receives support from the work of Epp, *Rights Revolution*, who has shown that during the mid-1930s, fewer than 10 percent of the cases of the Supreme Court's decisions involved individual rights (other than property rights) and that by the late 1960s almost 70 percent of decisions concerned individual rights (ibid., 2). See further, Richard L. Pacelle, Jr., *The Transformation of the Supreme Court's Agenda: From the New Deal to the Reagan Administration* (Boulder, CO: Westview Press, 1991).
66. Primus, *The American Language of Rights*, 179.
67. See, e.g., Ronald Dworkin, *Taking Rights Seriously* (Cambridge, MA: Harvard University Press, 1977); Robert H. Bork, *The Tempting of America: The Political Seduction of the Law* (London: Sinclair-Stevenson, 1990); Mary Ann Glendon, *Rights Talk: The Impoverishment of Political Discourse* (New York: Free Press, 1991).
68. See, e.g., Epp, *Rights Revolution*, chaps. 5–10; David Beatty, ed., *Human Rights and Judicial Review: A Comparative Perspective* (Dordrecht: Martinus Nijhoff, 1994); Philip Alston, ed., *The EU and*

Human Rights (Oxford: Oxford University Press, 1999); Tom
Campbell, K. D. Ewing, and Adam Tomkins, eds., *Sceptical Essays on
Human Rights* (Oxford: Oxford University Press, 2001), pt. III.

69. Michael Hardt and Antonio Negri, *Empire* (Cambridge, MA: Harvard
    University Press, 2000). Hardt and Negri argue that the emerging
    world order which they call Empire is expressed as a juridical formation
    and that the concept of right—albeit understood as a transforma-
    tive notion of "imperial right"(62)—lies at the core of this global
    constitution.

70. See, e.g., Maurice Cranston, *Human Rights Today* (London:
    Ampersand, 1955), 20: human rights refers to "what Locke and other
    theorists meant by 'natural rights,' but without any specific reference
    to a concept of nature." See also John Finnis, *Natural Law and
    Natural Rights* (Oxford: Clarendon Press, 1980), 198: "this book is
    about human rights ('human rights' being a contemporary idiom for
    'natural rights': I use the terms synonymously.)"

71. Hannah Arendt, *The Origins of Totalitarianism*, 2nd. ed. (San Diego:
    Harcourt Brace Jovanovich, 1968), ix.

72. Ignatieff, *Rights Revolution*, 28. In response to de Maistre's famous
    quip that, while he had met many people in his life—Spanish,
    Portuguese, and English—he had never met Man, Ignatieff observes,
    "We have met Man. He is us. Human rights derive their force in our
    conscience from this sense that we belong to one species, and that we
    recognize ourselves in every single human being we meet" (Ignatieff,
    Rights Revolution, 39–40). Cf. ibid., 299: "The conception of human
    rights, based upon the assumed existence of a human being as such,
    broke down at the very moment when those who professed to believe
    in it were for the first time confronted with people who had lost all
    other qualities and specific relationships—except that they were still
    human. The world found nothing sacred in the abstract nakedness of
    being human." For this reason Arendt asserts the critical importance
    of "the right to have rights (and that means to live in a framework
    where one is judged by one's actions and opinions) and a right to
    belong to some kind of organized community" (ibid., 296–297).
    "Our political life," she elaborates, "rests on the assumption that we
    can produce equality through organization" (ibid., 301).

73. See, e.g., Georg Jellinek, *The Rights of Minorities*, trans. A. M. Baty
    and T. Baty (London: P. S. King and Son, 1912). More recently, see
    Will Kymlicka, *Multicultural Citizenship: A Liberal Theory of Minority
    Rights* (Oxford: Clarendon Press, 1995).

74. See Jürgen Habermas, *Between Facts and Norms: Contributions to a
    Discourse Theory of Law and Democracy*, trans. William Rehg
    (Cambridge: Polity Press, 1996), 247–248. This seems also to be the
    implication of the thesis of Robert Alexy, arguing that constitutional
    rights are optimalization requirements of a legal order: Robert Alexy,

A Theory of Constitutional Rights, trans. Julian Rivers (Oxford: Oxford University Press, 2002).

75. See, e.g., Fernando Tesón, *A Philosophy of International Law* (Boulder, CO: Westview Press, 1998); Antonio Cassesse, *Self-Determination of Peoples: A Legal Reappraisal* (Cambridge: Cambridge University Press, 1995); Henry Steiner and Philip Alston, *International Human Rights in Context: Law, Politics, Morals*, 2nd ed. (Oxford: Oxford University Press, 2000).

76. This argument is made in Martin Loughlin, *The Idea of Public Law* (Oxford: Oxford University Press, 2003).

77. Hobbes, *On the Citizen*, 150–151.

78. Michael Ignatieff, *Human Rights as Politics and Idolatry* (Princeton, NJ: Princeton University Press, 2001), 9.

79. Ibid. See further Antonio Cassesse, "Are Human Rights Truly Universal?" in Obrad Savć, ed., *The Politics of Human Rights* (London: Verso, 1999), 149–165.

80. See Arendt, *Origins of Totalitarianism*, 298: "Man of the twentieth century has become just as emancipated from nature as eighteenth-century man was from history. History and nature have become equally alien to us, namely, in the sense that the essence of man can no longer be comprehended in terms of either category."

81. Ignatieff, *Human Rights*.

82. For a discussion of this issue, see Thomas L. Haskell, "The Curious Persistence of Rights Talk in the 'Age of Interpretation,' " *Journal of American History* 74 (1987): 984–1012.

83. See Martti Koskenniemi, "The Effect of Rights on Political Culture," in *The EU and Human Rights*, ed. Philip Alston (Oxford: Oxford University Press, 1999), 99–116, esp. 107–110.

84. Ronald Dworkin, *Taking Rights Seriously* (Cambridge, MA: Harvard University Press, 1977), 126: determining "the right answer" involves "identif[ying] a particular conception of community morality as decisive of legal issues; that conception holds that community morality is the political morality presupposed by the laws and institutions of the community."

85. This remains the case, notwithstanding the development of sophisticated theories, such as that of Alexy in *Theory of Constitutional Rights* that argue that balancing does not lead to radical openness.

86. Alexis de Tocqueville, *Democracy in America* (1835), trans. Henry Reeve, 2 vols. (New York: Vintage Books, 1990), 1:272.

87. Ibid., 273.

88. Ibid., 278.

89. Ibid.

90. *Federalist Papers*, no. 78 (Hamilton).

91. Pierre Manent, *Naissance de la politique moderne* (Paris: Payot, 1977), 11: "To base the legitimacy of society (human relationships)

on the autonomy of the individual is to base it on the most asocial principle" (cited in Ferry, *Rights*, 59).

92. Koskenniemi, "Effect of Rights," 100. For some, this issue is linked to the fact that today, as a consequence of rationalization and specialization, lawyers and judges no longer possess the deliberative and political skills to be able sensitively to handle these tasks: see Anthony T. Kronman, *The Lost Lawyer: Failing Ideals of the Legal Profession* (Cambridge: Belknap Press, 1993).

93. For an analytical assessment see Cécile Fabre, *Social Rights under the Constitution: Government and the Decent Life* (Oxford: Oxford University Press, 1999).

94. Cf. Louis Hartz, "The Whig Tradition in America and Europe," *American Political Science Review* 46 (1952): 989–1002, 997 n. 10: "When half a nation believes in Locke and half in Filmer or Marx, the result is not law but philosophy. *Inter arma leges silent* . . . America's famous legalism is thus the reverse side of its philosophic poverty in politics." See also John Gray, *Enlightenment's Wake: Politics and Culture at the Close of the Modern Age* (London: Routledge, 1995), 76: "liberal legalism . . . is, perhaps, only an especially unambiguous example of an older liberal project, or illusion, of *abolishing politics*, or of so constraining it by legal and constitutional formulae that it no longer matters what are the outcomes of political deliberation."

95. Kant, "An Answer to the Question: 'What is Enlightenment?' " in *Political Writings*, 54–60, 54.

Chapter 3

Epicureanism and the Enlightenment

Frederick Rosen

Probably the doctrine most subversive of traditional morality and the so-called monkish virtues was that of modern Epicureanism, which developed in the seventeenth century and has been closely associated with what we call "the Enlightenment." The doctrine engaged many writers not only due to its moral and political ideas but also because its essentially materialist view of nature seemed relevant to modern scientific enquiry and also appeared to banish fear of torment and suffering after death.

Ancient Epicureanism is usually associated with Epicurus himself (341BC–271BC) who established his school in Athens in 306BC, with the majestic Latin poem of Lucretius (99BC–55BC), *De Rerum Natura*, and with the discussion of Epicureanism in the first and second books of Cicero's *De Finibus* (45BC). It was a system of "uncompromising egoistic hedonism"[1] with the only perfect pleasure, the condition of *ataraxia*, where one lived serenely in bodily health and with as little physical and psychological distress as possible. The most important virtue was prudence and while emphasis was placed on the egoistic pleasures connected with friendship, there was little attention paid to social values and instincts. As one commentator has written, "[J]ust as the Epicurean community practiced economic self-sufficiency within the walls of its garden, the Epicurean man cultivates an inner self-sufficiency, a contentment in his own physical and mental states and a suppression of unnecessary desires."[2] Justice is not a virtue in the sense that we can discover its unchanging and immutable properties in the human soul, as in Plato's *Republic*, but it is something devised by artifice for human convenience. It is the means to achieve security from the attacks of other people: "a pledge of mutual advantage to restrain men from harming one another and save them from being harmed."[3]

Modern Epicureanism developed in the seventeenth century as part of the challenge to conceptions of nature and morality in scholastic philosophy, a challenge usually associated in France with Rene Descartes and Pierre Gassendi. Gassendi played a crucial role in restating the doctrines of Epicurus, especially his atomism, and in influencing numerous philosophers in France and Britain.[4] One scholar has noted that at least thirteen books were published in England between 1650 and 1700 dealing specifically with Epicurus or Lucretius and other ancient Epicureans.[5] Others have commented on Gassendi's influence on both Hobbes and Locke.[6] Hobbes knew Gassendi personally, and although Hobbes and Epicurus differed on numerous points, there was considerable affinity between Hobbes's asocial and apolitical individual, acting on the basis of self-interest and seeking to preserve oneself, and the portrait of humanity presented by Epicurus and particularly by Lucretius in the fifth book of *De Rerum Natura*.[7]

Although the revival of Epicureanism and its presentation in a modern form took place mainly in the latter half of the seventeenth and into the eighteenth century, there was an ongoing dialogue between numerous writers from the Renaissance (Erasmus and Bacon are often cited) in which Stoic and Epicurean themes were interwoven.[8] At first Epicurean doctrines were somewhat hidden beneath Stoic themes, but by the end of the seventeenth century Epicurean themes seemed to be the more prominent not only among the writers I have mentioned but also among the French moralists, natural jurists, writers such as Bayle and Mandeville, and among some representatives of the Scottish Enlightenment. In fact, what is generally presumed to be the Enlightenment, mainly European thought in the eighteenth century, does not fit in easily with modern Epicureanism, as modern Epicureanism extended over a longer period from the Renaissance to the present day. Although well-known Enlightenment figures, such as Helvétius and Voltaire embraced Epicurean doctrines (Helvétius's *De L'Esprit* begins with a quotation from Lucretius on the title page, and Voltaire's *Candide* ends with the Epicurean injunction, "let us cultivate our garden"), they were drawing on ideas already present in modern European thought from the Renaissance.

Numerous figures that we commonly associate with the European Enlightenment invoked pleasure and pain when writing of human motivation and action, and in most instances several common assumptions, taken from the Epicurean tradition, were employed. For example, there was a clear distinction between pleasure as a good and pain as an evil.[9] Unlike Plato and Aristotle, for example, few writers in the Epicurean tradition wrote of good and bad pleasures or good and bad pains, and to say that an act or institution gave pleasure meant that it was considered good. Similarly, there was no neutral state between pleasure and pain,[10] but generally an acceptance that pleasure was a normal part of life, with pain being abnormal in the same sense that disease was considered abnormal.

Furthermore, unlike Plato and Aristotle, there was no belief in "an ascending series of pleasures," which depended on the organ affected so that the pleasures of a full stomach would be inferior to the enjoyment of intellectual contemplation.[11] This is not to deny that one might obtain greater pleasure from contemplation than from eating (from the satisfactions of Socrates as opposed to those of a pig), but it is to say that there are not different levels of pleasure related to different parts of the body. Most modern Epicureans thus subscribed to the Epicurean doctrine of the unity of pleasure.[12]

If one examines the writings of two distinctive figures of the Enlightenment, Hume and Bentham, for example, the employment of these assumptions is clearly evident. In Hume's empiricism and its regard for ordinary life, its pleasures and pains, and virtues and vices, he never paused to consider different kinds of pleasure and pain. If utility pleased (see section 5 of *Enquiry Concerning the Principles of Morals*), the pleasure it provided was like any other pleasure. The various categories of pleasure considered by Bentham in *An Introduction to the Principles of Morals and Legislation* also led to no conclusions that some pleasures were superior to others.[13] Furthermore, not only did Hume's empiricism and attention to the virtues and vices that were praised and deplored in ordinary life depend on the doctrine of the unity of pleasure, but also ideas of sympathy and humanity seemed to require it for their coherence and force. The party of humankind might be regarded as the party of pleasure; the party of vice and disorder might be depicted also as the party of pain.[14] I am not claiming that Hume and Bentham used pleasure in the same way in every respect, but I do contend that they shared several important assumptions about pleasure and pain derived from the Epicurean tradition that made other aspects of their thought coherent.

When John Stuart Mill published *Utilitarianism* in 1861, he was also consciously carrying on the Epicurean tradition and accepted the account of pain and pleasure he had inherited. At the beginning of chapter 2 of his book he wrote of "every writer from Epicurus to Bentham, who maintained the theory of utility, meant by it, not something to be contradistinguished from pleasure, but pleasure

itself, together with exemption from pain . . . ."[15] He invoked
Epicurus, Epicureans, and Epicurean life six times in the opening
paragraphs of this chapter.[16] Mill's important essay seldom receives
much attention from students of the European Enlightenment. It is
usually treated as a critique of the doctrines of Bentham and James
Mill (as in the remarks concerning higher pleasures and that it is better to be Socrates dissatisfied than a pig satisfied) and hence a critique
of key figures in the later Enlightenment period in Britain. I take the
view that Mill's *Utilitarianism* was written not as a critique of earlier
hedonism, but as a defense of it, and as a defense of Epicureanism
against the sustained attack of Thomas Carlyle and a new form of
Puritanism, which he thought was then being introduced into Britain.

When Mill began *Utilitarianism* in 1854 he was also writing about
Carlyle's views on hero worship in a diary that he briefly kept, and the
following entry appeared:

> Moral regenerators in this age mostly aim at setting up a new form
> either of Stoicism or Puritanism—persuading men to sink altogether
> earthly happiness as a pursuit. . . . What is now wanted is the creed of
> Epicurus warmed by the additional element of an enthusiastic love of
> the general good.[17]

According to Carlyle one should look beyond pleasure, love, and
happiness to blessedness and God. "Love not Pleasure," he proclaimed, "love God."[18] He insisted that the path to God was not
through the calculation of pleasures, but through renunciation. "It is
only with Renunciation (*Entsagen*) that Life, properly speaking, can
be said to begin":

> What Act of Legislature was there that *thou* shouldst be Happy? A little
> while ago thou hadst no right to *be* at all. What if thou wert born and
> predestined not to be Happy, but to be Unhappy![19]

Carlyle had been Mill's friend for many years, and Mill gave him
credit for enlarging the narrow creed he inherited from his father. But
he never adopted Carlyle's doctrines and in his *Autobiography* he
explained just what was at stake:

> They seemed a haze of poetry and German metaphysics, in which
> almost the only clear thing was a strong animosity to most of the opin-
> ions which were the basis of my mode of thought; religious scepticism,
> utilitarianism, the doctrine of circumstances, the attaching of any
> importance to democracy, logic, or political economy.[20]

Mill was well aware of the differences between ancient and modern Epicureanism, and particularly of the extension of the aspiration to happiness from its confinement to "the wise" to all members of society. Working within this modern Epicurean framework where rules of justice secured basic rights to life and liberty, Mill considered what sort of happiness was appropriate to human aspirations. In reply to Carlyle's ringing denunciation of happiness, he first admitted that most people lived in a state of unhappiness, and this condition, he believed, was due to numerous factors such as inadequate laws, corrupt government, poverty, disease, selfishness, ignorance, and the absence of liberty. Nevertheless, he felt that the main elements of a happy life could be achieved. Every satisfied life required moments of tranquility intermingled with moments of excitement. It required the opportunity to care for others and for mental cultivation, not in order for everyone to become philosophers, but to develop interests in the world around them. In the exercise of one's faculties, one finds "sources of inexhaustible interest": "in the objects of nature, the achievements of art, the imaginations of poetry, the incidents of history, the ways of mankind past and present, and their prospects in the future."[21] Mill was convinced that poverty could be overcome by society and that science, together with good habits of physical and moral education, could enable mankind to tackle much debilitating disease. He was not setting forth utopia as being within the immediate grasp of humankind. On the one hand he believed that "all the grand sources . . . of human suffering are in a great degree, many of them almost entirely, conquerable by human care and effort." But on the other hand he recognized that the removal of these sources of suffering would be "grievously slow" and "a long succession of generations will perish in the breach before the conquest is completed."[22] He could appreciate that vast numbers of people were living without happiness and that in so-called civilized societies only a small percentage lived happily.[23] This recognition of widespread unhappiness did not lead him to abandon utilitarianism nor to restrict happiness to the life of the Epicurean sage, but to see the importance of sacrifice and duty in order to achieve happiness for everyone.

Mill's conception of human happiness thus required a high standard of virtue, which might include sacrifice and the acceptance of great pain. The pain was only legitimate, however, when its ultimate object was greater pleasure and happiness either at the time or in the future. He sought to join Stoic and Epicurean themes with the former subsidiary to the latter. In this respect Mill was faithfully following the Epicurean project at least from the seventeenth century. He and many others in the Epicurean tradition did not expect enlightenment through reason but through feelings—feelings fed by sensations of pleasure and feelings connected with sympathy with other human beings in similar circumstances.

Besides the emphasis on pleasure and happiness, and human feeling, modern Epicureanism emerged as a distinctive moral and political doctrine. This doctrine was evident in a number of works in the seventeenth century, but the most important was collected from Gassendi's writings by Francois Bernier.[24] The influential English version of Gassendi's moral philosophy, produced by Bernier, *Three Discourses of Happiness, Virtue, and Liberty*, was published in 1699, and in summarizing the doctrine of Epicurus, Gassendi wrote,

> Therefore to speak properly Right or natural Equity is nothing else but what is mark'd out by Utility or Profit, or that Utility which, by common Agreement, hath been appointed that Men might not injure one another, nor receive any wrong, but live in security, which is a real Good, and therefore naturally desired of every one.[25]

In Gassendi's account of the connection between utility and justice a number of important arguments were stated and developed. First, he dismissed the role of retaliation in any of the forms of justice. It had no place in distributive justice that was concerned with a person's worth, in corrective justice, where talionic punishments (an eye for an eye) were often unjust in their operation and consequences in bringing great pain into the system, and in matters of equity where the strict letter of the law was often unjust.[26] Nevertheless, he did not assume that justice was in itself desirable (as its operations were painful), but it became desirable in so far as it secured the basic tie without which a society could not exist.[27]

Second, Gassendi argued that for a law or practice to be just, it not only had to be useful but it also had to be "prescribed and ordained by the common Consent of the Society."[28] Two important consequences followed from this position. The first was that because justice was based on utility, a given law or practice could be just in one society though not in another, or just and then unjust in the same society when circumstances changed. These changes would depend on whether or not the law or practice was and remained useful in a social sense. This qualification was important, as the question to be asked of a given law was whether or not it secured the lives, liberties, and goods of the members of a society and prevented some members from harming others. The question was not whether this particular law was useful to me today in so far as it might enable me to profit from it, even though it would have to be rejected tomorrow because others were profiting and not me. The changes in laws and practices from society to society and from time to time should be based on whether or not they were useful to society. Many laws and practices would not be just or unjust, either because they did not raise issues of justice or because they were not useful to society in this fundamental sense. But how could one determine whether a given fundamental practice concerning human lives and property was just? This takes us to the second consequence: that the basic principles were approved by the common consent of members of society, or, as Gassendi put it at another point,

> [i]n a word, a thing is and ought to be reputed Just, or to have the Qualities of Just in a Society, *if its Usefulness respects all the Individuals associated*; but if it be not so 'tis not properly to be called Just, nor deserves to be so esteemed.[29]

For Gassendi, what made utility the basis of justice was not that "the wise" or the rich or the poor found a law useful and had the power to adopt and enforce it, but that all members found it useful by common consent or that the utility was such as the law or practice "respects all the individuals associated." On this account, there was no opposition between utility and justice and no sacrifice of some for the sake of a greater overall utility. Utility itself was a distributive principle, involving compact or agreement, and defined what counted as just and unjust. What made it distributive was that it was grounded in the common consent of the members of society, ultimately on their pleasures and pains, and applied equally to all members of society. Utility, then, became in Gassendi's account of Epicurean justice a technical term, referring to the nature and distribution of pains and pleasures and providing criteria to assess the justice of laws and practices.

Third, there could not be justice between human beings and animals and between human beings in different societies, because no mutual agreement existed to support that justice. Although there was no suggestion that animals should be maltreated, Gassendi stated bluntly, "So that to secure our selves, there remains for us no other means than to make use of that Power that we have, either to kill them, or to force them to obey us."[30] As between humans in different societies, he denied that one could appeal to a law of nations (*jus gentium*) but at the same time he recognized a "common precept": "*Thou shalt not do to another, what thou wilt not that another shalt do to thee.*" He gave to this precept the status of the "first natural Law." He argued that as nothing was more natural than society and that as society was unable to exist without this precept, then the precept was rightly termed "natural."[31] Thus, while people in different societies who did not live under a common agreement were not bound by justice, they could appeal to this common precept or first natural law not to harm others.

Fourth, as we have seen, following Epicurus, Gassendi introduced a new way of looking at nature both in his science and in his account of justice. Although he rejected the Stoic and Thomistic doctrines of natural law, and founded society on utility, he grafted the concept of nature on to the idea of common utility and found that these firm bonds warranted the term "natural." As Gassendi put it, "as to what *Epicurus* says, *That a true Law supposeth a mutual Compact, or every Law is a kind of Agreement*, 'tis no more than what *Plato, Aristotle, Demosthenes, Aristides*, and several others assert' "[32] (emphasis in original). In other words, Gassendi believed that Epicurus's view of the compact did not necessarily contradict the idea of natural justice found in Plato and Aristotle.

Finally, Gassendi attempted to deal with the satisfaction achieved by the unjust person who gained within society from his or her injustice. He rejected the view that the unjust person could be happy because he or she obtained what was desired, and called attention to the disordered *psyche* following the commission of acts of injustice: "full of Troubles, Jealousies and Fears, Gripings of Conscience and Anxiety of Mind. . . ."[33] Thus, the members of society resisted the temptation to be unjust, because of the anxieties concerning discovery and punishment, which persisted even if there was no serious possibility of punishment.

Bernier's compilation of Gassendi's writings on Epicurus was widely read and similar ideas appeared in other writers. For example, Thomas Stanley's *History of Philosophy* contained a substantial essay on Epicurus (part XIII), which restated the important connection between utility and justice:

> Wherefore to speak properly, Natural Right or Just is no other than a Symbol of Utility, or such an Utility agreed upon by Concurrence of Votes, as may keep Men from hurting, or being hurt by one another, so that they may live securely: A Good which every Man is taught by Nature to desire.[34]

Stanley went on to stipulate two conditions for the existence of justice: first, that "it be profitable or respect the common Utility, that is Security," and second, that "it be prescribed by the common Consent of Society; for nothing is completely just, but what the Society by common Consent or Agreement hath decreed to be observed."[35] In Stanley's account (as earlier in Gassendi's) great emphasis was placed not only on utility as the foundation of justice, but also on the importance of agreement and common consent as a condition for its existence. This agreement not to harm others was what in many respects determined utility. Stanley did not provide for any other test of utility nor did he invoke a "Legislator" to determine one. The system was bottom-up, so to speak: what was agreeable to humanity and accepted by members of society was just, because it was useful to them. Stanley developed this position one step further by emphasizing that the utility of a law or practice must extend to all:

> [W]hatsoever is by Experience found profitable to a mutual Society, or the common Participation of such Things as are esteemed just, that Thing hath the Nature of Just or Right, if it be such as its Utility extends unto all. But if any Man shall establish such a thing for just, and yet it shall happen not to be profitable to the mutual Society, it hath not the true Nature of Just or Right.[36]

Beyond the two conditions previously mentioned, that justice was based on utility as security and that the agreement not to harm others was based on common consent, he seems here to be suggesting a third, that the usefulness of any given law or practice *extends* to all members of that society. These tests were not conceived in addition to utility as the foundation of society, they were conceived based on what utility meant in the context of justice. To answer the question, is this law just, one rather would first ascertain if it was based on utility. One would then find out if it enhanced security (not harming or being harmed), was based on common consent, and extended to all. This determination would allow one to decide if the law was based on utility and thereby just. There is no discussion here or among other writers on Epicurean themes of the question of whether or not utility would allow some people to be sacrificed to increase the happiness or pleasure of others. Such sacrifice would be precluded by the three conditions listed above. Furthermore, none of these writers envisaged a particular system of government that would enable these conditions to be realized in practice, and their interest (like that of Epicurus) was simply to explore this doctrine as a contribution to moral philosophy. That Hobbes, Locke, Montesquieu, Rousseau, Helvétius, Hume, and Bentham might reach very different conclusions with regard to sovereignty and the institutions of government was not precluded by the arguments concerning the dependence of justice on utility. What these arguments achieved, however, was to establish that justice in society arose not from natural or divine law that could only with difficulty be ascertained by ordinary people, but from the common agreement of the individuals that comprised society. Furthermore, the object of government as a matter of justice was only to enhance the security of the lives, liberties, and properties of its members. From this point of view the virtue of justice was to play an important role in the development of theories of the modern state.

Stanley repeated a number of the doctrines already found in Gassendi, such as that there could not be justice between men and animals, because there could not be mutual agreement.[37] He also noted that the account of justice and utility did not limit or deny the importance of the other virtues such as beneficence or goodwill, which were concerned with the good of others.[38]

In *Epicurus's Morals* John Digby also restated the close connection Epicurus established between justice and utility:

> Justice is nothing in it self: Mankind united in Society discover'd the Utility and the Advantage of agreeing among themselves, to observe certain Conditions for their living inoffensively one towards another.[39]

Digby discussed other Epicurean themes such as the importance of prudence and friendship, and stressed how all of the virtues, such as temperance, magnanimity, prudence, and justice, were sought because of their "Consequences and Effects," that is to say, their utility to individuals and society.[40] He also emphasized that the studies Epicurus made of nature were not done for their own sake only but in order for him to become a moral philosopher.[41] He distinguished between Epicurus and Socrates by noting that Socrates despised the study of nature and turned to human matters only. On the contrary, Epicurus

> will have us pry and search into the Secrets of Physick, not for her own sake, but because it enlightens the Mind, discusses and examines the Causes and the End of all, makes us despise Death, and supplies us with Remedies against Fear; Which are Certain and sure Means to live and die peaceable.[42]

In contrasting the Stoics and Epicureans, Digby criticized the Stoics for believing that there were natural principles of justice, but when it came to discerning them the ancient Legislator, such as Lycurgus at Sparta, had to turn to divine authority (e.g., the oracle at Delphi) to do so. The Epicureans believed that a primitive people had no idea of justice, as it was developed only in society by those who could grasp its utility.[43]

In the Epicurean tradition, as we have seen, justice meant not harming others. This principle was secured by the social contract or by conventions and customs, and its utility was recognized by the civil peace and security for individuals that such a principle provided. The idea of liberty was closely related to that of justice, in so far as individuals in civil society were free to act as they pleased so long as they did not harm each other. This conception of justice opened the door for liberty in numerous spheres from religious toleration to freedom of speech, free trade, and the freedom to act generally where no harm was caused to others—culminating in the striking principle of John Stuart Mill's *On Liberty*. In this development or, more accurately, shift of focus from justice to liberty, an equally important shift took place through an orientation toward the future and future happiness. The economic freedom which emerged from this conception of justice entailed not only that security of persons and property would enable people to plan and invest for the future, secure in the belief that these plans and investments would survive prior to their maturity, but also that the economic growth necessary for this development would not be stifled by ideas opposed to risk and sacrifice.

An important debate within the Epicurean tradition took place between Smith and Bentham over the extent to which the existing usury laws were or were not a barrier to such liberty. Although Smith defended the existing laws in *An Inquiry into the Nature and Causes of the Wealth of Nations*,[44] Bentham provided a striking attack in his famous pamphlet *Defence of Usury*.[45] Both Bentham and Smith believed in economic freedom and both shared an orientation toward happiness in the future as part of economic development. Bentham described the act of money lending so that "putting money out at interest, is exchanging present money for future."[46] When he referred to the example of the envy of children who still had their portion of birthday cake after the others had eaten theirs, he noted that "those who have the resolution to sacrifice the present to the future, are natural objects of envy to those who have sacrificed the future to the present."[47] At the end of his work Bentham referred to projectors (or entrepreneurs) as "the race of those with which the womb of futurity is still pregnant."[48] For Bentham, the projector held the key to human progress, and his defense of projectors and a free market in money contained a special emphasis on an orientation toward the future. Furthermore, Bentham linked utility to the projector's aim at improvement in the future in producing new articles, reducing expense, meliorating existing practices, et cetera.

Smith also recognized the importance of the future, which can be seen in a famous passage in *The Theory of Moral Sentiments* where he linked prudence, frugality, and the impartial spectator:

> In the steadiness of his industry and frugality, in his steadily sacrificing the ease and enjoyment of the present moment for the probable expectation of the still greater ease and enjoyment of a more distant but more lasting period of time, the prudent man is always both supported and rewarded by the entire approbation of the impartial spectator, and of the representative of the impartial spectator, the man within the breast.[49]

For Smith, the impartial spectator regarded the present and the future in the same manner, and could applaud those who sacrificed present comfort and ease to achieve a greater comfort and ease in the future. As one can see in the passage just quoted, prudence was closely linked with frugality, self-command, parsimony, and sacrifice—all of which were supposed to lead gradually to greater enjoyment and happiness in the future.

Smith described the prudent person at length and distinguished between the superior wisdom and judiciousness that represented (with other virtues) the prudence of the great statesmen and legislators (as presented by Plato and Aristotle) from an inferior prudence that he found depicted in the Epicurean tradition.[50] If the superior prudence combined all the moral and intellectual virtues, the inferior prudence seemed to act differently. The person of prudence in this more limited sense lived within his or her income and was content with his or her situation. Through frugality, small accumulations were made, and "ease and enjoyment" gradually increased. "He has no anxiety to change so comfortable a situation," Smith continued, "and does not go in quest of new enterprises and adventures which might endanger . . . the secure tranquility." He is not wholly adverse to new enterprises, but "if he enters into any new projects and enterprises, they are likely to be well concerted and well prepared."[51] "In the bottom of his heart," Smith concluded his picture of the man of prudence in this inferior form, "he would prefer the undisturbed enjoyment of secure tranquillity, not only to all the vain splendour of successful ambition, but to the real and solid glory of performing the greatest and most magnanimous actions."[52]

According to Bentham, prudence consisted of discharging one's duties to oneself and was distinguished from probity and beneficence, the two virtues concerned with duties to others. Of these, probity was concerned with not harming others and beneficence was concerned more positively with doing them good.[53] In making these distinctions, Bentham was clearly attempting to construct a fairly simple and neutral account of the virtues. Unlike Smith, for example, his account of prudence did not include references to frugality or sacrifice, but simply to the idea that prudence was concerned with duties to oneself. He was also aware of other senses in which prudence was used (such as a synonym for intellectual virtue or practical wisdom[54]) and could be treated as an extra-regarding as well as a self-regarding quality.[55]

Bentham's key point regarding prudence was its connection with the principle of utility and thus with pleasure and pain. The future orientation of prudence might well require the sacrifice of immediate satisfaction in the hope of greater future pleasure or the relief of pain. If no attempt was made to promote the future happiness of the agent, the result was "asceticism"—"the offspring of delusion: the very opposite of prudence."[56] Bentham was aware that a good deal of human happiness depended on one's expectations of happiness in the future, and that a good part of the civil law was concerned with securing future expectations.[57] One reason for securing property to the proprietor rather than making a different distribution according to some other principle (such as merit or equality) was that pleasures acquired via the redistribution could never match (except in a few circumstances) the pain of disappointment in losing the property one possessed.[58]

Bentham had two arguments against Smith's attempt to link prudence, frugality, and the future. The first was that he came close to adopting asceticism, so that the life of prudent self-denial—for oneself and especially for others—seemed good in itself. Even though Smith insisted that the sacrifices of the present moment were intended to lead to greater ease and enjoyment, the prudent man did not admire or approve of the person who was "a bustler in business," who managed other people's affairs, and who listened "to the voice even of noble and great ambition."[59] His virtue of prudence in the Epicurean tradition (the inferior form) was not considered "the most endearing" or "the most ennobling" of the virtues.[60] If Smith thought that future happiness rather than asceticism should be the object of prudence, he seemed to exclude the happiness and particularly the future happiness of the projector who seemed to be portrayed as the one who most threatened to disturb the quiet enjoyment of the future by the frugal and prudent individual.

The second argument is based on the first in that unlike Smith, Bentham did not link frugality to the acquisition of wealth. The frugal and parsimonious person, saving and building up one's capital, was not the key to economic growth and the wealth of nations. For Bentham, the term "frugality," like that of "economy," was concerned with the preservation of wealth rather than with its acquisition.[61] The prudent person in Smith's conception was in fact the child who still possessed his or her piece of birthday cake after the others had eaten theirs, and although this piece of cake might represent wealth preserved, it was not wealth acquired. Bentham challenged Smith to revise his conception of the acquisition of wealth. He realized that such a revision would have to be extensive and at the outset would include the abolition of the usury laws and a celebration (rather than a denigration) of the projector or entrepreneur.

In one of his philosophical essays ("Of the External Senses"), Smith referred to the philosophy of Leucippus, Democritus, and Epicurus, as "revived by Gassendi" and "adopted by Newton," as "the established system, or as the system that is most in fashion, and most approved of by the greater part of the philosophers of Europe."[62] To this system he contrasted another that he depicted somewhat vaguely as "drawn from that species of metaphysics which confounds every thing and explains nothing."[63] Smith's recognition of modern Epicureanism has been supported here by arguments and doctrines taken from Epicurean writers in the fields of ethics and politics. The emphasis on tranquility of spirit finds its external manifestation in security of persons and property, and a freedom to act as one pleases without causing harm to others. The double helix of justice and liberty from which ideas of the social contract, utility, economic development, and progress emerge is at the heart of modern Epicureanism. To these ideas one might add the view that there could be considerable flexibility in the institutions of government in a society so long as they achieved security on which justice and liberty depended. Here was a unique focus on constitutional provisions that served primarily as securities against the abuse of power by rulers. The object of government was one of enhancing human happiness partly by allowing and securing various liberties and partly by reducing pain in supplying subsistence and basic welfare. At a deeper level is the importance of maintaining the distinctive orientation toward the future necessary for economic growth and human happiness, which is achieved partly by maintaining security and partly by removing obstacles that might otherwise prevent the entrepreneur from taking risks and sacrificing immediate pleasures for a greater happiness in the future.

It has herein been suggested that Epicureanism runs like a rich vein of precious metal through modern thought. It is often obscured in accounts of the European Enlightenment, which tends to be confined to the eighteenth century and is distinguished by a somewhat utopian emphasis on human rationality. The writers discussed here who drew on the Epicurean tradition emphasized instead the importance of feeling and its connection with pleasure and pain. The Enlightenment, as the Age of Reason, seems to be more a Kantian or even post-Kantian invention, which, while reflecting the emphasis on freedom and particularly freedom of religious belief, which is found in the eighteenth century, also brings with it a similar emphasis on enlightened despotism and civil obedience that is foreign to the Epicurean tradition. In the latter a moderate constitutionalism is emphasized with an acceptance of a variety of institutions of government so long as civil liberty and, particularly, security of life and property are respected, and individuals are secure against the abuse of power by others and by government. Its foundations are in the direct human experience of pleasure and pain and, in this sense, is a bottom-up theory in which ordinary feelings of happiness, utility, and virtue count for more than systems of ethics and politics imposed from above.

Notes

This article is based on arguments and materials more fully developed in Frederick Rosen, *Classical Utilitarianism from Hume to Mill* (London: Routledge, 2003).

1. Cyril Bailey, *The Greek Atomists and Epicurus* (Oxford: Clarendon Press, 1928), 526.
2. Geoffrey Scarre, "Epicurus as a Forerunner of Utilitarianism," *Utilitas* 6 (1994): 219–231, 219, 222.
3. Epicurus, KD, sec. xxxi, 102–103, in Epicurus, *The Extant Remains*, trans. Cyril Bailey (Oxford: Clarendon Press, 1926). See also sec. xxxvi, 102–103.
4. See Frederick Vaughan, *The Tradition of Political Hedonism from Hobbes to J. S. Mill* (New York: Fordham University Press, 1982), 43; and John Stephenson Spink, *French Free Thought from Gassendi to Voltaire* (London: Athlone Press, 1960), 85–102.
5. Vaughan, *Tradition of Political Hedonism*, 53; quoting Thomas Franklin Mayo, *Epicurus in England, 1650–1725* (Dallas: Southwest Press, 1934), xi.
6. See Lisa T. Sarasohn, *Gassendi's Ethics: Freedom in a Mechanistic Universe* (Ithaca: Cornell University Press, 1996), 202; and Howard Jones, *Pierre Gassendi: An Intellectual Biography* (Nieuwkoop: B. DeGraaf, 1981), 7.

7. See Sarasohn, *Gassendi's Ethics*, 142; Vaughan, *Tradition of Political Hedonism*, 69–70; and H. Nichols, Jr., *Epicurean Political Philosophy* (Ithaca: Cornell University Press, 1976), 183–190.

8. See Reid Barbour, *English Epicures and Stoics: Ancient Legacies in Early Stuart Culture* (Amherst: University of Massachusetts Press, 1998).

9. See Norman Wentworth De Witt, *Epicurus and his Philosophy* (Minneapolis: University of Minnesota Press, 1954), 217.

10. See Marcus Tullius Cicero, *De Finibus Bonorum et Malorum*, ed. H. Rackham (Cambridge, MA: Harvard University Press, 1999), I.xi, 42–43.

11. See De Witt, *Epicurus and his Philosophy*, 236.

12. See ibid., 235.

13. Jeremy Bentham, *An Introduction to the Principles of Morals and Legislation*, ed. J. H. Burns and H. L. A. Hart, with a new introduction by Frederick Rosen, *The Collected Works of Jeremy Bentham* (Oxford: Oxford University Press, 1996), 42–50.

14. See David Hume, *An Enquiry Concerning the Principles of Morals*, ed. Tom L. Beauchamp (Oxford: Clarendon Press, 1998), 9.9.

15. John Stuart Mill, *Utilitarianism*, ed. Roger Crisp, (Oxford: Oxford University Press, 1998), 54.

16. Ibid., 54–57.

17. John Stuart Mill, *Journals and Debating Speeches*, ed. John M. Robson, Collected Works of John Stuart Mill, 33 vols. (Toronto: University of Toronto Press, 1988), 27: 666.

18. Thomas Carlyle, *Sartor Resartus: The Life and Opinions of Herr Teufelsdrockh in Three Books*, ed. Rodger L. Tarr (Berkeley and Los Angeles: University of California Press, 2000), 143.

19. Ibid., 142–143.

20. John Stuart Mill, *Autobiography and Literary Essays*, ed. John M. Robson and Jack Stillinger, Collected Works of John Stuart Mill (Toronto: University of Toronto Press, 1981), 181.

21. Mill, *Utilitarianism*, ed. Crisp, 61.

22. Ibid., 62.

23. Ibid., 62–63.

24. See Spink, *French Free Thought from Gassendi to Voltaire*, 106–108.

25. Pierre Gassendi, *Three Discourses of Happiness, Virtue, and Liberty, Collected from the works of the Learn'd Gassendi, by Monsieur Bernier* (London: Awnsham and John Churchill, 1699), 315.

26. Ibid., 308–310.

27. Ibid., 312.

28. Ibid., 315.

29. Ibid., 316; italics added.

30. Ibid., 321.

31. Ibid., 327.

32. Ibid., 325.

33. Ibid., 333.
34. Thomas Stanley, *The History of Philosophy: Containing the Lives, Opinions, Actions, and Discourses of the Philosophers of Every Sect*, 4th ed. (London: A. Miller, 1743), 707.
35. Ibid.
36. Ibid.
37. Ibid., 710.
38. Ibid., 712.
39. John Digby, *Epicurus's Morals* (London: Sam. Briscoe, 1712), 146.
40. Ibid., 45–46, 57, 122.
41. Ibid., 80.
42. Ibid., 125–126.
43. Ibid., 143, 144.
44. See Adam Smith, *An Inquiry into the Nature and Causes of the Wealth of Nations*, Glasgow Edition of the Works and Correspondence of Adam Smith, ed. R. H. Campbell, A. S. Skinner, and W. B. Todd, 7 vols. (Indianapolis: Liberty Classics, 1981), 2: 2.iv.15, 357.
45. Jeremy Bentham, *Jeremy Bentham's Economic Writings*, ed. W. Stark, 3 vols. (London: George Allen and Unwin, 1952–1954), 1: 123–207.
46. Ibid., 1: 132.
47. Ibid., 1: 159.
48. Ibid., 1: 180.
49. Adam Smith, *The Theory of Moral Sentiments*, ed. D. D. Raphael and A. L. Macfie, Glasgow Edition of the Works and Correspondence of Adam Smith, 7 vols. (Indianapolis: Liberty Classics, 1982), 1: VI.i.11, 215.
50. Ibid., 1: VI.i.15, 216.
51. Ibid., 1: VI.i.12, 215.
52. Ibid., 1: VI.i.13, 216. See also Gloria Vivenza, *Adam Smith and the Classics: The Classical Heritage in Adam Smith's Thought* (Oxford: Oxford University Press, 2001), 54–57.
53. See Bentham, *Introduction to the Principles of Morals and Legislation*, 284.
54. Jeremy Bentham, *Deontology Together with a Table of the Springs of Action and Article on Utilitarianism*, ed. Amnon Goldworth, The Collected Works of Jeremy Bentham (Oxford: Oxford University Press, 1983), 127n.
55. Ibid., 187–188.
56. Ibid., 188.
57. See Paul J. Kelly, *Utilitarianism and Distributive Justice: Jeremy Bentham and the Civil Law* (Oxford: Oxford University Press, 1990), 71–103.
58. See Bentham, *Deontology*, 188–190.
59. Smith, *Theory of Moral Sentiments*, 1: VI.i.13, 215–216.
60. Ibid., 216.

61. Bentham, *Deontology*, 104.
62. Adam Smith, *Essays on Philosophical Subjects*, ed. W. P. D. Wightman and J. C. Bryce, Glasgow Edition of the Works and Correspondence of Adam Smith, 7 vols. (Indianapolis: Liberty Classics, 1982), 3: 140.
63. Ibid.

Chapter 4

Preface to Liberalism: Locke's First Treatise and the Bible

Robert Faulkner

Question: Is Human Law Primary?

A modern constitution is a man-made fundamental law, and it sets up a supreme government as agent of the people. What, however, of the commandments of the supreme God? How in face of Him can a man-made law and government be fundamental and supreme?[1]

This is the political-theological problem, we will argue, at the deepest level of John Locke's *First Treatise of Government*. At that level the *First Treatise* chiefly undermines, although it also revises. It undermines the primacy of the biblical God, of both His providence and His law, and it also revises biblical fundamentals so as to permit a more rational and civil faith. These are the two leading contentions of this study. If they prove to be true, the *First Treatise* is much more important to Locke's liberalism than is commonly believed. It is the precondition for his works on toleration and Christianity, the writings setting forth the liberal religion that can abide the primacy of civil government and of "civil interests" generally. It is also, then, the precondition for the *Second Treatise of Civil Government*. The famous *Second Treatise* may be the seminal articulation of modern representative government, but the neglected *First Treatise* proves to be its necessary preface. So we will contend. In this contention we supplement a growing body of more comprehensive treatments.[2] Nevertheless, this remains a rather uncommon and much controverted view. We will first address the many present-day scholars who deny the importance of the work, of its political-theological problem, and of Locke's originality in such matters.

The serious reason why the *First Treatise* has been neglected is the supposition that it is philosophically obsolete. After centuries of Enlightenment and post-Enlightenment, few commentators in the English-speaking world take seriously the primacy of revealed truth. Those who do often equate "Judeo-Christian values" with rational principles of human rights and liberal democracy. But is not such confidence in enlightened principles now itself obsolete? What of that congeries of skeptical attitudes loosely called "postmodernism"? Up-to-date intellectuals and scholars indict scientific rationalism as but "instrumental" to enlightened values, and they indict enlightened values as but preferences relative and indeed repressive. Whatever the cogency of all this, it is undeniable that a self-devouring disillusion-ment with reason now besets the late stages of modern rationalism. Some such relativism besets the guardians of liberalism itself. A John Rawls or a Richard Rorty may strive to keep the great cause afloat, but it is as merely a "political" conception or faith, as the "we believes" or "public reason" present in the practices of contemporary liberal society.[3] Rawls as well as Rorty have been brought to deny or to doubt demonstrable knowledge of rational foundations and thus of liberal foundations in particular. They in effect question whether any "com-prehensive understanding" can provide sufficient reason for liberal society. Nevertheless, "we" in liberal democracies are told that we must hold to our own faith. But why this "must"? Why the necessity so to believe in liberalism? The reason cannot be simply common belief, contrary to Rawls's assertions. For his (and Rorty's) version of liberalism is distinctive and thus partisan and partial. There are property-rights liberals as well as equal dignity liberals, not to speak of blue-collar democrats. And then there is in some liberal democracies the embarrassing prominence of conservatives, including the so-called religious fundamentalists who believe in neither equal dignity nor postmodern skepticism as to foundations. The question recurs almost naturally: why believe in a liberalism that doubts its reasonableness, especially in preference to a faith confident of its source in God's word and command? There is some reason for the new confidence of the orthodox.[4] There is a corresponding necessity for liberals to remind themselves of the reasons for liberalism and to see whether the difficulties now alleged are real.

Among a few of those concerned for liberalism's plight one now finds a renewed appreciation for Locke's efforts. A recent example is Jeremy Waldron, who has called upon scholars to look past historical circumstance and to learn from the deeper reasons that Locke supplied. The "*First Treatise* is an indispensable resource" in the recovery of an adequate theory of liberal equality, for it wrestles with "the general problems posed by divine law," not merely with the peculiarities of Robert Filmer.[5] Still, Waldron gets only a little way into Locke's reasoning. Looking for the "Christian foundations" of liberal equality, he slights the challenge to human freedom and equality posed by Christian foundations and by divine superiority and divine law in general. Waldron slights in particular the *First Treatise*'s many-sided and continuous efforts at critique and reform, even if he shows now and then, as in Locke's treatment of Adam and Eve, the remarkable liberation of women. Waldron seeks the Christian foundations of liberalism, but he has to acknowledge that the actual text of the *Two Treatises* "barely mentions" Jesus, St. Paul, and the New Testament. He almost has to acknowledge, that is, the liberal foundations of Locke's liberalism. Nevertheless, one must be grateful to a scholar who helps show a way back into what might seem a lost territory.

Still, for too many present-day readers the *First Treatise* will appear not only obsolete but also irretrievably parochial. Can one learn about a perennial problem from a work addressing Sir Robert Filmer's strange theory of the divine right of kings? Filmer had contended for a patriarchal monarchy derived from Father Adam, and it has long been a question why Locke spent such "pains" and pages in refuting someone whom the *First Treatise* itself calls no great "arguer" and one already "confuted." Did Locke have but a modest goal, as many contend? Was he merely defending against a second-rater the moderately monarchical and Protestant Britain of his time? Locke was rather conventional, politically and religiously, and certainly not a protagonist of "radical Enlightenment"—that remains a very influential opinion even among serious scholars.[6]

But this picture of a Locke immured in his times cannot account for Locke's startling innovations, especially the *First Treatise's* radical criticism of both monarchy and aristocracy. What of the biting attacks on all hereditary rule, whether of kings, dukes, or gentry, and on primogeniture, the economic prerequisite of hereditary monarchy and hereditary aristocracy alike (I.86–100)?[7] And what of the innovative creed that underlies this political-economic razor, that is, Locke's unBiblical doctrines of equal rights to life, liberty, and property? To come to the point that we will endeavor to prove, the conventional view neglects Locke's radical criticism of all religion and thus of all Christianity. It neglects in particular that in spearing Filmer, Locke hits the Bible.[8]

Precisely in the *First Treatise*, at almost its literal center, Locke expressly goes his own way ("But not to follow our A—too far out of the way . . . " I.86). There follows what is perhaps the clearest Lockean account of the foundation of the rights of man—and of the corresponding right of each person equally to subsistence and hence to inheritance.

Let us admit, nevertheless, that the attack on all monarchy, like most of Locke's attacks, is cautious and muted, that the attack on all aristocracy is especially muted, and, especially, that the new rational foundation appears in a theology. But we will insist that this last is a rationally transformed theology that highlights not God's law but man's needs and his rights, especially his right to enlightened self-reliance. "Reason," not revelation or grace, is the "*Voice of God*" in man (I.86). The basic "principle" is the "first and strongest desire" for "Self-Preservation," not some traditional law of nature or command-ment of God. This may be philosophic and rational individualism, reminding even of the Hobbist version. It is not Protestantism—unless so eviscerated as to omit justification by faith alone and by Christ's saving grace.

If this is reformation, it is not Protestant Reformation but the enlightened reform consistent with Locke's other formulations of liberal and civil religion. The most important formulation is the famous *Letter Concerning Toleration*, which in effect elevates freedom over truth in matters of worship. "[N]atural Rights are not forfeitable on account of Religion"; Locke takes pride in having "at length freed men from all Dominion over one another in matters of Religion."[9] The *Letter* begins by calling "Toleration," not faith in Jesus, the "chief Characteristical Mark of the True Church." It then proceeds to scat-ter little skeptical daggers at any supposedly "true church"—but a "name"—and at "truth of Religion"—"every Church is Orthodox to it self." Indeed, "the Religion of every Prince is Orthodox to himself." Whatever Locke's concern for sincerity of faith and the independence of churches, his brand of toleration ends up tolerating only religions tolerant and civil. It does not tolerate others, that is, all religions hitherto. Religions must "lay down toleration as the foundation of their own liberty" and advance no opinions contrary to the "moral Rules" needed for "Civil Society." True, "all the Life and power of true reli-gion" consists in the "inward and full persuasion of the mind." But it is also true that in the absence of orthodoxy and a true church, this famous Lockean doctrine of sincerity frees the believer to believe whatever he chances to believe. Does it not breed what grew in liberal lands: subjectivity of belief, inevitable self-doubt, and a multitude of weak and competing sects? Yet "the Civil Power is the same in every place." While retaining familiar-sounding but diluted beliefs, the

Letter Concerning Toleration leads the believer to depart the universal church for the realm of universal liberty and civil government. It leads believers to depart Christendom for liberalism. The innovations of the *First Treatise* are basic to the project of the *Letter*.

While the *First Treatise* is chiefly critical rather than constructive, it is comprehensively critical. It thrusts through Filmer at such biblical doctrines as God's creation of the world, His donation of the creatures to man, original sin, paternal power, inheritance by the eldest, and a chosen people. Filmer used these doctrines to support patriarchal monarchy in the world. Locke strikes not only at monarchy in the world but also at the King of kings, the Father of fathers. As the subtitle tells us, he addresses not only Filmer's "Principles" but also their "Foundation." That foundation proves to be finally the God of the Bible, supplemented by certain philosophic teachings as to nature and the nature of fatherhood in particular.[10] Nor should one suppose that Locke's conclusions apply only to the Old Testament, even if the *First Treatise* is chiefly about the Old Testament. For in discoursing on the Old Testament Locke refutes claims for the paternal and providential God who governs also in the New. The argument of the *First Treatise* is thus more relevant and more shocking than might appear, partly because it is more complete than might appear.

We will even speculate that the *Two Treatises*' strange incompleteness in form is part of its veiling of this critique. At the start of the work is a conspicuous tease: the famous missing middle. Locke confesses to "missing" middle pages, more than "all the rest," which will not be missed if "these Papers have that evidence" that Locke believes to be "in them" (Preface). What exactly is missing Locke does not say, except for a matter of procedure: to replace this bulk he would have to trace Filmer again "through all the Windings and Obscurities" in the "several branches of his wonderful System." But the *First Treatise* does much (all too much) of that tedious tracing. So what is missing? Suppose that we try to put two and two together. Might the substance of this missing middle be intimated by a missing portion at the end of the *First Treatise* (which is the most obvious middle between the treatises)? The final paragraph of the *First Treatise* recounts the "destruction" of the Jews by the Romans (I.169) and hence their demise as "God's peculiar People." Consider. Jews, Chosen by God, could never agree that their divine significance had been erased by a political event. And Christians, who are of course Locke's chief audience, would expect a turn from the defects of Jehovah to the saving Messiah. Yet the suppositions of a righteous God and a saving Jesus are missing. They are missing from both the end of the *First Treatise* and the beginning of the *Second*. Instead, Jews and Christians alike get Locke's *Second Treatise*, that is, the civil government that can protect men from destruction. If this admittedly risky speculation is true, then the veiled disappearance of the biblical God is the truth hidden by the missing middle, but indicated by "evidence" elsewhere in the *Treatises*, and the central teachings of Christians as well as Jews are replaced by Locke's central teachings of natural freedom and civil government. One is then led to wonder, then, whether it is merely coincidence that the argument for natural freedom begins just after the central section of the first *Treatise* (I.86), and the argument for "Dominion and Control" by government, at the central section of the second (II.223).

Still, speculations as to literary form cannot be more than secondary complements to the primary thing, which is an account of the substance of Locke's intention as to biblical essentials. That intention, I think, appears in the problems for reason, for political reasonableness in particular, that he finds in Filmer's political theology.

According to Locke, Filmer was in his way an innovator, and his innovation consisted in adding a rational standard of political right to the Bible's own account of God's workings. To the Bible's characteristic suggestion that all power is from God, Filmer added a standard for rightful power: inheritance from God's instrument Adam. "He, affirming that *the Assignment of Civil Power is by Divine Institution*, hath made the conveyance as well as the Power it self Sacred" (I.107, cf. 106). But Filmer's attempt to explain the conveyance of God's power by inheritance, Locke shows, is incoherent. Contrary to Filmer's hypothesis, the effort to deduce political right from the Bible falls back into deference to the mysterious providence of God. The attempt at a biblical politics falls back into an impolitic passivity before the powers that be. We will fill out this summary.

Filmer's doctrine was a biblically based patriarchalism. Since fathers should by nature rule their families, and since Adam according to God's word is the father of all fathers, Adam had a natural and divine authority over his children and descendants. But his children and descendants amount to all mankind. His heirs, Filmer concludes, are entitled to a lord-like power over mankind.

The surface argument of the *First Treatise* demonstrates in three stages that Filmer's theory, despite his assurances, cannot define who or what should be rightly obeyed. First, Adam was never considered in the Bible as lord of mankind (chapters III–VI). Second, even if he had been lord, it is impossible to tell from the Bible to whom by the laws of God or nature he conveyed his authority (chapters VII–IX).

And, third, even if one could know to whom he conveyed it, one certainly cannot know who now has it (chapters X–XI). The result of Filmer's counsel of obedience to the lord's heir, then, is two extremes: either anarchy or subservience. His patriarchalism either unsettles all governments, in favor of a true heir who cannot be known, or acquiesces in all existing authorities, including commonwealths and usurpers as well as kings. The unsettling contradicts Filmer's insistence upon obedience to established authority; the acquiescence contradicts his insistence upon paternal monarchy. Filmer chooses to acquiesce. To be "Properly a King," Locke concludes of Filmer's doctrine, needs no more than holding "Supreme Power," and "it matters not by what Means he came of it" (I.79). Filmer "resolves all into present possession" (I.21; cf. I.134) and in effect baptizes present possession with divine right.

Locke had complained early of Filmer's failures to define "fatherhood," to set forth the question, and to argue in clear words and propositions. Instead there appeared a "story" of a "strange kind of domineering Phantom," a "Gigantic Form," which "whoever could catch, got Empire, and unlimited absolute Power" (I.6, 7, 10, 13, 20). The mixing of rational right with mysterious providence ends by worshipping absolute authority and deferring to any authority.

Locke himself, however, is inclined to neither mere absolutism nor mere subservience. He insists upon knowing by reason who should by right govern, and the insistence informs his whole treatise. Else there is "an end to all Civil Government," as well as to "humane prudence, or consent" (I.126). This question, the political question of "what Persons have a Right to be obeyed," is "the great Question" (I.122; cf. I.106, Preface). Eventually, if laconically, Locke explicitly indicts quietism before what men call Providence. "If any one will say, that what happens in Providence to be preserved, God is careful to preserve as a thing therefore to be esteemed by Men as necessary or useful, 'tis a peculiar Propriety of Speech; which not every one will think fit to imitate" (I.147). This question as to "what Person or Persons" are to be obeyed has implications in the world, then, far beyond political governance. Indeed, Locke's insistence on rational warrant rather than providential sign may extend to even religious authority. At least he intimates a denial of belief in someone with the "Name of Priest" whose only credential is a claim to inherited divine power, but who offers nevertheless to supply "good absolution" upon confession of "Sins" (I.125). Locke's insistence on reason in choosing governors may be radical enough to undermine priests and miracles as well as kings and aristocrats. It seems to be some such effort, to establish the authority of reason over God's grace and over those who claim to inherit God's grace, that underlies the civil reformulations in the *Letter Concerning Toleration* and the *Reasonableness of Christianity*. What we can prove here is that such an effort suffuses the *First Treatise*'s reinterpretation of the Bible itself.

Reforming Genesis: Lordly Rule Made Reasonable

Locke's attacks on the primacy of God's righteousness and of man's corresponding duties are characteristically indirect, occur as he rebuts Filmerian proofs of Adam's authority over mankind, and are chiefly quiet reformulations. Should we expect much more? "[C]ertainly Propriety of speech is necessary in a Discourse of this Nature" (I.109), not least as to "words and names that have obtained in the World" (II.52). Still, both *First Treatise* and *Second* are willing to change customs and words when "the old are apt to lead Men into Mistakes, as this of Paternal Power probably has done" (II.52). Apparent respect yields to veiled reform.

(1) The Lord may have created Adam, but that creation, according to Locke, gave Adam no special power over men. For creating is merely begetting, and begetting by itself gives no special authority to the one first begat. Else the lion might rule all, since it was created earlier (I.15). This may be biblical-sounding language, but it varnishes unbiblical omissions and connotations. What of Adam's special stature, not created like the animals, "according to their kind," but "in the image of God" with "dominion" over the others (Gen. 1: 26)? What too of Adam's corresponding duty to subordinate himself and his progeny to the Lord's righteous commands—to abstain, for example, from "knowledge of good and evil" (Gen. 1: 27)? Silence. Later, Locke will equate creation in "the Image of God" with an "intellectual" creature (I.30), rather than one of lordly righteousness. Later still, his own account finds the foundation of justice in man's knowledge of his necessities, not in any revelation of God's righteousness (I.86, 87–100; cf. II.26–33). At most, the "Voice of reason" is "confirmed by Inspiration" (II.31). What too of the unbounded gratitude that one might think owed to God for the "blessing" of creation? Silence again. In the crucial context Locke avoids equating God's creation of the creatures with a "blessing," speaking so only later and inconsequentially (e.g., I.30, 33). Elsewhere, especially in the *Second Treatise's* decisive treatment of property, Locke gradually advances the

suggestion that nature is less a nursing mother than a niggardly stepmother, providing no blessing but rather bare materials that must be transformed to be useful. It is human effort that contributes 9/10, or rather 99/100, or rather 999/1000, of the value for man (II.37, 40, 41, 43). The first enigmatic reconstructions of the Bible begin to accustom us to a rational morality of industrious self-reliance.

(2) Worldly improvement, political as well as economic, takes priority over humble gratitude, and this becomes more visible when Locke reinterprets God's Donation of the creatures to Adam (Gen. 1: 28ff.). First Locke illuminates Filmer's tendentiousness, and then he practices his own. The focus is the Lord's injunction: "be Fruitful and Multiply" (I.23ff ; cf. Gen. 1: 28). This, we are eventually instructed, implies "the improvement too of Arts and Sciences, and the conveniences of Life" (I.33). It also implies, "by the by," the abolition of Absolute Monarchy. Large and rich states governed by monarchies, especially Turkish-style monarchies, will not have 1/3, nay 1/30, nay 1/100, of the "Conveniences of Life and Multitudes of People" possible under other laws (I.41, 33). There is a corresponding "by the by" in the *Second Treatise*. A "prince" who by "established laws of liberty" protects and encourages the "honest industry of mankind," will "quickly be too hard for his neighbors" (II.42). Locke's Bible becomes a complement to liberal political economy, that is, to his scheme for the wealth of nations. The Bible itself had prescribed use in reverence of the creatures and of one's gains, as George Windstrup has pointed out—in reverence, that is, for creation and the Lord whose property we all are.[11]

There occurs in this context one of the *First Treatise*'s only two quotations from the New Testament: according to "the Apostle," God "gives us all things richly to enjoy" (I.40; cf. 1 Tim. 6: 17). Still, the biblical original directs to piety and gratitude, not to riches and acquisitions. The wealthy should not "set their hopes on uncertain riches but on God who richly furnishes us with all things to enjoy." Locke's reinterpretation, then, is not Protestantism but enlightened acquisitive Protestantism. One sees in process the rhetoric of enlightening. Later, when Locke has located the origin of right in man's natural necessities, he is less subtle. Man had "a right" to "the creatures" without God's "Verbal Donation," and Locke allows himself to doubt in print, albeit parenthetically, whether God's words "must be understood literally to have been spoken" (I.86).

(3) Liberation from God and His righteousness breaks the surface in Locke's account of Eve, which, as Jeremy Waldron observed, frees woman from divine punishment for any supposed original sin. But the

argument is even more radical: Locke's version seems to free all mankind. God's curse did not condemn Eve to subjection in marriage, if her "Condition or Contract with her Husband" should exempt her (I.47). It did not condemn women in childbirth to "those multiplied Pains God threatens her" with, "if there should be a Remedy for it" (I.47, 67). It did not condemn women to a general subjugation to men (I.67, 29, 44, 99). Moreover, original sin in general is only a "curse" for all mankind, not a state of fallen and guilty nature, and a curse to be overcome as much as possible by human remedies. Reason, law, and labor are the remedies. The implication is that a Creator-God must have been uncaring, since His creation left mankind in pain, exploitation, and poverty. The possibility of grace goes unmentioned by Locke, as does any significant distinction between nature created and nature fallen. All this is consistent with Locke's orientation by a "state of nature," which, if not Hobbist, nevertheless in some formulations is an "ill condition" from which men are "quickly driven" (II.127; cf. 123–127). It is consistent too with his turn to man-made arts, including not only the arts of enterprise but also such other arts of free society as contractual marriage with the possibility of divorce (II.78–83).

(4) Filmer seemed to think the argument from the "natural dominion" of fathers to be "the Main Basis of all his frame," according to Locke (I.50; cf. 73, 6, 9), and Locke's corresponding rebuttal comprises his most bitter denunciations and the longest of the chapters refuting Adamic dominion. This is strange. For the argument is from nature, not revelation, and yet it is treated as decisive for the biblical patriarchalists. Do biblical teachings as to patriarchs and God the father presuppose an untutored deference, an unenlightened common sense, a complacent acquiescence, with respect to fathers (cf. I.50)? There is reason to think that this is Locke's concern. The most scathing attack in either *Treatise* focuses on the supposition of paternal superiority, on philosophic defenses of this superiority as natural (I.51–58; cf. I.154), and on its manifestations in "religion," even in "Holy Writ" (I.58).

"What Father of a Thousand, when he begets a Child, thinks farther than the satisfying of his present Appetite" (I.54)? Locke unlimbers his rhetorical artillery. Fathers do not give to children "*Life and Being*," because God or nature does; or if fathers do, they do not intend the benefit, because they are moved merely by "present Appetite" (I.54); or if nature plays a part, it is not for a higher good, but out of lust. Locke inveighs especially against a natural teleology as to fatherly authority. He tacitly denies any natural tendency to immortality through offspring, as well as any fatherly inclination to govern well in the light of some superior portion of intellect. Instead he focuses on abuses, not least those occasioned by unenlightened mind. In the uncivilized world whole tribes of fathers abuse and even dine on their offspring (I.57), and the inhumanities are not restricted to primitives. It is precisely the "busie mind of man," "whose thoughts are more than the Sands, and wider than the Ocean," that exacerbates inhumane domination (I.58). What is needed is not a turn to the intellect, as if it were some divine guide to divine "*Being*," but a turn to reason, as tied by enlightened planning to human necessities. Otherwise fashion rules, spurred on by imagination and passion, and "Custom" makes it "Sacred." This leads Locke to slash away at "Reverence" in "Religions," as well as in "Governments" and "Manners," and then at "holy writ" itself for stories of sacrifices of children by their fathers (I.58). It is a parade of horribles, and the horribles follow from the most natural kind of rule—if "reason" is not man's "only star and compass" (I.58). Mastery of nature by science involves mastery of a natural tendency, especially in fathers, to imitate divine being. Mastery of nature begins at home.

Both treatises of Locke's political science dwell on reforming the family. The chief purpose of Lockean marriage is to bring up children able to be "most useful to themselves and others" and especially "to shift for themselves" (II.55–56; cf. I.129). Locke makes the family private, secular, nuclear, and child-oriented; he denies to paternal authority any role in governing those outside the nucleus. This liberal family is not a shaper of worshipful sons but an instrument of society. It is to be the agency most responsible for supporting and educating self-reliant "members" of civil society. In *Some Thoughts Concerning Education* Locke urges education at home, not in schools. Thus, perhaps, one avoids church schools, ancient authors, and even the "dead" languages such as Latin ("long since dead everywhere," 172, 189; cf. 164ff., 168–169, 195). His home schooling has a cast chiefly economic and civil. It promotes especially a rather economic education in the practical and useful arts, for "a man of business" (164–167, 169–171, 174, 177, 181). In this spirit Locke encourages toughening of the body, a tutor who seems to be no clergyman, learning "a trade" (even a "manual" trade, 201–202), and fatherly instruction in business affairs and notably in accounting (210–212). So men learn to shift for themselves, and "their own reason" is substituted for "old custom" (216).

It is also true that Locke's reform of marriage is intended to protect the wife, freeing her from patriarchal males and allowing for divorce after the children have been raised (II.81). Also, Locke conspicuously replaces "paternal" with "parental" authority. This equalizing dominates, despite qualifications for the sake of domestic government. One authority is necessary in the family, as Locke says in the fashion of his politics, and he would rest it in the father as "naturally" the "abler and stronger" (II.82). He seems to think males the superior fighters, acquirers, and providers (cf. II.72–76); he says explicitly that female "tenderness" is a disadvantage in disciplining the "unruly and disordered appetites" of children.[12] As to sexual activity apart from marriage, Locke says little (in passing he mentions sodomy, adultery, and incest, I.129). He may intimate that this is amongst the private things as to which we are at liberty, and as to which men will be disciplined by the industriousness, and credit with others, that they need in society. Still, the big reform is the making of the family into something merely private and secular as well as child-oriented, rather equal, and more self-reliant than worshipful. The priority of education in the faith disappears, and political greatness is denied to the heads of great families per se. But all this requires replacement of the extended and patriarchal family, ensconced in the family property and obedient to superior lords, by the nuclear family, with the young trained up to "shift for themselves" (II.83). Liberal society requires a liberal family.

Against Inherited Privilege

The final chapters of the *First Treatise* target the extended or patriarchal family, biblical or no, and then the institutions of ancient Israel. These discussions are parts of a larger critique, starting at the end of chapter VI, as to the problem of conveying divine authority. Even if Filmer had established Adam's lordship over the human race, which Locke's four rebuttals have denied, he did not show how Adam conveyed it, or to whom. Locke alludes to the general problem of determining who on earth obtained the Lord's authority (occasionally he shows Filmer equating Adam with "Absolute Monarch and Lord of the Whole World," I.80). It seems that in practice biblical patriarchalism leads to worldly authority in powerful families, who inherit riches and rule through the eldest son, and to an unworldly void in political authority, as exemplified by the Lord's chosen people. The title of chapter IX is "Of Monarchy, by Inheritance from Adam," of chapter XI, on the Jews, "Who Heir?"

Filmer had found two modes by which divine authority is conveyed, fatherhood and inheritance. Fathers have Adam's superiority; eldest sons may inherit it. But two titles to the same authority can lead to contradictory results. The title from property, whether arrived at by inheritance or not, leads to rulers who may not be fathers. The argument of chapters VII and VIII focuses on this contradiction. But incoherence is also inherent in conveyance by fatherhood itself, which is treated at the end of VI.

If fatherhood is title to rule, does the first father retain it, or do all his sons obtain it as they become fathers? This problem, inherent in patriarchalism, is exacerbated by the *"Absolute, Unlimited*, nay, *Unlimitable Power"* of the lordly father (I.69). Thus Adam has title (along with his heirs), or all of his children who are fathers have it (and thus all fathers in the world). Locke draws the two impolitic consequences for politics: unlimited monarchy or unlimited anarchy. The attempt to derive government from Adam's paternal authority either unsettles every ruler who cannot show that he is Adam's one true heir, or enfranchises every ruler, including every usurper such as an "Oliver," who can claim the mantle of being a father (I.79). Filmer's paternal defense of the divine right of kings proves but a phantom, a "new nothing" that cannot distinguish kings from usurpers (I.72, 79). In this context Locke indicts not only Filmer but also "his Disciples" (I.71). The Preface had identified Filmer's followers with churchmen ("the Pulpit," the "Drum Ecclesiastic") and his doctrine with "the Current Divinity of the Times." However that may be, the discussion has obvious ecclesiastical implications. Consider the incongruity of "Oliver" Cromwell as prince of a priesthood of all believers, or the duality of pope and all believers as inheritors of Christ's mantle.

Even if the title by fatherhood were without difficulty because of the ubiquity of fathers, incoherence enters with Filmer's second title. An eldest son's right by inheritance, for example, clashes with the right of any other sons who are fathers. In the Bible one sees the very sons of Adam ruling over different private dominions, and yet Cain, according to Filmer, ruled Abel as older son and with the authority of his father (I.75–77). Was Adam, lord of the world as both father of mankind and possessor of mankind, himself incoherent as to who was to succeed to his authority?

These internal difficulties with paternalism "might well excuse me" from further consideration of Filmer's doctrine, Locke says, since the contradictions are visible to "any ordinary understanding" (I.80). Nevertheless, Locke proceeds. He proceeds from theory to practice, from an incoherent but influential doctrine to how the world is in fact influenced by it. How might one "make out" a government from Filmer's "principles," however contradictory, or how might a "right of empire" be derived nevertheless from a "Lord of the whole World" (I.80; cf. 74)?

If one judges by the Lockean discussions that follow, the effects on worldly politics of the mysterious Lord tend to the inhumane or to the ineffectual. A government seems to be "made out," first, by supposing rule to be inherited as property by the eldest son, just as wealth is. This mix of divine warrant and inherited rule results in a particular sort of aristocracy. It is, if one can surmise from admittedly small hints, perhaps something like feudal lords (cf. "vassals," I.42, 43). But such lordly authorities do not take care for men generally. Alternatively, government is made out, second, by supposing governance in God the Father, or at least in His anointed such as priests and the "judges" of ancient Israel. But pious government slights politic government; it too fails to care for the governed. The final chapter XI has the most mysterious title in the *Two Treatises* and the only one in the form of a question ("Who Heir?"). It seems that neither Adam nor the Lord provided an heir who took care of men in the world. Whether there be absolute inherited government or an absence of politic government, the result in neither case is rightful government, that is, government for the "Preservation of Every Man's Right and Property" (I.92).

In light of this, it is not surprising that Locke develops his alternative foundation of government precisely as he rebuts Filmer's account of worldly inheritance. He suddenly turns from theological intricacies to "the plain of the Case" (I.86), not a revealed God's law but man's reasonable rights, and in light of that he proceeds to reform inheritance and government too (I.87ff.).

Locke had become visibly more insistent after he had demonstrated Filmer's hopeless incoherence. He did retain biblical premises at first, supposing not only that there ought to be governments in the world (as the Bible asserts), but also that these are descendants of Adam or the Lord (as "our A_" asserts). Still, he had insisted that one must "know the person" of this governor in order that he be obeyed (for "it may be myself," I.81). One must know the person "by right" invested with power, Locke then insists. The primacy of knowing and of justice leads away from the mysterious Lord to Locke's special kind of rational justice: man's right to provide for himself without the prior approval of God or anyone (I.86 ff.).

In Locke's enlightened theology, then, man can know God's will by "reason and sense" applied to one's "strong desires" for what one needs. Accordingly, man has a right to the creatures even without God's revealed Donation (I.86). Nor should moral scruples stand in the way, any more than religious scruples. The natural freedom to acquire is not subject to human consent, that is, to any law or opinion as to fairness, decency, or *honestum*. Any such *juris gentium* is secondary to mankind's actual consent, and even if mankind or its decent portion had consented to such a moral opinion, it is not fundamental. Such agreement is but a "positive and not Natural Right" (I.88). The *First Treatise* thus presupposes the critique of common moral ideas developed by the *Essay Concerning Human Understanding* (I.iii, esp. 2–9, 12). In place of pious reverence or equitable opinion, the *First Treatise* establishes the primacy of an individual right to "Self-preservation." If man had to wait upon others' acquiescence he "had starved, not withstanding the Plenty God had given him" (I.86, II.28).

This new and humane measurement of right lays an axe to any inheritance whatsoever of political power and to all exclusive inheritance by the eldest son. The edge of the axe is partly the demand for a reason, which puts all privilege by mere inheritance into question. It is chiefly the demand for a reason rooted in equal rights to the necessities of life. While Locke later allows fathers to bequeath estates to those of his children "who please them best" (II.72, 73), this gives no peculiar privilege to the eldest child. Nor does it gainsay the "ordinar[y]" principle of equal desert, which is what the *First Treatise* quietly establishes and the *Second Treatise* builds upon (II.4–15, 22–24, 72, etc.).

Younger children have "an equal title" to inherit by "that right they have to maintenance, support and comfort from their Parents" (I.93). That is Locke's new principle of family life: the principle of human rights, not fatherly or parental right and duty. The consequences are political as well as familial. Property is not to go to the firstborn, and this negative by itself tends to democratize holdings. And "dominion" and "empire" are not to go by inheritance at all. Inheritance is restricted to property in Locke's sense, which is an instrument of private needs, and dominion is restricted to government in Locke's sense, which is an agent of all. Government is to preserve every man "from the Violence or Injury of Others" (I.92). Thus Locke achieves his famously sharp distinction between private and public. He uses it here to exclude government as the prerogative of some person or class. Government is turned from prerogative, especially one belonging to the head of a family, into responsibility for a collective. Locke calls government a "Terror to Evil Doers," and while this might remind of an instrument of God's righteousness, he corrects any such inference by turning first toward "public" good and then toward individuals as such. Government is "for the good of every particular Member of that Society" as far as possible (I.92). Given this measure of right, Locke can prescribe in the *Second Treatise* his universal politics: the artificial representative of "the people," which is the one government that in every society all are to obey.

In short, a foundation in individual rights cuts into the arrangements typical of all premodern family relations, especially aristocratic and monarchical family relations. All in the family have the right to inherit equally (I.87–91). Down with inheritance by the eldest son and by sons alone. Since property is only for private needs, and government is to protect all equally as individuals in "society" (I.91–97), governing is an abstract "power," not a regime of a certain class of human being. Down with patriarchal rule, any inherited rule, and proud expectations complemented by deference from lower orders. Since fatherly power is only to provide for others, it is a duty to children rather than a power of the father, and it is an authority "forfeited" to some "Foster-Father" if the natural father does not provide care (I.88–90, 93, 97, 100). Down with any strict version of honor thy father (or thy mother). To exaggerate somewhat (since Locke reforms the natural family without replacing it and emphasizes discipline as well as provision): "Honor thy caregiver."

Providence

Filmer had attempted a biblical answer to the question of rightful power, and this led him to the more worldly Old Testament. "This is the book of the generations of Adam" (Gen. 5:1). It led too to the model of ancient Israel. Locke's concluding argument shows that Israel's practices do not bear out Filmer's deductions. Still, the target of the *First Treatise*'s final chapter (XI, "Who Heir") is less faulty deductions than the Bible itself. For Filmer's confusions and dangers mirror somehow the Bible's, especially his crucial failures to specify political rule and to make politics primary. Here Locke more directly if still circumspectly takes on the God of the Bible, the dark "Providence" who did not provide even for His chosen people. The chapter having the most mysterious title is the longest chapter in either *Treatise*.

The "Great Question which in all Ages has disturbed Mankind" is not whether there should be power, nor the origin of it, but "who should have it" (I.106). So the last chapter begins. Who "by right" should have power, Locke adds once again. He adds now an unmysterious definition of political right: "Peace and Tranquillity, which is the business of Government and the end of Humane Society" (I.106). The final chapter begins with Locke's own pronouncement of *the* decisive question. Evidently the right answer has not been revealed. The chapter ends by intimating part of the answer: whoever should rule, God should not. The revealed answer is wrong. The chapter's final paragraph notes the Jews' "captivity" and then "destruction" (I.169); the chapter appears inconclusive and even unfinished. But the final remarks conclude an argument suggesting that God not only failed to provide kings, contra Filmer, but also failed to provide for the people, *contra* right. The Jews had kings for "not one third" of their existence (I.169; cf. 150–153, 164–169). What kingship they had originated not only in political necessity but also in the teeth of God's opposition, as appears from the biblical passages to which Locke alludes. The people said: "Give us a king like all nations" who will "govern us" and "go out and fight our battles" (1 Sam. 8:5, 20, 7). But the Lord said: "they have rejected me from being King over them"; they are "forsaking me and serving other gods" (1 Sam. 8:5, 7, 8; cf. 1 Sam. 12:17). The Lord was the Jews' king, and His law prescribed above all obedience to Him.

The problem of an otherworldly judge showed itself especially in the worldly business of war. Judges, Locke says of a certain period, "were all the governors they then had"; they were "men of valor, whom they made their generals to defend them in time of peril" (I.158). The incongruity between name and function suggests what is the case: Locke's abstraction from the biblical function. The judges were to "judge Israel," as Locke later states (I.163), which meant establishing righteousness, which meant keeping the Israelites "in the way of the Lord" and away from "other gods." If so, God would provide. If not, their sins and God's wrath caused their sufferings. War and captivity were punishments, and righteousness, not generalship, was the chief remedy (Judges 2:16–19; 2:22; 3:7; 6:10; 10:6–8).

Although Locke intimates this theme more than he expounds it, it occasionally surfaces, notably in Locke's retelling of the incident of the Tower of Babel. In Genesis the lesson is of mankind's impious pride ("to make a name for themselves"). The people challenged God with a tower to the heavens (Gen. 11:4–9). Locke's reinterpretation takes the people's side. The lesson is of a "Free People" who institute political governance: "Let us build us a City" (I.146; cf. Gen. 11:4). For their presumption God had punished men, dividing them by languages and into warring peoples. Locke has the presumption to defend man against such a God, albeit in a quick remark easily missed amidst virtually interminable turgidities. Only in such obscurity does he venture to attack the "Propriety" of presuming that man must esteem "what happens in Providence to be preserved" as if "God is careful to preserve a thing" (I.147). In the name of politics and humanity Locke compels us to wonder whether Israel suffered from an inflated but parochial paternal power, a "domineering phantom" on a cosmic scale.

In short, the *First Treatise of Government* concludes with a train of criticism that prepares the *Essay Concerning Civil Government*. Perhaps the old and metaphoric characterization of the *Second Treatise*, as a Bible of free government, is more apt than is now supposed. At the least one can say that Locke thought that his plan, and not the old Bible, should have primary power in the world.

A Question Still

Does the *First Treatise* succeed in its extraordinary task? Does Locke refute the claims of his opponents? That Locke showed Filmer's claims to be inconsistent and contradictory—of this there can be no doubt. Adamic monarchy is not supported by the example of biblical Israel, which is Filmer's own political-religious model. The argument for monarchy by divine right seems unable to avoid justifying governments elective, popular, and usurped, as well as monarchical, and it cannot identify Adam's heir in any politically relevant sense. On his own premises, then, Filmer's divine political right seems neither divine, nor political, nor a standard of right.

But might Filmer and his followers have a rejoinder? Might he and they argue that Filmer has come as close to coherence on these topics as a man can—given the unexpected ways of our unfathomable Lord and the flaws in our fallen capacities? Reason should acknowledge its deficiencies. Perhaps mystery is part of our fate, and full clarity is impossible before an inscrutable providence.

From this point of view Locke fails to confront the Bible's own claim to be the voice of a mysterious God; he merely holds it to a rational standard foreign to it. When God "vouchsafes to speak to *Men*," Locke supposes that he would not cross "the Rules of language in use amongst them" (I.46). When Locke directly confronts "Providence," it is with respect to the "Propriety" of reason and right (I.147). When he reinterprets biblical doctrines of creation, original sin, and so forth, it is with a view to his own account of human nature and nature itself. His argument seems "foundational," as postmodernists say. When the *First Treatise* turns from what "our Author" says to what "I have said" (I.86, 97), it turns to the fundamental force of self-preservation and to the ensuing natural rights to life and the means of life (I.86–100). What, however, of a God able to overrule nature and to govern human thoughts by his mysterious will? That God's creation was not mere physical begetting (in Locke's sense), that Adam and Eve fell, that God intended His creation used in reverence to him and intended that fathers obey His righteous governance— these biblical doctrines are displaced by Locke. But they are not refuted, at least by the arguments we have set forth. Of course, if Locke's theories of language, nature, and justice were self-evidently true and good, or otherwise obviously well founded, we might follow his critique accordingly. After two and a half centuries of political and philosophic refutation, however, who can knowingly or confidently claim that? If the foundational argument were all of the *First Treatise*'s critique of religion, the critique fails.

But there is more to Locke's critique. To begin with, one would have to reconsider Locke's other political-theological works. And even if the arguments of the *First Treatise* are on this topic authoritative, as I suspect, a more theologically literate reading than mine may discern a more telling critique.[13] Filmer had fallen into contradiction when he tried to marry clear argument to mysterious providence. Is this a difficulty that the Bible shares? The Bible too advances rational descriptions, commandments, and assurances. He who appeared to Adam and Moses with promises and laws is not simply mysterious. When God speaks to men, must he not necessarily observe "the Rules of language in use amongst them"? Might a closer reading show that the *First Treatise* brings out contradictions among the assurances and promises? Locke supplies many biblical passages, summaries, and citations, and these no doubt signify more than the reformulations that appear on the surface. Is Locke indicating how the Word of God on its own terms contradicts itself or offers contradictory commands? Is "the infinite deity" nevertheless definitely confined by "Promises and Oaths" (I.6), or does God promise the same honor and empire to descendants of different patriarchs (I.74–78, 123–156), or promise prosperity and yet permit "bondage," "captivity," and "disaster" (I.169)? Locke moves toward refutations on the Bible's grounds as well as his own.

Nevertheless, this movement is truncated, secondary, and inconclusive. A dialectical refutation would have to take very seriously the Bible's speech and in particular the Lord's speeches. But the *First Treatise*, whatever its occasional allusions, tends to explain away intimations of the divine by reference to "imagination," "Fashion," and "Custom" (I.58). This reductionism seems similar to that pervading Locke's epistemological dismissals of "spirits" in the *Essay Concerning Human Understanding*. It presupposes a foundational psychology and perhaps even a rather materialistic physics.[14] But it is hard to take seriously what one supposes to be imaginary. In general the *First Treatise* does not much engage the Bible's decisive speeches except to object on Locke's own grounds. While occasionally characterizing the Bible as the sacred word of God, Locke from the start chiefly interprets the work according to ordinary rules of language and even as a "history" or "story" (I.113, 117, etc.). He eventually if tacitly equates the Jews, their Bible, and their prophets with other civil societies and their "men of renown" and poets (I.141, 153). He portrays the Jews' fate as political failure. Locke thus abstracts from the Jews' own understanding, that is, from the miraculous drama of God's chosen people as the vehicle of God's righteousness and law. His is a slighting treatment of prophets, prophecy, and the Messiah, to say nothing of Christ as Savior,[15] and he slights in particular the crucial expression of Jehovah's peculiar rationality, the Mosaic law. Locke never treats expressly of the two principal commandments. While he wields part of the fifth commandment against fatherly power ("Honor your father and your mother"), his quotations always omit the words indicating the Lord's superiority and man's corresponding dependence: "Honor your father and your mother, that your days may be long in the land which the Lord your God gives you."

In short, Locke's arguments are of this form: if duty to God comes before the right to property, men would have starved; if God were the ruler of Israel, he did not provide the care that a ruler should. Whatever Locke's humane justice (no small quality), such arguments do not refute or even address the revealed claim that human misfortune results from sin against God's righteousness. One sees a determined skepticism and a determined humanitarianism, as well as a reasonable distrust of hopes unsupported by "common sense and experience" (I.137). But determination is by itself willfulness, and Locke's turn to nature and epistemology prevents him from relying consistently on ordinary reasonableness as to prudence and experience. Not addressing his opponents' extraordinary hopes in their own terms, he only secondarily engages dialectically his extraordinary opponent.

If Locke's rebuttal is determined insistence rather than rational refutation, how can one understand this? Might he have believed such a refutation impossible? That explanation, it seems, was one contention of Leo Strauss, not only as to Locke but as to the great philosophers of Enlightenment generally. What could Strauss have meant? According to his *Philosophy and Law*, the early modern philosophers suspected or at least "felt" that the possibility of a mysterious deity was itself impossible to refute.[16] They turned instead to new ways, to antireligious mockery and, more seriously, to a hypothetical-activist "Napoleonic strategy." Determined to defeat the Bible's immense challenge to prudence and reason, suspecting the impossibility of refutation, Hobbes, Spinoza, and the rest saw "no other way" than to "attempt a complete understanding of the world and life without the assumption of an unfathomable God." If this comprehensive effort succeeded, man would have proved himself "theoretically and practically the lord of the world and the lord of his life." The proof would be in the progress. The biblical God would be "outlived" if not exactly refuted. His world would be superseded in theory and in practice by a man-made enlightened world.

Might one find evidence for such a project in certain distinctive characteristics of the *Two Treatises*? In the *First Treatise* the "foundation" of Filmer's system is "detected and overthrown," as the subtitle puts it. The foundation is the God of the Bible, and the phrase bespeaks victory rather than refutation. Also, we have seen that Locke's theoretical doctrine explains revelation by a certain natural psychology and physics—with an intention to explain it away. In effect, epistemology explains away the possibility of revelation. Similarly, the measure of all doctrine, including religious doctrine, is humane provision. The *Second Treatise*, accordingly, seems to be the social and political project that follows upon these new standards of reasoning. It is an *Essay:* an attempt, in an old and still familiar sense of the word "essay."[17] It seems an attempt at a man-made system that provides for human necessities and weakens human longings for a divine provider.

How Locke's project of overcoming biblical religion can be defended by reason, I conclude, is a question entered upon, but not adequately answered, by his *First Treatise of Government*.

Notes

1. For comments on this essay I am grateful to Christopher Bruell, Robert Eden, and Susan Shell, and also to the anonymous readers for the *Review of Politics*, in which the essay first appeared in print (Summer, 2005). I am grateful to the *Review* for permission to republish, and I am especially grateful to Proffesor Gary McDowell for the original opportunity to develop this topic.
2. Thomas Pangle, *The Spirit of Modern Republicanism* (Chicago and London: University of Chicago Press, 1988), 131–275; Michael Zuckert, *Launching Liberalism, On Lockean Political Philosophy* (Lawrence: University Press of Kansas, 2002), 129–168; Peter C. Myers,

Our Only Star and Compass, Locke and the Struggle for Political Rationality (Lanham: Rowman and Littlefield, 1998), 1–65; Nathan Tarcov, *Locke's Education for Liberty* (Chicago: University of Chicago Press, 1984), 9–76; Leo Strauss, *Natural Right and History* (Chicago: University of Chicago Press, 1953), 202–251. The quotation in the text is from Locke, *A Letter Concerning Toleration*, ed. James H. Tully (Indianapolis: Hackett Publishing Company, 1986), 26.

3. Richard Rorty, "The Priority of Democracy to Philosophy," in *Objectivity, Relativism, and Truth* (Cambridge: Cambridge University Press, 1991), 175–196. For two of the latest of Rawls' reformulations, and for his muffling of the religious challenge, see "Justice as Fairness: Political not Metaphysical," "The Idea of Public Reason Revisited," and *"Commonweal* Interview with John Rawls," all in John Rawls, *Collected Papers*, ed. Samuel Freeman (Cambridge, MA: Harvard University Press, 2001), 388–414, 573–615, 616–627. The problem is clarified and plumbed in J. Judd Owen, *Religion and the Demise of Liberal Rationalism* (Chicago and London: University of Chicago Press, 2001).

4. Ernest L. Fortin, *Human Rights, Virtue, and the Common Good, Untimely Meditations on Religion and Politics* (Lanham: Rowman and Littlefield, 1996), 55.

5. Jeremy Waldron, *God, Locke, and Equality, Christian Foundations of John Locke's Political Thought* (Cambridge: Cambridge University Press, 2002); on the postmodern void and the superior depth of Locke, 1–15, for the passages quoted or referred to, see 1–28, especially 13, 18–19.

6. Consider Jonathan I. Israel, *Radical Enlightenment, Philosophy and the Making of Modernity 1650–1750* (Oxford: Oxford University Press, 2001), esp. 516, but see also 468–460, 470, 265–270, 70, 78, 259, 583. John Dunn is a chief authority for the view that as to politics Locke's works are philosophically irrelevant; they are merely "historical," that is, confusedly Calvinist and wrapped within the "tradition and change" of his own time. *The Political Thought of John Locke* (Cambridge: Cambridge University Press, 1969). For refutations see Tarcov, *Locke's Education*, 90, 127, 142–144, and Myers, *Political Rationality*, 14–23, 32. n. 66, 107, 135 n. 52.

7. All such references to the *Treatises* are to *Two Treatises of Government*, ed. Peter Laslett (Cambridge: Cambridge University Press, 1997). As for the parenthetical references within the text, the roman numerals I and II refer to the First and Second Treatises, respectively, and the Arabic numerals to the sections therein.

8. See Zuckert, "An Introduction to Locke's First Treatise," in *Launching Liberalism*, 137, and in general the works cited before in note 2.

9. Locke, *Letter*, 38, 55; the ensuing quotations in the text are from 23, 26, 32, 37, 42, 49, 51, 52.

10. As to Locke's acknowledgment of Filmer's foundation in divine providence, see Tarcov, *Locke's Education*, 13–21; and Zuckert, "An Introduction to Locke's First Treatise," 129–146.

11. As to Locke's two quotations from the New Testament, other allusions, and the pattern of distortion, see George Alan Windstrup, "Politic Christianity: Locke's Theology of Liberalism," PhD Dissertation, Princeton University, Department of Politics, 1977, 255. Windstrup's little known work is among the most tenacious and extensive inquiries into Locke's political theology.

12. *Some Thoughts Concerning Education*, ed. Ruth W. Grant and Nathan Tarcov (Indianapolis: Hackett Publishing Company, 1996), secs. 4, 5, 7, 39, 41; cf. 34, 35, esp. 78.

13. Consider the examinations by Pangle, in *Modern Republicanism*, 136–149; and in *Political Philosophy and the God of the Bible* (Baltimore and London: Johns Hopkins University Press, 2002), 10–11.

14. *Essay Concerning Human Understanding*, IV.xi.12 and also IV.iii.27.

15. Laslett's index to both *Treatises* has no entries for prophets, prophecy, Messiah, Christ, or Savior.

16. Leo Strauss, "Introduction," in *Philosophy and Law*, trans. Fred Baumann (New York: Jewish Publication Society, 1987), 10–14. See also Matthew Davis, "Locke and the Problem of the Biblical God," chapter 2 of "Ancient and Modern Approaches to the Problem of Relativism: A Study of Husserl, Locke and Plato," PhD Dissertation, Boston College, Department of Political Science, 1995, 25–85.

17. As to the definition of "essay" and the political significance of the essay form, see Robert Faulkner, "Francis Bacon," in *Encyclopedia of the Essay*, ed. Tracy Chevalier (London: Fitzroy Dearborn Publishers, 1997).

Chapter 5

Montesquieu and the Constitution of Liberty

Paul A. Rahe

Thirty-five years ago, in *The Ideological Origins of the American Revolution*, Bernard Bailyn surveyed the intellectual traditions that exercised influence in the American colonies on the eve of the American Revolution and argued that the English commonwealthmen identified by Caroline Robbins had a greater substantive impact than did the writers of classical antiquity and the Enlightenment, the exponents of the common law, and the Puritan divines. Of the writers who fell within the last three categories, he did not repeat what he had said concerning "the classics of the ancient world"—that they

> are everywhere in the literature of the Revolution, but they are everywhere illustrative, not determinative, of thought. They contributed a vivid vocabulary but not the logic or grammar of thought, a universally respected personification but not the source of political and social beliefs. They heightened the colonists' sensitivity to ideas and attitudes otherwise derived.

To the Enlightenment, the common law, and the colonists' Puritan heritage he attributed greater substantive influence. He merely insisted that "these clusters of ideas . . . did not in themselves form a coherent intellectual pattern"; that "among them" there were, "in fact, striking incongruities and contradictions"; and that "what brought these disparate strands of thought together, what dominated the colonists' miscellaneous learning and shaped it into a coherent whole, was the influence" of Robbins's commonwealthmen, "whose thought overlapped with that of those already mentioned but which was yet distinct in its essential characteristics and unique in its determinative power."[1]

That John Trenchard and Thomas Gordon, Benjamin Hoadly, Robert Molesworth, Lord Bolingbroke, James Burgh, Paul de Rapin-Thoyras, and the like, as well as their predecessors among the republicans and radical Whigs of the seventeenth century, did much to shape the political culture of the American colonies prior to the 1760s we need not doubt. That the English Whig tradition helped form the expectations and attitudes of the colonists is clear. If, however, we are to judge the influence of writers by the frequency in which they were cited in the political literature of the Revolutionary epoch stretching from 1760 to 1805, Bailyn cannot quite be right, for the French philosophe Montesquieu, the jurist William Blackstone, the philosopher John Locke, and the historian and essayist David Hume were all cited much more frequently than the authors of *Cato's Letters*, and no other figure in the English radical tradition is to be found in the top fifteen. Even in the first two decades of the period Locke and Montesquieu take precedence.[2]

Nor can one argue that these citations were mere window-dressing. When the colonists deliberated with regard to the ultimate significance of their quarrel with the mother country, it was Locke's *Two Treatises of Government* that they consulted. When they pondered the character of the British Constitution and considered what sort of institutions to forge for themselves, they pored over Montesquieu, Blackstone, and Hume. These figures were for the colonists of the late eighteenth century authorities unrivaled. Apart from Locke, they were latecomers, to be sure, preaching to colonists living within a political ethos largely already formed by an interplay between their own experience of self-government in the wilderness and the classical, religious, and Whig authors they read. But, as outsiders— a Frenchman, a student of jurisprudence, a Scot—Montesquieu, Blackstone, and Hume seemed to stand above the political fray, and they commanded a respect and enjoyed an authority that no commonwealthman or partisan Whig, apart from the renowned author of *An Essay Concerning Human Understanding*, ever secured.

Montesquieu, the figure most often cited in the political literature of this period, reigned supreme.[3] When his name is mentioned, there is nearly always a generous epithet attached. Letters written in 1763 to newspapers in Boston speak of him as "a great writer," as "this great writer," and as "the great Montesquieu." They term him "the admired writer" and "the very justly celebrated author of *The Spirit of the Laws*." They call him the "penetrating Montesquieu."[4] Two years later, in a pamphlet published in Newport, Rhode Island, Martin Howard dubs him "the admired Secondat."[5] As John Dickinson readily acknowledges in his *Letters from a Farmer in Pennsylvania*, the French philosophe is "a very learned author."[6] His colleagues in the Continental Congress agreed. In an address to the inhabitants of Quebec that he drafted, they speak of the Frenchman as "an illustrious author of your nation" and term him "the immortal *Montesquieu*" (emphasis in original). His is, they explain, "a name which all Europe reveres," for he is a "truly great man," a renowned "advocate of freedom and humanity."[7]

Similarly, for Carter Braxton, writing in 1776, the author of *The Spirit of the Laws* was "the learned Montesquieu."[8] A contributor to the *Massachusetts Spy* that same year called him "the judicious MONTESQUIEU" and termed him "a great *authority*."[9] He was, as both James Madison and Alexander Hamilton took occasion to remark in *The Federalist*, "the celebrated Montesquieu."[10] As such, he was an authority for Federalists and Anti-Federalists alike.[11] He could even be described as an "oracle."[12]

Of course, those who cited Montesquieu generally did so for rhetorical effect, but a great many appear to have studied him with care as well. In 1763, T. Q. and J., though rival correspondents to the Boston press, agreed on one thing: that a proper interpretation of *The Spirit of the Laws* was the key to understanding whether multiple office-holding by members of the legislature was a threat to liberty in Massachusetts.[13] When Benjamin Rush argued against slavery in a pamphlet penned a decade later, he displayed a detailed knowledge of Montesquieu's great work.[14] When Worcestriensis wrote to the *Boston Massachusetts Spy* in September 1776 to oppose religious persecution and yet advocate public support for a religious establishment, he did so as well.[15] The same can be said for the anonymous South Carolinian who published his *Rudiments of Law and Government Deduced from the Law of Nature* in 1783.[16] Even those who found it necessary to disagree with Montesquieu took it for granted that *The Spirit of the Laws* was the appropriate starting point for reflection on the political question under consideration. On such occasions, even when his name passes unmentioned, one can often detect his presence.[17] No one did more to shape American thinking with respect to the constitution of liberty in modern times.

For Montesquieu's preeminence, there was an obvious reason. His *Spirit of the Laws*, which first appeared in French in 1748 and was translated into English two years thereafter, is arguably the greatest work in constitutional prudence penned in modern times, and almost instantly upon publication it was recognized as such. In 1749, David Hume informed its author that his book would be "the wonder of the centuries."[18] Two years later, in his *Enquiry Concerning the Principles of Morals*, he alerted the public to the fact that Montesquieu was "an author of great genius, as well as extensive learning," and he described *The Spirit of the Laws* as "the best system of political knowledge that, perhaps, has ever yet been communicated to the world."[19] In 1750, in his correspondence, Horace Walpole described that work as "the best book that ever was written."[20] Seven years later, in his *Abridgment of English History*, Edmund Burke hailed its author as "the greatest genius, which has enlightened this age."[21] Not since Aristotle composed *The Politics* had anyone so thoroughly surveyed the variety of polities to be found in the known world, examined the conditions under which they thrived, and pondered their virtues, vices, and propensities.[22]

Moreover, Montesquieu took political liberty and the institutions and circumstances conducive to its flourishing as his principal theme, and he singled out as a form of government that had liberty as its direct object the very polity from which the American colonists derived their own institutions. As James Madison put it in *The Federalist*, "The British constitution was to Montesquieu, what Homer has been to the didactic writers on epic poetry. As the latter have considered the work of the immortal Bard, as the perfect model from which the principles and rules of the epic art were to be drawn, and by which all similar works were to be judged; so this great political critic appears to have viewed the Constitution of England, as the standard, or to use his own expression, as the mirror of political Liberty; and to have delivered in the form of elementary truths, the several characteristic principles of that particular system."[23] How and why Montesquieu came to admire the English political system in such a manner deserve more than a passing glance.

A Nation Ignored

Had that Charles-Louis de Secondat who would in due course become baron de La Bréde et de Montesquieu been born on January 18, 1649, precisely fifty years before he was, in fact, born—that is, had he been born on the eve of Charles I's execution—it is inconceivable that half a century later he would have devoted the two longest chapters of a mammoth work on government to a study of the English polity. In the seventeenth century, Frenchmen evinced very little interest in England. The regicide caught their attention, of course, but it evoked little but horror; and apart from the handful of years in which Oliver Cromwell was in the ascendancy, England played no very prominent role in the affairs of Europe or the New World.

From the perspective of Louis XIV, England was a mere pawn—a relatively inconsequential island state prone to faction and civil strife, virtually begging for manipulation. He is said once to have asked the ambassador to Paris from the kingdom that had so recently produced Shakespeare and Milton whether there had ever been any writers of note in his country. In this regard, the Sun King was not peculiar. When the dramatic poet Corneille was sent an English translation of *Le Cid*, he purportedly shelved it in his cabinet where it apparently belonged: between the work's translations into other barbaric tongues such as Slavonic and Turkish.[24] In seventeenth-century France, no one thought England, the English, their language, their literature, their philosophy, their institutions, their mode of conduct, their accomplishments in science, and their way of seeing the world a proper object for contemplation.

In the course of Montesquieu's childhood and youth, all of this abruptly changed. As a consequence of the Glorious Revolution, which reached its denouement within a month of Montesquieu's birth with the promulgation of the Declaration of Rights and the coronation of William of Orange and Mary Stuart as king and queen of England in succession to the latter's father James,[25] England, having thereby secured a government commanding popular trust, found its footing for the first time and suddenly and unexpectedly presented itself to the world as a great power. In the War of the League of Augsburg, William, in his joint capacity as stadholder of the United Provinces of Holland and king of England, managed to marshal the resources of the English and the Dutch and to forge a coalition sufficient to thwart, at least for a time, the ambitions of Louis XIV. Then, in the War of the Spanish Succession, England's duke of Marlborough marshaled the same resources, forged an even more formidable coalition, and gave Louis XIV a thrashing the likes of which the French had not seen in many a year. No longer was it conceivable that the Sun King would upset the balance of power in Europe, establish his hegemony over the Holy Roman Empire by installing his nominee on its throne, make Spain his satellite, and institute a universal monarchy in Europe and French dominion in the New World. From this setback, administered to France by a country that had hitherto seemed negligible, the ancien régime never fully recovered.

Prior to the battle of Blenheim, which took place when Montesquieu was not yet sixteen, France had enjoyed a preeminence on the field of the sword that no one dared deny. The French had occasionally been checked, but on no occasion in the preceding 150 years had an army of France suffered a genuinely decisive defeat. It, thus, came as a shock when all of Europe learned that on August 13, 1704 an army commanded by the duke of Marlborough and Prince Eugene of Savoy had annihilated a much larger French force and captured Commander Marshal Tallard.[26]

Of course, had the battle of Blenheim been a fluke, had it been a genuine anomaly, as everyone at first assumed, Louis's defeat on this particular occasion would not have much mattered. At most, it would have marked a temporary, if severe setback for French arms. In the event, however, this great struggle was but the first of a series of French defeats meted out by armies captained by duke of Marlborough, and it foreshadowed the series of setbacks that would bedevil the French as the century wore on. If we are today ill informed concerning the events that took place at Ramillies, Oudenarde, Lille, and Malplaquet in the brief span of years stretching from 1706 to 1709,[27] just before the young baron de La Bréde took up residence in his nation's capital, it is because we are inclined to resolutely ignore the fundamental realities of political life.[28] "Battles are," as Winston Churchill observed with regard to the events of this very period, "the principal milestones in secular history. . . . Great battles, won or lost, change the entire course of events, create new standards of values, new moods, new atmospheres, in armies and in nations, to which all must conform."[29]

Thus it was after Marlborough's great victories that attitudes toward England changed, and young Frenchmen of penetrating intelligence thought it necessary to read about and even visit the country that had put together, funded, and lead the coalition that had inflicted on the Sun King so signal a defeat. It is within this context that we must situate Montesquieu as a writer; it is within this context that we must read his *Spirit of the Laws*.[30]

Montesquieu's Discovery of England

Of course, Montesquieu was never primarily concerned with England as such. As a Frenchman, quite naturally he cared most for France. In 1709, when he was twenty, he journeyed from his native Bordeaux to Paris, and there he continued his studies in the law until his father died in 1713, the year when the Treaty of Utrecht brought the War of the Spanish Succession to an end. In those years, by dint of diplomatic skill and a canny exploitation of the partisan strife that erupted in

England, Louis XIV had managed to preserve his kingdom intact and even to secure the Spanish throne for his younger son.[31] But this did not alter the fact that his great project had proved unattainable. Nor did this fortunate turn of events disguise the fact that overreaching on his part had bankrupted France and very nearly brought down the polity. A sense of foreboding gripped Montesquieu's countrymen as they slowly digested what there was to be learned from their repeated defeats on the field of the sword. It is no accident that, as a thinker, Bishop Bossuet had no real heirs in France. Nor should it seem odd that the Regency, which followed King Louis's death in 1715, came to be synonymous with decay. It was no longer possible to thrill to the vision that had informed Louis's great effort, and no one at the time had an alternative vision to proffer.

By 1717, when the twenty-eight-year-old baron de La Bréde et de Montesquieu set out to write the *Persian Letters*, it was perfectly clear to anyone with a discerning eye that the ancien régime was bankrupt in more than one way. In his little book, Montesquieu explored this state of affairs in a circumspect fashion that enabled him to escape the clutches of the censor, gently satirizing the foibles of his contemporaries, subverting inherited mores, obliquely criticizing both the Roman Catholic Church and the ambitions and despotic inclinations of Louis XIV, and intimating to all who cared to read between the lines that the ancien régime was on its last legs.[32] If he eventually turned to England, it was only after laying out a preliminary analysis of the predicament of his native France.

Montesquieu was not the first Frenchman to make England an object of study. That honor belonged to his younger contemporary, the poet François-Marie Arouet, whom we know best by his pen-name Voltaire. The latter sojourned in England from May 1726 to October or November 1728 and then returned to France. In April 1734 he paved the way for his banishment by publishing on the subject of England and the English the incendiary *Lettres philosophiques*, which presented to his compatriots, by way of invidious comparison, a savage critique of the political and religious regime under which they lived.[33] As the marquis de Condorcet would some years later observe in his biography of the poet, this brief work marked "the epoch of a revolution." It caused in France "the birth of a taste for English philosophy and literature." It initiated French "interest in the mores, the politics, the commercial understanding of this people." It even induced Voltaire's compatriots to familiarize themselves with the barbarous English tongue.[34]

Montesquieu journeyed to England in November 1729, roughly a year after his younger compatriot's departure, and he departed early in 1731. His sojourn there was much shorter than Voltaire's. In contrast with the poet, he made no great effort fully to master the language and become an English author, and he made much less of an impression on those with whom he sojourned. But he did circulate within aristocratic circles, and he paid close attention to everything that he was told. Montesquieu was well connected. He had known Bolingbroke in France; he set out on his European tour in the company of the earl of Waldegrave; he met King George II in Hanover; and he arrived in England on the yacht of the earl of Chesterfield. While in the British Isles, he spent time with the king and with Queen Caroline, and he put together a collection of French ballads for their son Frederick, the prince of Wales. He almost certainly met the dowager duchess of Marlborough; he listened carefully when the future earl of Bath told stories concerning the deceased duke; and he befriended the husband of Marlborough's eldest daughter the duke of Montagu. He also attended Parliament and paid close attention to the debates. He read with care Bolingbroke's *Craftsman*, and he perused the periodical press. He was elected to the Royal Society and inducted into the Free Masons. In sum, he used his time well.[35]

England and Rome

When he returned to France, Montesquieu retreated to his chateau in Bordeaux and devoted two years to writing. It was in this period of self-imposed, solitary confinement that he composed his *Considerations on the Causes of the Greatness of the Romans and their Decline*, the work that he was to publish in Holland in the latter part of 1734, not long after the public hangman, on instructions from the parliament of Paris, had with all due ceremony lacerated and burned Voltaire's *Lettres philosophiques.*

On the face of it, Montesquieu's *Considerations* would appear to have next to nothing to do with his extended sojourn in England. In its pages, to be sure, if only for comparative purposes, there is occasional mention of the English and of the government under which they then lived, but neither the people nor the polity looms especially large. Montesquieu's chosen subject was Rome, after all, and for the most part he stuck to his last.[36] When viewed in this light alone, Montesquieu's *Considerations* must be judged a minor masterpiece. There is no work on Roman history of comparable length, written before its author's time or since, that is as penetrating.

It remains unclear, however, just why Montesquieu thought it worth his time to write the book. It has neither a preface nor an introduction to inform us concerning his intentions;[37] and though it foreshadows in some respects the themes of *The Spirit of Laws*, it evidences little to suggest a pertinence to public policy of the sort that was so central to the concerns that inspired the latter work. It would be tempting to conclude that in the early 1730s Montesquieu was an antiquarian, intent on establishing his reputation within the republic of letters by writing a scholarly work on a noble theme.

More can, however, be said, for in 1886 a second work, known from Montesquieu's catalogue but thought to be forever lost, a work that was almost certainly composed at the same time as his little book on Rome, came to light: it was entitled *Reflections on Universal Monarchy in Europe*, and it survived only in printed form.[38] This brief essay, we learn from a note in Montesquieu's own hand placed at the top of the manuscript of yet another unpublished work, its author had originally had "printed with" his *Considerations on the Causes of the Greatness of the Romans and their Decline*. It had evidently been his purpose to publish the two together within the pages of a single volume. In fact, the paper on which the *Reflections* is printed is of the same stock as that used by Montesquieu's publisher Desbordes in the first impression of *Considerations*. But, as Montesquieu goes on to indicate in his marginal note, certain "reasons caused" him "to suppress" *Reflections*. These reasons he does not, in this particular marginal note, spell out. Elsewhere, however, in a note he penned on the first page of the printed copy of his *Reflections*, he is more forthcoming: he "suppressed" this work, he says, "for fear that certain passages would be interpreted ill."

This was not, however, the end of the matter—for there survives yet another manuscript of significance for understanding Montesquieu's intentions in this regard, the so-called Bodmer manuscript—which is written partly in the hand of Montesquieu and partly in the hand of an amanuensis known to have worked for him in the period stretching from 1733 or shortly before that date to 1738 or shortly thereafter. Within this manuscript, one finds a set of corrections laid out in preparation for the publication of a new, improved, and substantially expanded edition of the *Considerations*. This revised version of the *Considerations* was to contain two additional chapters not in the original version published in 1734, and these were to be drawn in their entirety from the *Reflections*. Moreover, in the manuscript of Montesquieu's *Pensées*, there are three entries graced with marginal notes indicating that they had been inserted in the *Considerations*—entries that, in fact, appear nowhere except in the chapters of the *Reflections* that Montesquieu attempted to find place for in the revised version of his little book on Rome.[39]

There can, then, be no doubt that Montesquieu originally intended to publish his *Reflections on Universal Monarchy in Europe* as a companion piece and sequel to his *Considerations on the Causes of the Greatness of the Romans and their Decline* and that he was dissuaded from doing so not by a change of opinion concerning their appropriateness for one another but solely by fear that a publication of the former work would cause him the sort of difficulties that Voltaire had so recently brought on himself with his *Lettres philosophiques*. Moreover, as we have also seen, there is evidence that, in the aftermath of 1734, Montesquieu persisted in wanting to supplement the argument of the *Considerations* with that of the *Reflections* and that he sought to incorporate much of the latter work within a revised edition of the former. In short, the two works are really one and need to be read in tandem. When they are, Montesquieu's intentions become, in at least one crucial regard, much more clear.

Montesquieu's *Reflections on Universal Monarchy in Europe* have a simple, straightforward aim—to dispel once and for all the notion, entertained by Louis XIV and all who admired him, that, in "the state in which Europe actually subsists, it could happen that one people could possess, as the Romans did, a lasting superiority over the others."[40] To this end, he advances three historical arguments—that progress in the art of war, exemplified by the invention of artillery and firearms, has rendered individual soldiers equal in their capacity to wreak harm and done the same thereby for the nations to which they belong; that an alteration in the *ius gentium* has ruled out the enslavement of conquered peoples and the seizure and sale of their property in such a manner that war tends to bankrupt rather than enrich conquerors; and that money has become the sinews of war to such a degree that, insofar as it interrupts the commerce of the those engaged and promotes that of neutrals, armed conflict reduces its participants' longterm capacity to project power.[41]

Had Louis XIV "succeeded" in "the project of a universal monarchy" attributed to him, Montesquieu insists,

> [N]othing would have been more fatal to Europe, to his old subjects, to himself, to his family. Heaven, which knows that which is really advantageous, served him better in his defeats than it would have done with victories; and, instead of rendering him the sole king of Europe, it favored him more by rendering him the most powerful of all.

Indeed, had Louis won the battle of Blenheim, "the famous battle in which he received his first check, the work would have been far from achieved; it would have barely begun. It would have been necessary to stretch further his forces and frontiers. Germany, which had participated in the war almost solely by renting out soldiers, would have made it its chief concern; the North would have aroused itself; all the neutral powers would have intervened; and his allies would have changed sides."[42]

When considered in light of its intended sequel, Montesquieu's *Considerations on the Causes of the Greatness of the Romans and their Decline* reads like an introduction,[43] written in such a manner as to attract those inclined to an excessive veneration for ancient Rome, and designed in such a fashion as to wean them, step by step, from that fatal attraction by making their admiration give way to disgust and horror at the inhumanity inherent in the imperial project undertaken by Rome.[44] It is not fortuitous that the work was originally entitled *Considérations sur les causes de l'agrandissement des Romains et de leur décadence.*[45] Nor is it an accident that *grandeur* was, in the end, substituted for *agrandissement*. If Rome's reputation for grandeur was deployed by Montesquieu to attract readers, its aggrandizement was, in fact, his theme.

Montesquieu's *Considerations on the Greatness of the Romans and their Decline* was, as should now be clear, part of a larger project—to which his *Reflections on Universal Monarchy in Europe* was also a contribution. Together, they constitute his *Essay Concerning Human Understanding*, which was, like them, a ground-clearing operation designed to prepare the way for the construction of a lasting edifice. Together, they were intended to serve as an introduction to a third essay, which, we now know, Montesquieu at this time began drafting for inclusion in the same volume.

Not long after Montesquieu's death, his son delivered on his behalf a eulogy, in which, in passing, he revealed that his father's "book on the government of England, which had been inserted into *The Spirit of Laws,* was composed" in 1733 long before the publication of that great work and that his father had entertained "the notion of having it printed with" his treatise on "*the Romans*"[46] (emphasis in original). There is good reason to credit this claim.

The manuscript of *The Spirit of Laws* that Montesquieu dispatched to his publisher does not survive, but we do have an earlier version of the text replete with insertions and revisions in the author's hand and in the hands of his various amanuenses. Robert Shackleton's pioneering work on Montesquieu's secretaries makes it possible for us to date with some precision the handiwork of each.[47] Within this particular manuscript, as Shackleton points out, there are two chapters in a hand earlier than all of the others. One of these two (3.17.6) was originally composed for inclusion in Montesquieu's *Reflections on Universal Monarchy in Europe* and appears to be an extract from the missing manuscript of that suppressed work. The other (2.11.6) is a draft of the longest and most famous chapter of *The Spirit of the Laws:* Montesquieu's "Constitution of England." Both chapters are in the hand of the amanuensis who served Montesquieu from 1733 or shortly before until 1738 or shortly thereafter and who helped pen the Bodmer manuscript.[48] In short, the claim advanced by Montesquieu's son is not only plausible; it is a possibility that we would be inclined to entertain even if he had not suggested it.[49]

It is in this light that we need to read Montesquieu's *Considerations* and his *Reflections.* We should not want to imitate the Romans, and in his *Considerations* Montesquieu shows us why. And even if for some perverse reason we should want to imitate the Romans, he then demonstrates in his *Reflections*, we could not succeed. We are left to wonder what alternative to the policy hitherto followed by the states of Europe there might, in fact, be, and it is at this point that Montesquieu intended to direct our attention to the polity that had emerged on the other side of the English Channel—the polity responsible for Louis XIV's defeats at Blenheim, Ramillies, Oudenarde, Lille, and Malplaquet.

In the first impression of the first edition of his *Considerations*, before the censors weighed in and he decided to tone down the pertinent passage, Montesquieu allowed himself a revealing observation, remarking, "The government of England is one of the wisest in Europe, because there is a body there which examines that government continually and which continually examines itself; and such are that body's errors that they not only do not last long but are useful in giving the nation a spirit of attentiveness."[50] It was, we may surmise, to provide a frame for a study of this government, which he had initially drafted for inclusion in a volume containing his *Considerations* and his *Reflections*, that Montesquieu initially set out to write his *Spirit of the Laws.*

A Polity Without Principle?

As I have remarked elsewhere,[51] in part 1 of *The Spirit of the Laws*, Montesquieu introduces for the first time his novel typology of political forms, analyzing democratic and aristocratic republics, monarchies, and despotisms initially with an eye to the structure or "nature" of each (1.2.1–3) and, then, with regard to the "principle" or "human passions" that sets each "in motion" (1.3.1–11). Thereafter, in the second part of the same work, he introduces for our contemplation a form of government that appears to explode this typology, prefacing his discussion of what he has already obliquely referred to as "a republic concealed under the form of a monarchy" (1.5.19, p. 304) by introducing a category of distinction hitherto unmentioned: the "object" peculiar to each political community.[52] That "all states have the same object in general, which is to maintain themselves," Montesquieu readily concedes. But he insists, as well, that "each state has an object that is particular to it."

> Aggrandizement was the object of Rome; war, that of Lacedaemon; religion, that of the Jewish laws; commerce, that of Marseilles; public tranquillity, that of the laws of China; navigation, that of the laws of the Rhodians; natural liberty was the object of the police of the savages; in general, the delights of the prince, that of despotic states; his glory and that of the state, that of monarchies; the independence of each individual is the object of the laws of Poland, and what results from this is the oppression of all.

"There is also," he then adds, "one nation in the world which has for the direct object of its constitution political liberty," and he promises "to examine the principles [*les principes*] on which" this constitution "is founded" (2.11.5). This promise he keeps in the very next chapter by launching into an elaborate discussion of the "beautiful system" constituted by the pertinent nation's constitution and laws (2.11.6, esp. p. 407).[53] But neither here nor anywhere else does he tell us what is its "nature." Nor does he ever specify what is *the* "principle" and what are "the human passions that set in motion" what turns out to be the government of England.

Instead, Montesquieu leaves it to us to sort out this question for ourselves. To begin with, he invites us to contemplate a structure of government too complex to be defined simply in terms of the allocation of sovereign power (2.11.6), and, then, he asks us to consider the manner in which its "laws" help "form the mores, manners, and character of a nation" despite the fact that "all the passions are there left free" so that the principles predominant variously in democracies, monarchies, and despotisms (the love of equality, honor, and fear), being neither instilled by education nor elicited by the government's "nature" or structure, have no particular sway and, in their place, "hatred, envy, jealousy, the ardor to enrich and distinguish oneself appear to their full extent" (3.19.27, pp. 574–75). That a polity so favorable to psychological anarchy should, nonetheless, be "moderate" (1.7.17) and adept as well at the projection of power—this is the true mystery.

Moderation in Government

When he first introduces the notion of "moderate government," Montesquieu insists that it "is able, as much as it wishes and without peril, to relax its springs. It maintains itself by its laws and even by its momentum [*force*]."[54] Such is not the case, he points out, with despotism, the quintessence of immoderate government—for if there were to appear in such a polity a "good citizen" and if, out of love of country, he were "tempted to relax the springs of the government" and then actually "succeeded" in doing so, "he would run the risk of losing himself, it, the prince, and the empire" as well (1.3.9, 4.3).

Republics are equally incapable of relaxing their springs and can only within limits approximate moderation. Republics and despotic governments have this in common: they are fragile; they require apprehension; they must remain tense. "It is necessary," Montesquieu asserts, "that a republic dread something. The fear [*crainte*] of the Persians maintained the laws among the Greeks. Carthage and Rome threatened one another and rendered one another firm. It is a thing singular: the more these states have of security, the more, like waters excessively tranquil, they are subject to corruption" (1.8.5).

Moderate governments can profit from success and relax their springs because they encounter less friction than polities not in their nature moderate. Once set in motion, they possess a momentum all their own; like perpetual-motion machines, they do not run down. "To form a moderate government," Montesquieu tells us, "it is necessary to combine powers, to regulate them, to temper them, to make them act, to give, so to speak, a ballast to one in order to put it in a condition to resist another; this is a masterpiece of legislation, which chance rarely produces and prudence is rarely allowed to produce." It may be more difficult to sustain and stabilize the government of any given despot but it is much easier to institute despotic government in the first place. Though it constitutes an assault on human nature (1.2.4, 8.8, 21), despotism is, in a sense, natural. It "jumps up, so to speak, before our eyes; it is uniform throughout: as the passions alone are necessary for its establishment, the whole world is good enough for that" (1.5.14, p. 297).

In his initial discussion of moderate governments, Montesquieu is coy. For this, there is a reason. "I say it," he will later confess, "and it seems to me that I have composed this work solely to prove it: the spirit of moderation ought to be that of the legislator; the political good, like the moral good, is always to be found between two limits" (6.29.1). Political moderation is, in a sense, Montesquieu's cause. Already, in 1721, when he published his *Persian Letters*, he was prepared to float the notion that "the government most in conformity to reason" and "most perfect" is "a gentle [*doux*] government" free from unnecessary "severity," which "moves towards its end with minimal expense" by conducting "men in the manner that accords best with their propensities and inclinations."[55]

England interested Montesquieu in part because it was clearly viable in a way that his native France might well not be: the duke of Marlborough had proved as much at Blenheim, Ramillies, Oudenarde, Lille, and Malplaquet. He was interested in it also because, in leaving the passions free, it seemed to be "a gentle [*doux*] government" free from unnecessary "severity" and to move "towards its end with minimal expense" by conducting "men in the manner that accords best with their propensities and inclinations."

In this regard, the only rival to the species of government found in England would appear to be monarchy. According to Montesquieu, "monarchical government" can "maintain and sustain itself" without "much in the way of probity" because "the force" possessed by its "laws" is sufficient. Severe self-discipline is not required where "he who causes the laws to be executed judges himself above the laws." If "bad counsel or negligence" prevents the monarch from "causing the laws to be executed," he can easily repair the evil: he need only change his counsel or correct the negligence itself" (1.3.3).

"In monarchies," Montesquieu explains, "policy makes great things happen with as little of virtue as it can, just as in the most beautiful machines, art also employs as little of movement, of forces, of wheels as is possible. The state subsists independently of love of the fatherland, of desire for true glory, of self-renunciation, of the sacrifice of one's dearest interests, and of all those heroic virtues which we find in the ancients and know only from hearing them spoken of." If virtue can be discarded, it is because in a monarchy "the laws take the place of all these virtues, for which there is no need; the state confers on you a dispensation from them."

It is a good thing, Montesquieu adds, that monarchies have no need for the virtuous because therein "it is very difficult for the people to be so." Consider, he urges, "the miserable character of courtiers. . . . Ambition in idleness, baseness in pride, a desire to enrich oneself without work, an aversion for truth, flattery, treason, perfidy, the abandonment of all one's engagements, contempt for the duties of the citizen, fear of the virtue of the prince, hope looking to his weaknesses, and, more than that, the perpetual ridicule cast on virtue form, I believe, the character of the greatest number of courtiers, as is remarked in all places and times" (1.3.5).

If monarchy can nonetheless produce good government, it is because in it honor "takes the place of the political virtue" grounded in the love of equality that is to be found in republics. The honor that Montesquieu has in mind is artificial: if it gives rise not to civic virtue but to the vices characteristic of courtiers, it is because it is a "false honor," more consonant with "vanity" than with "pride," which demands artificial "preferences and distinctions" and is grounded in "the prejudice of each person and condition." The consequences of this all-pervasive "prejudice" are paradoxical but undeniable. "In well-regulated monarchies," Montesquieu contends, "everyone will be something like a good citizen while one will rarely find someone who is a good man." Monarchy he compares to Newton's "system of the universe, where there is a force which ceaselessly repels all bodies from the center and a force of gravity which draws them to it. Honor makes all the parts of the body politic move; it binds them by its own actions; and it happens that each pursues the common good while believing that he is pursuing his own particular interests" (1.3.6–7, 5.19, 2.19.9, 5.24.6).[56] Monarchies are ruled by something like Adam Smith's "invisible hand."[57]

Something of the sort applies also in England, where, Montesquieu tells us, political liberty is "established by" the "laws" (2.11.6, p. 407). There too as in monarchy, "policy makes great things happen with as little of virtue as it can." There too "just as in the most beautiful machines, art also employs as little of movement, of forces, of wheels as is possible"; and one can say that "the state subsists independently of love of the fatherland, of desire for true glory, of self-renunciation, of the sacrifice of one's dearest interests, and of all those heroic virtues which we find in the ancients and know only from hearing them spoken of."

The Constitution of Liberty

Montesquieu prefaces his initial discussion of the English polity with an account of the nature of "liberty," which he carefully distinguishes from "independence" of the sort possessed by those in the state of nature. His point is that the former is much more valuable than the latter. He begins, however, with a puzzling claim—that "liberty," properly understood, consists in "being able to do what one ought to want and in not being constrained to do what one ought not to want." Then, Montesquieu explains what this cryptic formula actually means—first, that "liberty is the right to do what the laws permit,"[58] and, then, that it is incompatible with genuine independence, for if a man is "able to do what the laws forbid, he no longer has liberty since the others would likewise possess this same power" and obstruct his freedom to do what the laws allow (2.11.3).[59] To prevent those most likely to strive for this species of independence from being "able to abuse power," he soon adds, "it is necessary that in the disposition of things power check power." It is his contention that "a constitution can be such that no one will be constrained to do things that the law does not require or prevented from doing those which the law permits him to do" (2.11.4). This would appear to be the object of the English polity, and it evidently constitutes what Montesquieu has in mind when he devotes the eleventh book of his tome to the laws which form "political liberty in its relation with the constitution" (2.11).[60] The government of England pursues this end chiefly through what eventually came to be called the separation of powers.[61] In its relation with the constitution, Montesquieu tells us, political liberty "is formed by a certain distribution of the three powers" (2.12.1).[62]

Montesquieu distinguishes "political liberty in its relation with the constitution" from "political liberty in its relation with the citizen." The latter is the subject of the twelfth book of *The Spirit of Laws*. But because it is the central focus of Montesquieu's concern, it intrudes on that book's immediate predecessor as well. "In a citizen," Montesquieu explains therein, "political liberty is that tranquillity of mind [*esprit*] which comes from the opinion that each has of his security." If he is to possess "this liberty, it is necessary that the government be such that one citizen be unable to fear [*craindre*] another citizen" (2.11.6, p. 397). The separation of powers is as essential to the elimination of this fear as it is to the guarantee that "no one will be constrained to do things that the law does not require or prevented from doing those which the law permits him to do."[63]

On the face of it, the two forms of liberty would appear to be inseparable. Where the executive and the legislative power are united in the hands of a single individual or corporate body, as they are in despotisms and tend to be in republics, one has reason "to fear [*craindre*]" that the individual or body that "makes tyrannical laws" will "execute them in a tyrannical manner." In similar fashion, if "the power of judging" is not somehow "kept separate from the legislative power and the executive power, there is no liberty." If it is united with the legislative power, "the judge would be the legislator" and the citizen's life and property would be subject to "arbitrary power." If it is united with the executive power, "the judge would have the strength [*force*] of an oppressor." If the power "of making the laws" were united with "that of executing public resolutions and with that of judging crimes or the disputes of particular citizens," Montesquieu exclaims, "all would be lost" (2.11.6, p. 397).

In the end, however, it is unclear to what degree "political liberty in its relation with the constitution" and "political liberty in its relation with the citizen" are mutually supportive. To begin with, Montesquieu tells us that "only the disposition of the laws, and even the fundamental laws" can give rise to the former, while the latter seems to depend more on "the mores, the manners, and the received examples" prevalent within a political community, and this species of liberty is more effectively promoted by "certain civil laws" than by political arrangements. Moreover, he goes out of his way to tell us that "it can happen that the constitution will be free and the citizen not" and that "the citizen will be free and the constitution not" (2.12.1).

When he is discussing the citizen's liberty, Montesquieu's focus seems almost entirely psychological.[64] This helps explain why he can claim that "the knowledge which one has acquired in some countries and which one will acquire in others with regard to the surest regulations that one can hold to in criminal judgments interests human kind more than anything else that there is in the world" (2.12.2). And it makes sense of his otherwise inexplicable concern with the psychological impact of taxation and his association of "duties," such as those "on commodities," that "the people least feel" with both "moderate government" and "the spirit of liberty" (2.13.7–8, 14).[65] If he asserts that "in our monarchies, all felicity consists in the opinion that the people have of the gentleness [*la douceur*] of the government" (2.12.25), it is because human happiness and, therefore, "political liberty in its relation with the citizen" is a state of mind.

Nowhere does Montesquieu suggest that "tranquillity of mind" is an attribute of the English. In fact, he intimates the opposite. This "nation" is, he concedes, "always inflamed." Precisely because "all the passions" are in England left "free," the Englishman tends to follow "his caprices and his fantasies." Moreover, because he and his countrymen are inclined "not to care to please anyone," they often "abandon themselves to their own humors." And frequently, they switch parties and abandon one set of friends for another, having forgotten "the laws of love and those of hatred" (3.19.27, pp. 575, 577).

Moreover, because the laws make no distinctions among men, each Englishman "regards himself as a monarch; and men, in that nation," are, in a sense, "confederates rather than fellow citizens." The fact that "no citizen ends up fearing [*craignant*] another" gives the Englishman a king-like "independence" that makes the English as a nation quite "proud." But, at the same time, "living," as they do "much among themselves" in a state of "retirement" or "retreat [*retraite*]," they "often find themselves in the midst of those whom they do not know." This renders them "timid," like those men in the state of nature truly graced with independence, but the recognition of "reciprocal fright [*une crainte réciproque*]" does not have on them the effect that it has on men in their natural state: it does not cause them to draw near, to take "pleasure" in the approach of "an animal" of their "own sort," and to become sociable. They are similarly immune to "the charm" of sexual "difference" and to "the natural appeal" that draws women and men to one another even in that aboriginal state.[66] Instead of friendliness and longing, "one sees in" the "eyes" of these Englishmen, "the better part of the time, a strange [*bizarre*] mixture of ill-mannered shame and pride." Their "character" as a "nation" most clearly appears in the products of their minds—which reveal them as "people collected within themselves" who are inclined to "think each entirely on his own" (3.19.27, pp. 582–583). In short, Montesquieu's Englishman is very much alone.

That so solitary a man should have an "uneasy spirit [*esprit inquiet*]" stands to reason (3.19.27, p. 582). Nor is it surprising that, unprompted by genuine peril or even by false alarm, he should nonetheless "fear [*crainte*] the escape of a good" that he "feels," that he "hardly knows," and that "can be hidden from us," and that this "fear [*crainte*]" should "always magnify objects" and render him "uneasy [*inquiet*] in his situation" and inclined to "believe" that he is "in danger even in those moments when" he is "most secure" (3.19.27, pp. 575–576). The liberation of the passions does not give rise to joy. "Political liberty in its relation with the constitution" may well be "established" for the English "by their laws," but this does not mean that they "actually enjoy" what Montesquieu calls "political liberty in its relation with the citizen"—for the latter is constituted by "that tranquillity of mind which comes from the opinion that each has of his security" (2.11.1 and 6, pp. 397, 407), and the English are anything but tranquil of mind.

"Uneasiness [*inquiétude*]" without "a certain object" would appear to be the Englishman's normal state of mind. He is rarely given reason to fear another citizen: fear is not deployed to secure his obedience as it is in a despotism. But he is anxious and fearful nonetheless. Moreover, in such a country, "the majority of those who possess wit and intelligence (*esprit*) would be tormented by that very *esprit*: in the disdain or disgust" that they would feel with regard "to all things, they would be unhappy with so many reasons not to be so" (3.19.27, pp. 576, 582). As a settled disposition, *inquiétude* would appear to be the distinguishing feature of Englishmen.

England's constitution exploits this disposition to good effect by providing a focus for the *inquiétude* that makes the Englishman so inclined to "fear the escape of a good" that he "feels," that he "hardly knows," and that "can be hidden from us," and so prone to "believe" that he is "in danger even in those moments when" he is "most secure" (3.19.27, pp. 575–576). In the political realm, Montesquieu observes, the characteristic uneasiness of the English gives rise to occasional panic, and the separation of powers gives direction to these popular fears. It does so by way of the partisanship that it fosters.

Partisanship is, in Montesquieu's judgment, the fundamental fact of English life. In consequence, it is with this fact that he begins his analysis of the influence of the laws on English mores, manners, and character: partisanship is the premise from which his argument unfolds. "Given that in this state, there would be two visible powers, the legislative and the executive power," he observes at the outset, "and given that every citizen would have a will of his own and would value his independence according to his own pleasure, the majority of people would have more affection for one of these powers than for the other, since the great number is not ordinarily equitable or sensible enough to hold the two in equal affection." This propensity would only be exacerbated by the fact that the executive had offices in his gift, for his dispensing of patronage would alienate those denied favor as it turned those employed into adherents (3.19.27, p. 575).

"The hatred" existing between the two parties "would endure," Montesquieu tells us, "because it would always be powerless," and it would forever be powerless because "the parties" would be "composed of free men" who would be inclined to switch sides if one party or the other appeared to have "secured too much." The monarch would himself be caught in the toils of partisan strife: "contrary to the ordinary maxims of prudence, he would often be obliged to give his confidence to those who have most offended him and to disgrace those who have best served him, doing out of necessity what other princes do by choice." Not even the historians would escape with their judgment intact: "in states extremely free, they betray the truth on account of their liberty itself, which always produces divisions" such that "each becomes as much the slave of the prejudices of his faction as he would be of a despot" in an absolute monarchy (3.19.27, pp. 575, 583).

Montesquieu finds this spectacle droll but in no way distressing. In a polity so caught up in partisanship, he notes that "every man would, in his way, take part in the administration of the state," and "the constitution would give everyone . . . political interests." One consequence of this widespread political participation would be that "this nation would love its liberty prodigiously since this liberty would be true." To "defend" its freedom, as it had in Montesquieu's youth at the time of the War of the League of Augsburg and the War of the Spanish Succession, "it would sacrifice its well-being, its ease, its interests," subjecting itself to taxes that no prince, however absolute, would dare impose, and deploying against its enemies in the form of a national debt owed its own citizens "an immense fictional wealth that the confidence and nature of its government would render real" (3.19.27, p. 577).

This marshaling of resources is no small matter. Although the English were "inclined to become commercial" and "always occupied with their own interests," though they preferred "gain" to "conquest" and "peace" to "war and aggrandizement" and were, therefore, "pacific on principle," they were in no way weak. Their outlook was, in fact, a source of strength. Because they had no truck with "the arbitrary principle of glory" and were "free from destructive prejudices," they simply refused to sacrifice "the real needs of the people" to "the imaginary needs of the state." They lived on an island and, for their defense, maintained an "empire of the sea." Though they might think it essential to their security that Scotland be absorbed and Ireland kept in thrall, they had no other territorial ambitions and, therefore, no great need for "strongholds, fortresses, and armies on land." Even when they sent out colonies, they did so "more for the purpose of extending their commerce than for domination." They were, in consequence, free from the "new malady" that had "extended itself across Europe," for they had no need to maintain "an inordinate number of troops" in peacetime and did not suffer a "perpetual augmentation of taxes" therefrom. "Poor with the wealth and commerce of the entire universe" the English certainly were not (2.10.2, 13.1, 17; 3.19.27, pp. 578–579; 4.20.8).

Of course, England did have "need of an army at sea" to protect its commerce and "guarantee it against invasions," and it maintained "every sort of facility" to sustain its "forces at sea." But it was relatively easy for the English to field "a navy superior to that of all the other powers," for the latter "had need to employ their finances for war on land" and "had not enough for war on the sea" as well. This left the English in the position that Xenophon had once imagined for his fellow Athenians: blessed with "the power to injure others without being subject to injury themselves." In consequence, they displayed "a haughtiness [*fierté*] natural" in men who are "capable of giving insult everywhere" and who believe "that their power has no more limits than the ocean" itself (3.19.27, pp. 578–579; 4.21.7).

England's capacity to project power at sea gave it "a great influence in the affairs of its neighbors." The fact that it generally "did not employ its power for conquest" caused those neighbors to "seek out its friendship" all the more and to "fear its hatred more than the inconstancy of its government and its internal agitation would seem to promise it." If it was "the destiny of its executive power" to be "almost always uneasy at home [*inquiétée au dedans*]," it was nonetheless "respected abroad," and with some frequency England found itself at "the center of negotiations in Europe," to which it brought "a greater measure of probity and good faith than the other participants" since "its ministers" were so "often obliged to justify their conduct before a popular council." The simple fact that they would be held "responsible [*garants*] for events" produced by "circuitous conduct [*une conduite detournée*]" on their part instilled in them the conviction that "it would be safest for them to take the straightest path" (3.19.27, pp. 579–580).

An equally salutary side effect of the party struggle, Montesquieu tells us, would be that, in England, everyone "would speak much of politics," and some would "pass their lives calculating events which, given the nature of things and the caprice of fortune, . . . would hardly submit to calculation." It matters little, he intimates, whether "particular individuals reason well or ill" concerning public affairs: in a nation that is free, "it suffices that they reason," for from their reasoning arises "the liberty" that provides them with protection against the unfortunate "effects of this same reasoning" (3.19.27, p. 582).[67]

In a country governed in this manner, Montesquieu hastens to add, the charges lodged by the party inclined to oppose the executive "would augment even more" than usual "the terrors of the people, who would never know really whether they were in danger or not." The "republic concealed under the form of a monarchy" is, however, superior to its ancient predecessor in that "the legislative power," which is distinct from the people, "has the confidence of the people" and can, in times of crisis, render them calm.[68] "In this fashion," Montesquieu observes, when "the terrors impressed" on the populace lack "a certain object, they would produce nothing but vain clamors and name-calling [*injures*]; and they would have this good effect: that they would stretch all the springs of government and render the citizens attentive" (3.19.27, p. 576).

In circumstances more dire, however, the English would comport themselves in a manner reminiscent of the various peoples of ancient Crete—who showed how "healthy principles" can cause even "bad laws" to have "the effect of good." In their zeal "to keep their magistrates in a state of dependence on the laws," the Cretans are said to have "employed a means quite singular: that of *insurrection*." In a procedure "supposed to be in conformity with the law," Montesquieu reports, "one part of the citizenry would rise up, put the magistrates to flight, and oblige them to re-enter private life." One would naturally presume that "such an institution, which established sedition for the purpose of preventing the abuse of power, would . . . overturn [*renverser*] any republic whatsoever," but Montesquieu insists that this was not the case in Crete because "the people possessed the greatest love for the fatherland" (1.8.11).

In England, where the citizens exhibit a love of liberty as prodigious as the patriotism of the citizens of Crete, something quite similar transpires. If the terrors fanned by the party opposed to the executive were ever "to appear on the occasion of an overturning [*renversement*] of the fundamental laws," Montesquieu observes, "they would be muted, lethal, excruciating and produce catastrophes: before long, one would see a frightful calm, during which the whole would unite itself against the power violating the laws." Moreover, if such "disputes took shape on the occasion of a violation of the fundamental laws, and if a foreign power appeared," as happened in 1688, "there would be a revolution, which would change neither the form of the government nor its constitution: for the revolutions to which liberty gives shape are nothing but a confirmation of liberty" (3.19.27, p. 576). As Montesquieu remarks elsewhere, the "impatience" characteristic of a people such as the English, "when it is joined with courage," gives rise to an "obstinacy [*l'opiniâtreté*]" that makes a "free nation" well suited "to disconcert the projects of tyranny." If their characteristic restlessness renders the English incapable of taking repose, it renders them vigilant at the same time (3.14.13).[69]

Paradoxically, then, the fact that Englishmen do not "actually enjoy" the sense of "security" and "tranquillity of mind," which Montesquieu describes as "political liberty in its relation with the citizen," helps account for the ethos of political distrust and the spirit of watchfulness and wariness that guarantee that "political liberty in its relation with the constitution" remains "established by their laws" (2.11.6, pp. 397, 407). The partisan conflict inspired by the separation of powers transforms the *inquiétude* characteristic of the English into a vigilance directed against all at home or abroad who might be tempted to encroach on their liberty. This vigilance is the passion that sets the English polity in motion, and it serves as a substitute for the republican virtue that the English need not and generally do not possess.

Montesquieu in America

No one in the British colonies in North America knew anything of Montesquieu's decision to censor his own work in 1734; none were aware that the Voltaire's fate had caused him to suppress his *Reflections on Universal Monarchy in Europe* and the little essay on the constitution of England that he had begun to draft. But they did profit from the book that he wrote in its stead, for a good many of those among the colonists who were educated did read *The Spirit of the Laws*, wherein he eventually published nearly all of the material excised. They thrilled with pride when they perused his celebration of the "beautiful system" that provided for English liberty. They were delighted that he had noticed that a country such as England would be inclined to "give to the people of its colonies the form of its own government," and those among them who had occasion to ponder the future of British North America, a number that increased dramatically with the passing of years, paused to savor his prediction that "as this government bears with it prosperity, one would see great peoples formed in the very forests which they had been sent to inhabit" (3.19.27, p. 578).[70]

It is hardly, then, an accident that, when the time came for the leaders of these "great peoples" to forge institutions for themselves, they reread *The Spirit of the Laws*. Almost everything that Montesquieu had written concerning the English and the potential inherent in the form of government on which they prided themselves could be applied in what became the United States of America, and, as should be obvious by now, it can still be applied today.

Notes

In citing the *Persian Letters* and *The Spirit of the Laws*, I have used the Pléiade edition: Charles de Secondat, baron de La Brède et de Montesquieu, *Oeuvres complètes de Montesquieu*, ed. Roger Caillois (Paris: Bibliothèque de la Pléiade, 1949–1951), 1: 131–373, 2: 225–995. All of the interlinear references in the text are to the parts, books, and chapters of Montesquieu's *Spirit of the Laws*; where the chapters are long, I have specified the pertinent page of the edition used. In general, the translations are my own. Where I found that I could not do better myself, I have not been hesitant to borrow phraseology from Montesquieu, *The Spirit of the Laws*, trans. Thomas Nugent (New York: Hafner, 1949) and from Montesquieu, *The Spirit of the Laws*, ed. and trans. Anne M. Cohler, Basia Carolyn Miller, and Harold Samuel Stone (Cambridge: Cambridge University Press, 1989).

1. Consider Bernard Bailyn, *The Ideological Origins of the American Revolution* (Cambridge, MA: Belknap Press, 1967), esp. 22–54, in light of Caroline Robbins, *The Eighteenth-Century Commonwealthman: Studies in the Transmission, Development and Circumstance of English Liberal Thought from the Restoration of Charles II until the War with the Thirteen Colonies* (Cambridge, MA: Harvard University Press, 1961). An earlier version of the former was published as the introduction to Bernard Bailyn, ed., *Pamphlets of the American Revolution, 1750–1766* (Cambridge, MA: Belknap Press, 1965–), 1: 1–202.

2. See Donald S. Lutz, "The Relative Influence of European Writers on Late Eighteenth-Century American Political Thought," *The American Political Science Review* 78 (1984): 189–197.

3. To date, there is no adequate account of Montesquieu's influence overall. One should begin, however, with Paul Merrill Spurlin, *Montesquieu in America, 1760–1801* (Baton Rouge: Louisiana State University Press, 1940). Regarding his influence on the framers of the American Constitution, more has been done: see Paul Merrill Spurlin, "Montesquieu and the American Constitution," in *The French Enlightenment in America: Essays on the Times of the Founding Fathers*, ed. Paul Merrill Spurlin (Athens: University of Georgia Press, 1984), 86–98; James W. Muller, "The American Framers' Debt to Montesquieu," in *The Revival of Constitutionalism*, ed. James W. Muller (Lincoln: Nebraska University Press, 1988), 87–102; and Anne M. Cohler, *Montesquieu's Comparative Politics and the Spirit of American Constitutionalism* (Lawrence: University Press of Kansas, 1988).

4. Letter by T. Q., *The Boston Gazette and Country Journal*, April 18, 1763; Letter by J., *The Boston Evening Post*, May 23, 1763; Letter by T. Q., *The Boston Gazette and Country Journal*, June 6, 1763; and Letter by U., *Boston Gazette*, August 1, 1763, in *American Political Writing during the Founding Era, 1760–1805*, ed. Charles S. Hyneman and Donald S. Lutz, 2 vols. (Indianapolis: Liberty Press, 1983), I: 19–37, 19–20, 23, 25–27, 37.

5. See Martin Howard, Jr., "A Letter from a Gentleman at Halifax" (1765), in *Pamphlets of the American Revolution*, I: 541.

6. See *Letters from a Farmer in Pennsylvania to the Inhabitants of the British Colonies*, no. VII, in *Empire and Nation*, ed. Forrest McDonald, 2nd ed. (Indianapolis: Liberty Fund, 1999), 42.

7. "Appeal to the Inhabitants of Quebec," October 26, 1774, in *Journals of the Continental Congress, 1774–1789*, ed. Worthington Chauncey Ford, 34 vols. (Washington, DC: U.S. Government Printing Office, 1904–1937), I: 107, 110–111.

8. A Native of this Colony, "An Address to the Convention of the Colony and Ancient Dominion of Virginia on the Subject of Government in General, and Recommending a Particular Form to Their Attention," *Virginia Gazette*, in *American Political Writing during the Foundation Era*, June 8 and 15, 1776, 328–339, 333.

9. Letter by Worcestriensis No. 4, *Boston Massachusetts Spy*, September 4, 1776, in *American Political Writing during the Founding Era*, 449–454, 450, 453.

10. See Jacob E. Cooke, ed., *The Federalist* (Middletown, CT: Wesleyan University Press, 1961), 324, 523.

11. Cf. *The Complete Anti-Federalist*, ed. Herbert J. Storing (Chicago: University of Chicago Press, 1981): Robert Yates and John Lansing, "Reasons of Dissent" (2.3.7); Luther Martin, "The Genuine Information Delivered to the Legislature of the State of Maryland" (2.4.44); Letters of Cato III (2.6.10–21, 25, 36, 43, 48); Letters of Centinel I (2.7.11, 17–19, 33, 73); Letters from the Federal Farmer II (2.8.15–19, 97, 148); Essays of Brutus (2.9.11–21, 39); Essays of an Old Whig IV (3.3.11, 20); A Review of the Constitution Proposed by the late Convention by a Federal Republican (3.6.8, 16, 19, 23); The Address and Reasons of Dissent of the Minority of the Convention of Pennsylvania To Their Constituents (3.11.16–17, 26, 44–45); Essays by William Penn (3.12.13); Letters of Agrippa IV (4.6.16–17); Letters of a Republican Federalist (4.13.21); Essays by a Farmer (4.17.22); Essays by a Farmer (5.1.13, 68, 93); Address of a Minority of the Maryland Ratifying Convention (5.4.10); Address by John Francis Mercer (5.5.5–6); Letter of Richard Henry Lee to Governor Edmund Randolph (5.6.1); Essays by Cato (5.10.4); Essay by Tamony (5.11.7); Reply to Cassius by Brutus (5.15.1); Speeches of Patrick Henry in the Virginia State Ratifying Convention (5.16.14); Speech of George Mason in the Virginia Ratifying Convention (5.17.1); James Monroe, *Some Observations on the Constitution* (5.21.12–13); Essays by Cincinnatus (6.1.12, 32); Essays by Sidney (6.8.17–19, 31, 35); Speeches by Melancton Smith in the New York Ratifying Convention (6.12.5), with Cooke, *Federalist*, 52–53, 56, 292, 295, 324–326, 328, 523 and with James Wilson, Speeches at the Pennsylvania Convention, November 24 and December 4, 1787; Cato, Poughkeepsie *Country Journal* and *Advertiser*, December 12, 1787; A Citizen of American [Noah Webster], *An Examination into the Leading Principles of the Federal Constitution*, October 17, 1787; and A Foreign Spectator [Nicholas Collin], "An Essay on the Means of Promoting Federal Sentiments in the United States," Philadelphia *Independent Gazetteer* August, 6, 10, 16–17, 24 and September 4,

12–13, 17, 1787, in *Friends of the Constitution: Writings of the "Other" Federalists, 1787–1788*, ed. Colleen A. Sheehan and Gary L. McDowell (Indianapolis: Liberty Fund, 1998) 74, 212, 237, 346, 386n, 400, 401n, 415, 425–426, 432. In the postscript dealing with the ratification of the Constitution that Bernard Bailyn added to the enlarged (but otherwise unrevised edition) of his book, Montesquieu plays a considerable role: see Bernard Bailyn, *The Ideological Origins of the American Revolution*, enlarged ed. (Cambridge: Belknap Press, 1992), 321–379.

12. See Cooke, *Federalist*, 324.

13. Letter by T. Q., *The Boston Gazette and Country Journal*, April 18, 1763, 19–22; Letter by J., *The Boston Evening Post*, May 23, 1763, 22–28; and Letter by T. Q., *The Boston Gazette and Country Journal*, June 6, 1763, 28–32, in *American Political Writing during the Founding Era*, I: 19–32.

14. A Pennsylvanian, "An Address to the Inhabitants of the British Settlements in America Upon Slave-Keeping" (1773), in *American Political Writing during the Founding Era*, I: 217–230, 218–219n, 225n, 228n.

15. See Worcestriensis No. 4, *Boston Massachusetts Spy*, September 4, 1776, in *American Political Writing during the Founding Era*, 449–454, 450, 453–454.

16. See "Rudiments of Law and Government Deduced from the Law of Nature" (1783), in *American Political Writing During the Founding Era*, 565–605, esp. 567n, 576n, 577n, 578n, 586n, 592n, 596n, 599n, 603n.

17. The federalism of John Dickinson is a case in point. First cf. *The Records of the Federal Convention of 1787*, ed. Max Farrand (New Haven: Yale University Press, 1911), I: 20–22 (May 29, 1787) with *The Records of the Federal Convention of 1787*, 235–237 (June 13, 1787); note *The Records of the Federal Convention of 1787*, 242–245 (June 15, 1787); and consider, with care, *Supplement to Max Farrand's The Records of the Federal Convention of 1787*, ed. James H. Hutson (New Haven: Yale University Press, 1987), 84–91. Then, consider *The Records of the Federal Convention*, I: 85–87 (June 2, 1787), 136 (June 6, 1787), 150, 152–153 (June 7, 1787); II: 114–115 (July 25, 1787), 123 (July 26, 1787), 202 (August 7, 1787), 278 (August 13, 1787), 292 (August 14, 1787), with an eye to *Supplement to The Records of the Federal Convention*, 128–129, 134–139. Finally, see Fabius, "Observations on the Constitution Proposed by the Federal Convention," no. 8, April 29, 1788, in *The Documentary History of the Ratification of the Constitution*, ed. Merrill Jensen et al. (Madison: State Historical Society of Wisconsin, 1976–), 17: 246–251, esp. 246–249, where Dickinson makes it clear that the so-called Connecticut Compromise embodied a set of constitutional principles inspired ultimately by Montesquieu and was no compromise at all.

18. See Louis Desgraves, "Aspects de la correspondance de Montesquieu en 1749," in *Lectures de Montesquieu*, ed. Edgar Mass and Alberto Postigiola (Naples: Liguori Editore, 1993), 66.

19. See David Hume, *An Enquiry Concerning the Principles of Morals* (London: A. Millar, 1751), 54–55; as cited in Robert Shackleton, *Montesquieu: A Critical Biography* (Oxford: Oxford University Press, 1961), 245.

20. Horace Walpole to H. Mann, January 10, 1750, in *Letters of Horace Walpole, Fourth Earl of Oxford*, ed. Paget Toynbee, 16 vols. (Oxford: Clarendon Press, 1903–1905), II: 419.

21. See Edmund Burke, "Abridgment of English History" (1757), in *Works of the Right Honourable Edmund Burke*, 8 vols. (London: H. G. Bohn, 1854–1859), VI: 297.

22. One can get a good sense of the work's scope from perusing the essays collected in *Montesquieu's Science of Politics: Essays on The Spirit of Laws*, ed. David W. Carrithers, Michael A. Mosher, and Paul A. Rahe (Lanham, MD: Rowman and Littlefield, 2001). There is much of value as well in *Montesquieu and the Spirit of Modernity*, ed. David W. Carrithers and Patrick Coleman (Oxford: Voltaire Foundation, 2002). The best attempt to date at a comprehensive analysis of Montesquieu's masterpiece is Thomas L. Pangle, *Montesquieu's Philosophy of Liberalism: A Commentary on The Spirit of the Laws* (Chicago: University of Chicago Press, 1973). Shackleton's *Montesquieu* is far more valuable for the light it casts on Montesquieu's life than for its analysis of his writings and thought.

23. See Cooke, *Federalist*, 324–325.

24. See C. P. Courtney, "Montesquieu and English Liberty," in *Montesquieu's Science of Politics*, 273–290, 273.

25. In this connection, see Lois G. Schwoerer, *The Declaration of Rights, 1689* (Baltimore: Johns Hopkins University Press, 1981).

26. For the details, see Winston S. Churchill, *Marlborough: His Life and Times* (London: George G. Harrap, 1947), I: 711–868.

27. See ibid., II: 95–627.

28. See Paul A. Rahe, "Averting Our Gaze," *The Journal of the Historical Society* 2 (2002): 145–151.

29. Churchill, *Marlborough*, II: 381.

30. For a more detailed argument along these lines than there is space for here, see Paul A. Rahe, "The Book That Never Was: Montesquieu's *Considerations on the Romans* in Historical Context," *History of Political Thought* 26 (2005): 43–89.

31. See Churchill, *Marlborough*, II: 628–1005.

32. The best introduction to this important, but neglected work is Diana J. Schaub, *Erotic Liberalism: Women and Revolution in Montesquieu's Persian Letters* (Lanham, MD: Rowman and Littlefield, 1995).

33. See Peter Gay, *Voltaire's Politics: The Poet as Realist* (New York: Vintage Books, 1965), 33–48, 66–68; and Theodore Besterman,

Voltaire, 3rd ed. (Chicago: University of Chicago Press, 1976), 113–128. For an earlier, more circumstantial, and ultimately less reliable account, see J. Churton Collins, *Voltaire, Montesquieu and Rousseau in England* (London: Eveleigh Nash, 1908), 1–116.

34. Jean-Antoine-Nicolas de Caritat, marquis de Condorcet, "Vie de Voltaire" (1791), in François Marieu Arouet de Voltaire, *Oeuvres complètes de Voltaire*, ed. Louis Émile Dierdonné Moland, 52 vols. (Paris: Garnier, 1877–1885), I: 208.

35. See Shackleton, *Montesquieu*, 117–145. For an earlier, still useful, if occasionally erroneous account, see Collins, *Voltaire, Montesquieu and Rousseau in England*, 117–181.

36. See Michel Baridon, "Rome et l'Angleterre dans les *Considérations*," in *Storia e ragione: Le Considérations sur les causes de la grandeur des Romains et de leur décadence di Montesquieu nel 250° della publicazione*, ed. Alberto Postigliola (Naples: Liguori, 1987), 293–309.

37. At one point, Montesquieu started to draft a preface, in which he explained that he had originally set out to describe the transition from the republic to the principate and that he had later decided to begin at the beginning, but he left the draft incomplete. See "Project de préface," in *Oeuvres complètes de Montesquieu*, ed. Jean Ehrard and Catherine Volpilhac-Auger (Oxford: Voltaire Foundation, 1998–), II: 315–316.

38. It was first published in *Deux opuscules de Montesquieu*, ed. Charles de Montesquieu (Bordeaux: G. Gounouilhou, 1891), 11–42.

39. See Patrick Andrivet and Catherine Volpilhac-Auger, "Introduction à *Considérations sur les causes de la grandeur des Romains et de leur decadence*," and Catherine Larrère and Françoise Weil, "Introduction à *Réflexions sur la monarchie universelle en Europe*," in *Oeuvres complètes de Montesquieu*, ed. Ehrard and Volpilhac-Auger, II: 40–86, esp. 41–42; 321–337, esp. 321–324, which should be read in light of the seminal work of Robert Shackleton, "Les secrétaires de Montesquieu," in *Essays on Montesquieu and the Enlightenment*, ed. David Gilson and Martin Smith (Oxford: Voltaire Foundation, 1988), 65–72.

40. See *Réflexions sur la monarchie universelle en Europe* I, in *Oeuvres complètes de Montesquieu*, ed. Ehrard and Volpilhac-Auger, II: 339–364, 339–340.

41. See *Réflexions sur la monarchie universelle en Europe* II–XVII, in *Oeuvres complètes de Montesquieu*, ed. Ehrard and Volpilhac-Auger, II: 341–359.

42. See *Réflexions sur la monarchie universelle en Europe* XVII, in *Oeuvres complètes de Montesquieu*, ed. Ehrard and Volpilhac-Auger, II: 358–359.

43. I find it astonishing that, in the introduction to the one recent English translation of this work, there is no mention of the *Reflections* at all: see David Lowenthal, "Introduction," in Montesquieu, *The Causes of the Greatness of the Romans and their Decline*, trans. David Lowenthal

(Ithaca: Cornell University Press, 1965), 1–20. This is not, however, an anomaly. Almost nowhere in the scholarship on Montesquieu's *Considerations* does anyone say a word concerning the original design of the book that Montesquieu had printed early in 1734: see, e.g., Roger B. Oake, "Montesquieu's Analysis of Roman History," *Journal of the History of Ideas* 16 (1955): 44–59; David Lowenthal, "The Design of Montesquieu's Considerations: Considerations on the Causes of the Greatness of the Romans and their Decline," *Interpretation: A Journal of Political Philosophy* 2 (1970): 144–166; Georges Benrekassa, *La politique et sa mémoire: Le politique et l'historique dans le pensée des lumières* (Paris: Payot, 1983), 37–89; the essays collected in *Storia e ragione*; and Richard Myers, "Montesquieu on the Causes of Roman Greatness," *History of Political Thought* 16 (1995): 37–47. Though the facts concerning Montesquieu's original intentions have been known for more than a century, I know of no discussion of their importance apart from the brief remarks in Andrivet and Volpilhac-Auger, "Introduction à *Considérations sur les causes de la grandeur des Romains et de leur décadence*," 3–86; and Larrère and Weil, "Introduction à *Réflexions sur la monarchie universelle en Europe*," 321–337.

44. For a more detailed discussion of these two texts than is possible here, see Paul A. Rahe, "The Book that Never Was: Montesquieu's *Considerations on the Romans* in Historical Context," *History of Political Thought* 26: 1 (Spring 2005): 43–89.

45. See Andrivet and Volpilhac-Auger, "Introduction à *Considérations sur les causes de la grandeur des Romains et de leur décadence*," 40.

46. Charles de Secondat, "Mémoire pour servir a l'éloge historique de M. de Montesquieu," in Louis Vian, *Histoire de Montesquieu: Sa vie et ses oeuvres* (Geneva: Slatkine Reprints, 1970), 396–407, 401.

47. Shackleton, "Les secrétaires de Montesquieu," 65–72.

48. See Robert Shackleton, "*L'Esprit des lois*: le manuscrit de la Bibliothèque nationale," in Gibson and Smith, *Essays on Montesquieu and the Enlightenment*, 85–92; and Larrère and Weil, "Introduction à *Réflexions sur la monarchie universelle en Europe*," 321–324.

49. Cf. Jean Jacques Granpre Molière, *La théorie de la constitution Anglaise chez Montesquieu* (Leiden: Presse Universitaire de Leyde, 1972), who fails to recognize the significance of the fact that the draft of *L'Esprit des lois* 2.11.6 is in the same hand as an extract from the missing manuscript of *Reflexions sur la monarchie universelle en Europe*.

50. See *Considérations sur les causes de la grandeur des Romains et de leur décadence* VIII, in *Oeuvres complètes de Montesquieu*, ed. Ehrard and Volpilhac-Auger, II: 152. In the second impression and in subsequent editions, Montesquieu tempered his praise for England considerably, substituting for his highly suggestive claim that its government "is one

of the wisest in Europe" the much milder observation that it is "wiser" than Carthage, Athens, and the republics of modern Italy.

51. What follows constitutes a restatement and amplification of part of my earlier discussion: see Paul A. Rahe, "Forms of Government: Structure, Principle, Object, and Aim," in *Montesquieu's Science of Politics*, 69–108.

52. Montesquieu's striking description of the English constitution echoes views long common in England. *Cf., e.g.*, Roger L'Estrange's claim, advanced on the eve of the Restoration, that "our former Government, eminently, included all the perfections of a Free-State, and was the Kernel, as it were, of a Common-wealth, in the shell of Monarchy." See [Roger L'Estrange], "A Plea for Limited Monarchy, As it Was Established in this Nation, Before the Late War" (1660), in *The Struggle for Sovereignty: Seventeenth-Century English Political Tracts*, ed. Joyce Lee Malcolm (Indianapolis: Liberty Press, 1999), I: 495–504, 499. This sort of claim was frequently heard from the late Tudor period onward: see Patrick Collinson, "The Monarchical Republic of Queen Elizabeth I," *Bulletin of the John Rylands Library of Manchester* 69 (1987): 394–424. Note also David Hume, "Of the Liberty of the Press," "Of the Independency of Parliament," and "Of the Parties of Great Britain," in *Essays Moral, Political, and Literary*, ed. Eugene F. Miller (Indianapolis: Liberty Classics, 1985), 9–13, 44–53, 64–72.

53. That he has discussed "the principles" of England's "constitution" in 2.11.6 Montesquieu specifies at 3.19.27, p. 574. In 2.11.5 and at 3.19.27, p. 574, he is evidently employing the plural term *principes* in the loose, nontechnical sense in which he uses it in the preface to his book (Preface), in the title of 3.19, and with some frequency elsewhere (1.4.2, p. 264; 4.8; 5.9; 8.14; 3.17.7, 19.5, 16–17; 6.28.6). As is suggested by Montesquieu's choice of words in 1.5.18, 8.11–12, 2.11.13, 16, the plural term as used in these passages quite often includes what he has in mind when he uses the singular term in its technical sense.

54. In this connection, see Bernard Manin, "Montesquieu et la politique moderne," *Cahiers de philosophie politique* 2–3 (issue nos.) (Reims: Université de Reims, 1985), 157–229 (esp. 182–229), and Cohler, *Montesquieu's Comparative Politics*, 66–97. Note also Walter Kuhfuss, *Mässigung und Politik: Studien zur politischen Sprache und Theorie Montesquieus* (Munich: Wilhelm Fink Verlag, 1975), 94–229.

55. See Montesquieu, *Lettres Persanes*, no. 80; in *Oeuvres Complètes de Montesquieu*, ed. Caillois, I: 252.

56. As Bertrand Binoche, *Introduction à De l'esprit des lois de Montesquieu* (Paris: Presses Universitaires de France, 1998), 125, points out, in these passages Montesquieu is alluding to Bossuet, who had juxtaposed the "false honor" arising from an ambition for the things of this world with the true honor sought by Christians.

57. Cf. Adam Smith, "The Theory of Moral Sentiments," IV.i.10 and "An Inquiry into The Nature and Causes of the Wealth of Nations," IV.ii.9, with "The History of Astronomy," III.2, in *Essays on Philosophical Subjects*—all to be found in *The Glasgow Edition of the Works and Correspondence of Adam Smith* (Oxford: Oxford University Press, 1976).

58. Cf. Arist. *Eth. Nic.*, 1138a5–7 with Thomas Hobbes, *Leviathan*, ed. Edwin Curley (Indianapolis: Hackett, 1994), II.xxi.1–18; and Thomas Hobbes, *A Dialogue between a Philosopher and a Student of the Common Laws of England*, ed. Joseph Cropsey (Chicago: University of Chicago Press, 1971), 73. For an example of the confusion to which Montesquieu's discussion of liberty has given rise, see David Spitz, "Montesquieu's Theory of Freedom," in *Essays in the Liberal Ideal of Freedom* (Tucson: University of Arizona Press, 1964), 28–35. Cf. Pierre Manent, *An Intellectual History of Liberalism*, trans. Rebecca Balinski (Princeton: Princeton University Press, 1994), 60–63.

59. For a further exploration of this point, see 5.26.15, 20. Cf. 5.24.2.

60. In this discussion (2.11.3–4), Montesquieu appears to be following John Locke: see the latter's *Two Treatises of Government: A Critical Edition with an Introduction and Apparatus Criticus*, ed. Peter Laslett, 2nd ed. (Cambridge: Cambridge University Press, 1970), II.iv.22, vi.57, ix.123.

61. See M. J. C. Vile, *Constitutionalism and the Separation of Powers* (Oxford: Clarendon Press, 1967). That Montesquieu is discussing the separation of powers without employing the phrase is evident, as James Madison had occasion to observe, both from his inclination to criticize polities in which two or more of the powers are "united" or "joined" and from his insistence that "the power of judging" be "separated" from both "the executive" and "the legislative power." Consider 2.11.6, 396–397, in light of Cooke, *Federalist*, 324–327. Cf., however, Charles Eisenmann, "*L'Esprit des Lois* et la séparation des pouvoirs" and "La pensées constitutionnelle de Montesquieu," and Michel Troper, "Charles Eisenmann contre le mythe de la séparation des pouvoirs," *Cahiers de philosophie politique* 2–3 (issue nos.) (Reims: Université de Reims, 1985), 3–79. As one would expect, Montesquieu owed his terminology, in part, to the 1691 French translation of John Locke's *Second Treatise of Civil Government*: see Shackleton, *Montesquieu*, 286. Note also Alberto Postigliola, "Sur quelques interprétations de la 'séparation des pouvoirs' chez Montesquieu," *Studies on Voltaire and the Eighteenth Century* 154 (1976): 1759–1775.

62. On this, see Pangle, *Montesquieu's Philosophy of Liberalism*, 117–138; Manent, *An Intellectual History of Liberalism*, 53–64; and Harvey C. Mansfield, Jr., *Taming the Prince: The Ambivalence of Modern Executive Power* (New York: Free Press, 1989), 213–246.

63. "Liberty," Montesquieu writes in his notebooks, "is that good which makes it possible to enjoy the other goods." It can be found in "well-regulated monarchies" and wherever one finds "good laws" functioning in the manner of "large nets" in which "the subjects" are like fish who "believe themselves free" because they do not "sense that they have been caught." For the pleasures associated with political participation, Montesquieu has little esteem: "I count," he writes, "as a very small thing the happiness of disputing furiously over the affairs of state and not ever saying one hundred words without pronouncing the word *liberty* as well as the privilege of hating half of the citizens." See *Mes pensées*, nos. 1797–1798, 1800, 1802, in *Oeuvres complètes de Montesquieu*, ed. Caillois, I: 1430–1432. If Montesquieu considers England "the freest country that there is in the world"—freer than "any republic"—it is not because there are elections in that country and debates in its Parliament but because "a man in England" can have "as many enemies as he has hairs on his head" and yet "nothing" will "on this account befall him." This last observation Montesquieu glosses with the remark that "this fact matters much because the health of the soul is as necessary as that of the body." See *Notes sur l'Angleterre*, in *Oeuvres complètes de Montesquieu*, ed. Caillois, I: 884.

64. See Pangle, *Montesquieu's Philosophy of Liberalism*, 139–142.

65. See ibid., 142–145.

66. Cf. 1.1.2.

67. For a strikingly similar account of the manner in which the separation of powers gives rise to a partisanship that explains many of the features of English life, see David Hume, "Of the Liberty of the Press," in *Essays Moral, Political, and Literary*, 9–13. Note also Hume, "Of Passive Obedience," in *Essays Moral, Political, and Literary*, 488–492, esp. 491–492.

68. Cf. Niccolò Machiavelli, *Discorsi sopra la prima deca di Tito Livio*, 1.4, in *Tutte le opere*, ed. Mario Martelli (Florence: Sansoni, 1971), 82–83.

69. In a much earlier work, Montesquieu has a character observe that in England's historians "one sees liberty constantly spring forth from the fires of discord and sedition" and that one finds "the Prince always tottering on a throne," which is itself "unshakeable." If the "nation" is "impatient," this character remarks, it is nonetheless "wise in its very fury." Consider *Lettres Persanes*, no. 136, in *Oeuvres complètes de Montesquieu*, ed. Caillois, 1: 336, in light of Neal Wood, "The Value of Asocial Sociability: Contributions of Machiavelli, Sidney and Montesquieu," in *Machiavelli and the Nature of Political Thought*, ed. Martin Fleisher (New York: Athenaeum, 1972), 282–307, esp. 298–305.

70. See, e.g., "Appeal to the Inhabitants of Quebec," October 26, 1774, *Journals of the Continental Congress* I: 107.

Part II

The Enlightenment and the Constitution in America

Chapter 6

The American Enlightenment

Gordon S. Wood

The ratification of the U.S. Constitution in 1788 was greeted with more excitement and more unanimity among the American people than at any time since the Declaration of Independence a decade earlier. " 'Tis done!" declared Benjamin Rush in July 1788. "We have become a nation." This was an extravagant claim, to say the least. Yet Rush thought that the new United States had become a nation virtually overnight. Everywhere in America, he said, there was "such a tide of joy as has seldom been felt in any age or country. . . . Justice has descended from heaven to dwell in our land, and ample restitution has at last been made to human nature by our new Constitution of all the injuries she has sustained in the old world from arbitrary government, false religions, and unlawful commerce." The new nation represented the "triumph of knowledge over ignorance, of virtue over vice, and of liberty over slavery."[1]

What gave Revolutionaries like Rush confidence in America's instant nationhood was their belief in America's enlightenment. As early as 1765 John Adams had declared that all of previous American history had pointed toward the eighteenth-century Enlightenment. The seventeenth-century settlement of America, he said, had opened up "a grand scene and design in Providence for the illumination of the ignorant, and the emancipation of the slavish part of mankind all over the earth."[2] The Revolution had become the climax of this great historic drama. Enlightenment was spreading everywhere in the Western world, but nowhere more so than in America. With the break from Great Britain complete and the Constitution ratified, many Americans in the 1790s thought that the United States had become the "most enlightened" nation in the world.[3]

For the people of these obscure provinces, "so recently," as Samuel
Bryan of Pennsylvania declared, "a rugged wilderness and the abode
of savages and wild beasts," for these provincial people to claim to be
the most enlightened nation on earth and to have "attained to a
degree of improvement and greatness . . . of which history furnishes
no parallel" seemed scarcely credible.[4] The United States in 1789, in
comparison with the former mother country, was still an underdevel-
oped country. Americans had no sophisticated court life, no magnificent
cities, no great concert halls, no lavish drawing rooms, and not much
to speak of in the way of the fine arts. Its economy was primitive.
There was as yet nothing comparable to the Bank of England; there
were no stock exchanges, no large trading companies, no great centers
of capital, and no readily available circulating medium of exchange.
Nineteen out of twenty Americans were still employed in agriculture,
and most of them lived in tiny rural communities. In 1790 there were
only twenty-four towns in the entire United States with a population
of 2,500 or more, and only five of these urban areas were cities with
populations over 10,000. It took over two months for news of a
foreign event in London to reach Philadelphia.[5] No wonder many
Europeans thought of the United States as a remote wilderness at the
very edges of Christendom, 3,000 miles from the centers of Western
civilization.

Nevertheless, as far removed from the centers of civilization as they
were, many Americans persisted in believing not only that they were
the most enlightened people on earth but also that because they were
enlightened they were by that fact alone a nation. Indeed, America
became the first nation in the world to base its nationhood solely on
Enlightenment values. Gertrude Stein may have been right when she
said that America was the oldest country in the world.

It was a strange kind of nationalism Revolutionary Americans
asserted. For Americans to identify their nation with the Enlightenment
was to identify it with transnational, indeed, universal, and ecumenical
standards. They had little sense that their devotion to the universal
principles of the Enlightenment was incompatible with loyalty to
their state or to the country as a whole. Historian David Ramsay
claimed he was "a citizen of the world and therefore despise[d]
national reflections." Nevertheless, he did not believe he was being
"inconsistent" in hoping that the professions would be "administered
to my country by its own sons." Joel Barlow did not think he was any
less American just because he was elected to the French National
Convention in 1792–1793. The many state histories written in the
aftermath of the Revolution were anything but celebrations of localism

and the diversity of the nation. Indeed, declared Ramsay, these histories were testimonies to the American commitment to enlightened
nationhood; they were designed to "wear away prejudices—rub off
asperities and mould us into an homogeneous people."[6]

Homogeneous people! This is a phrase that seems to separate us
most decisively from that different, distant eighteenth-century world.
Because we today can take our nationhood for granted, we can indulge
ourselves with the luxury of celebrating our multicultural diversity.
But 200 years ago Americans were trying to create a nation from
scratch and had no such luxury. They were desperately trying to make
themselves one people, and the best way they could do that was to
stress their remarkable degree of enlightenment. Since the
Enlightenment emphasized the value of homogeneity and of being a
single people, by describing themselves as the most enlightened
people in the world, Americans assumed that they would thereby be a
nation. More than anything else, their deep desire to be a nation is
what accounts for their impassioned insistence that they were especially
enlightened.

But why would they assume that they were especially enlightened?
Of course, they had many European radicals like Richard Price filling
their heads with the idea that they had actually created the
Enlightenment. "A Spirit" that had originated in America, Price told
Benjamin Franklin in 1787, was now spreading throughout the
Atlantic world. This spirit, said Price, promised "a State of Society more
favourable to peace, virtue, Science, and liberty (and consequently to
human happiness and dignity) than has yet been known. . . . The
minds of men are becoming more enlighten'd, and the silly despots of
the world are likely to be forced to respect human rights and to take
care not to govern too much lest they should not govern at all."[7]

But it was not simply compliments like Price's that made Americans
believe that they were the most enlightened people on earth. They
thought they had ample reasons for their confidence. They may not
have been correct in their reasoning, but it is important for us to know
why they thought as they did. By doing so we can understand not
only something about the origins of the United States but also something of what the Enlightenment meant to many people in the
eighteenth-century Atlantic world.

Americans had no doubt that they were living in an age of
Enlightenment. Everywhere the boundaries of darkness and ignorance
were being pushed back and light and reason were being extended
outward. More than most people in the Atlantic world Americans
were keenly aware that savagery and barbarism were giving way to

refinement and civilization. Precisely because they were provincials living on the periphery of civilization, living, as historian Franco Venturi once pointed out, in a place "where the contact between a backward world and modern world was chronologically more abrupt and geographically closer," they knew what the process of becoming enlightened really meant. The experience of becoming refined and civilized was more palpable and immediate for them than it was for those living in the metropolitan centers of the Old World.

Americans told themselves over and over that they were a young and forming people. And because they inhabited a New World and were in a plastic state, they were more capable of refinement and education than people stuck in the habits and prejudices of the Old World. In writings, orations, poetry—in every conceivable manner and in the most extravagant and rapturous rhetoric—Revolutionary Americans told themselves that they were more capable than any people in the world of making themselves over.

As republicans attempting to build a state from the bottom-up, they were necessarily committed to Lockean sensationalism—that knowledge came less from reason and more from sense experience. Not only did such Lockean sensationalism give a new significance to the capacities of ordinary people, since all people had senses, but it also opened up the possibility of people being educated and improved by changing the environments that operated on their senses.

These views lay behind the enlightened assumption that all men were created equal. Even those as aristocratic as William Byrd and Governor Francis Fauquier of Virginia now conceded that all men, even men of different nations and races, were born equal and that, as Byrd wrote, "the principal difference between one people and another proceeds only from the differing opportunities of improvement." "White, Red, or Black; polished or unpolished," declared Governor Fauquier in 1760, "Men are Men."[8]

The American Revolutionary leaders were primed to receive these ideas that culture was socially constructed and that only education and cultivation separated one man from another. In fact, their receptivity to these explosive ideas, which became the basis of all modern thinking, helps explain why they should have become the most remarkable generation of leaders in American history. Because they were men of high ambition and yet of relatively modest origins, they naturally were eager to promote the new enlightened standards of gentility and learning in opposition to the traditional importance of family and blood. They saw themselves sharply set apart from the older world of their fathers and grandfathers. They sought, often unsuccessfully but always sincerely, to be what Jefferson called "natural aristocrats"— aristocrats who measured their status not by birth or family but by enlightened values and benevolent behavior. To be a natural aristocrat meant being reasonable, tolerant, honest, virtuous, and candid. It also implied being cosmopolitan, standing on elevated ground in order to have a large view of human affairs, and being free of the prejudices, parochialism, and religious enthusiasm of the vulgar and barbaric. It meant, in short, having all those characteristics that we today sum up in the idea of a liberal arts education.

Almost all the Revolutionary leaders—even including the second and third tiers of leadership—were first-generation gentlemen. That is to say, almost all were the first in their families to attend college and to acquire a liberal arts education that was now the new mark of an enlightened eighteenth-century gentleman. Jefferson's father, Peter Jefferson, was a wealthy Virginia planter and surveyor who married successfully into the prestigious Randolph family. But he was not a refined and liberally educated gentleman: he did not read Latin, he did not know French, he did not play the violin, and, as far as we know, he never once questioned the idea of a religious establishment or the owning of slaves.

His son Thomas Jefferson was very different. Indeed, all the revolutionaries knew things that their fathers had not known, and they were eager to prove themselves by what they believed and valued and by their virtue and disinterestedness.

Most important, these Revolutionary leaders felt a greater affinity with the people they spoke for than did elites in Europe. Not for them "the withdrawal of the upper classes" from the uncultivated bulk of the population that historian Peter Burke speaks about. Because the American gentry were establishing republics, they necessarily had to have a more magnanimous view of human nature than their European counterparts. Republicanism required a society that was not only enlightened but was cohesive, virtuous, and egalitarian. Monarchies could comprehend large territories and composite kingdoms and rule over people who were corrupt and were diverse in interests and ethnicities. Monarchies had their unitary authority, kingly honors and patronage, hereditary aristocracies, established national churches, and standing armies to hold their diverse and corrupt societies together. Republics had none of these adhesive elements. Instead, republics were supposed to rely for cohesion on the moral qualities of their people—their virtue, their intelligence, and their natural sociability. Republicanism created citizens, and citizens were all equal to one another.

In fact, it was this emphasis on republican homogeneity and equality that drove the revolutionaries to exclude from citizenship in their new nation both the nearly 20 percent of the total population that was of African ancestry and the tens of thousands of Indians living within its borders. The British monarchy, where everyone but the king was dependent and unequal, had had no difficulty at all in embracing both slaves and Indians as subjects. But a republic of equal citizens was different.

As equal citizens, the American people necessarily possessed a unanimity and a oneness that other people did not have. As Joel Barlow noted in 1792, the "people" had come to mean something very different in America from what it did in Europe. In Europe the people remained only a portion of the society; they were the poor, the rabble, the miserables, the menu peuple, the Pöbel.[9] But in America the people were the whole society. In republican America there could be no subjects, no orders, no aristocracy, no estates separate from the people. The people had become everything.

Perhaps some American gentry in the privacy of their dining rooms continued to express the traditional elitist contempt for ordinary folk. But it was no longer possible in public for an American leader to refer to the people as the common "herd." During the Virginia ratifying convention in June 1788 Edmund Randolph had used just this term in reference to the people, and Patrick Henry had immediately jumped on him. By likening the people to a "herd," said Henry, Randolph had "levelled and degraded [them] to the lowest degree," reducing them "from respectable independent citizens, to abject, dependent subjects or slaves." Randolph was forced to rise at once and defensively declare "that he did not use that word to excite any odium, but merely to convey an idea of a multitude."[10]

From this moment no American political leader ever again dared in public to refer to the people in such disparaging terms. Instead in their orations and writings they exulted in the various ways the American people as a whole were more enlightened than the rest of mankind.

In these attempts to justify their enlightenment, Americans created the sources of their belief in their exceptionalism, in their difference from the people of the Old World. Americans, they told themselves, were without both the corrupting luxury of Europe and its great distinctions of wealth and poverty. "Here," said the French immigrant and author, Hector St. John Crèvecoeur, in one of his typical ecstatic celebrations of the distinctiveness of the New World, "are no aristocratical families, no courts, no kings, no bishops, no ecclesiastical dominion, no invisible power giving to a few a very visible one, no great manufactures employing thousands, no great refinements of luxury. The rich and the poor are not so far removed from each other as they are in Europe." There was nothing in America remotely resembling the wretched poverty and the gin-soaked slums of London. America, continued Crèvecoeur, was largely made up of "cultivators scattered over an immense territory," each of them working for himself. Nowhere in America, he said, ignoring for the moment the big houses of the Southern planters and the slave quarters of hundreds of thousands of black Africans, could one find "the hostile castle and the haughty mansion, contrasted with the clay-built hut and miserable cabin, where cattle and men help to keep each other warm and dwell in meanness, smoke and indigence."[11]

Precisely because Americans were separated from Europe and, as Jefferson said in 1787, "remote from all other aid, we are obliged to invent and execute; to find means within ourselves, and not to lean on others." The result of this American pragmatism, this ability, said Jefferson, "to surmount every difficulty by resolution and contrivance," was a general prosperity.[12] White Americans enjoyed the highest standard of living in the world, and goods of all sorts were widely diffused throughout the society. Indeed, the enlightenment of a society could be measured by the spread of material possessions, by seeing whether most people possessed what Jefferson called those things "applicable to our daily concerns." Did people eat with knives and forks instead of with their hands? Did they sleep on feather mattresses instead of straw? Did they drink out of china cups instead of wooden vessels? These were signs of prosperity, of happiness, of civilization. Jefferson believed that to know the real state of a society's enlightenment one "must ferret the people out of their hovels, . . . look into their kettle, eat their bread, loll on their beds under pretence of resting yourself, but in fact to find out if they are soft."[13]

The Revolution had made Americans a more intelligent people. It had given "a spring to the active powers of the inhabitants," said David Ramsay in 1789, "and set them on thinking, speaking, and acting far beyond that to which they had been accustomed."[14] Three-quarters of all the books and pamphlets published in America between 1640 and 1800 appeared in the last thirty-five years of the eighteenth century. By eighteenth-century standards, levels of literacy, at least for white Americans in the North, were higher than almost any other place on earth and were rapidly climbing, especially for white women. All their reading made them enlightened. Jefferson was convinced that an American farmer rather than an English farmer had conceived of making the rim of a wheel from a single piece of wood. He knew it had to be an American because the idea had been suggested by Homer, and "ours are the only farmers who can read Homer."[15]

Unlike in England where conservative aristocrats opposed educating the masses for fear of breeding dissatisfied employees and social instability, American elites wholeheartedly endorsed education for ordinary people. American leaders issued a torrent of speeches and writings on the importance of popular education that has rarely been matched in American history or in the history of any other country. Their goal, as Benjamin Rush put it, was not to release the talents of individuals as much as it was to produce "one general and uniform system of education" in order to "render the mass of the people more homogeneous, and thereby fit them more easily for uniform and peaceable government."[16]

Formal schooling was only part of the educational process of rendering the people more homogeneous and enlightened. Because information of all sorts had to be spread throughout the sprawling nation, Americans began creating post offices faster than any other people in the world. One of the consequences of this expanding postal system was an astonishing increase in the circulation of newspapers. "In no other country on earth, not even in Great Britain," said Noah Webster, "are Newspapers so generally circulated among the body of the people, as in America." By 1810 Americans were buying over 22 million copies of 376 newspapers annually—even though half the population was under the age of sixteen and one-fifth was enslaved and prevented from reading. This was the largest aggregate circulation of newspapers of any country in the world.[17]

Because republics, as Benjamin Rush said, were naturally "peaceful and benevolent forms of government," Americans inevitably took the lead in promoting humane reforms. Jefferson in fact thought that America was the most compassionate nation in the world. "There is not a country on earth," he said, "where there is greater tranquillity, where the laws are milder, or better obeyed . . ., where strangers are better received, more hospitably treated, & with a more sacred respect."[18] In the several decades following the Revolution, Americans took very seriously the idea that they were peculiarly a people of sentiment and sensibility, more honest, more generous, and more caring than other peoples.

They eagerly began creating charitable and humanitarian societies by the hundreds and thousands. Indeed, there were more such societies formed in the decade following the Revolution than were created in the entire colonial period. These multiplying societies treated the sick, aided the industrious poor, housed orphans, fed imprisoned debtors, built huts for shipwrecked sailors, and, in the case of the Massachusetts Humane Society, even attempted to resuscitate those suffering from "suspended animation," that is, those such as drowning victims who appeared to be dead but actually were not. The fear of being buried alive was a serious concern at this time. Many, like Washington on his death bed, asked that their bodies not be immediately interred in case they might be suffering from suspended animation.

The most notable of the humanitarian reforms coming out of the Revolution involved new systems of criminal punishment. Jefferson and other leaders drew up plans for liberalizing the harsh and bloody penal codes of the colonial period. Since people learned from what they saw, the cruel and barbaric punishments of monarchies carried out in public, said Thomas Paine, hardened the hearts of their subjects and made them bloodthirsty. "It is [monarchy's] sanguinary punishments which corrupt mankind."[19] Maybe it was sensible for Britain to have over 200 crimes punishable by death, for monarchies were based on fear and had to rely on harsh punishments. But, said Paine, republics were different. They were capable of producing a kinder and gentler people.

People were not born to be criminals, it was now said; they were taught to be criminals by sensuously experiencing the world around them. If the characters of people were produced by their environments, as Lockean liberal thinking suggested, perhaps criminals were not entirely responsible for their actions. Maybe impious and cruel parents of the criminal were at fault, or maybe even the whole society was to blame. "We all must plead guilty before the bar of conscience as having had some share in corrupting the morals of the community, and levelling the highway to the gallows," declared a New Hampshire minister in 1796.[20] If criminal behavior was learned, then perhaps it could be unlearned. "Let every criminal, then, be considered as a person laboring under an infectious disorder," said one writer in 1790. "Mental disease is the cause of all crimes."[21] If so, then it seemed that criminals could be salvaged and not simply mutilated or executed.

These enlightened sentiments spread everywhere and eroded support for capital punishment in the new republican states. Not that the reformers had become soft on crime. Although Jefferson's code called for the death penalty only for treason and murder, he did propose the *lex talionis*, the law of retaliation, for the punishment of other crimes. So the state would poison the criminal who poisoned his victim, and would castrate men guilty of rape or sodomy; guilty women would have a half-inch hole bored through their noses. In Massachusetts in

1785 a counterfeiter was no longer executed. Instead, he was set in the pillory, taken to the gallows where he stood with a rope around his neck for a time, whipped twenty stripes, had his left arm cut off, and finally was sentenced to three years' hard labor.

Although most states did something to change their codes of punishment, Pennsylvania led the way in the 1780s and 1790s in the enlightened effort, as its legislation put it, "to reclaim rather than destroy," "to correct and reform the offenders" rather than simply to mark or eliminate them. Pennsylvania abolished all bodily punishments such as "burning in the hand" and "cutting off the ears" and ended the death penalty for all crimes except murder. In their place the state proposed a scale of punishments based on fines and years of imprisonment. Criminals were now to feel their personal guilt by being confined in prisons apart from the excited environment of the outside world, in solitude where, declared a fascinated French observer, the "calm contemplation of mind which brings on penitence" could take place.[22]

Out of these efforts was created the penitentiary, which turned the prison into what Philadelphia officials called "a school of reformation." By 1805 New York, New Jersey, Connecticut, Virginia, and Massachusetts had followed Pennsylvania in constructing penitentiaries based on the principle of solitary confinement. Nowhere else in the Western world, as enlightened philosophers recognized, were such penal reforms carried as far as they were in America.[23]

Not only did the Americans believe that they possessed a more intelligent, more equal, more prosperous, and more compassionate society than those of other countries, but they also thought that they were less superstitious and more rational than the people of the Old World. They had actually destroyed religious establishments and created a degree of religious liberty that European liberals could only dream about. Many Americans thought that their Revolution, in the words of the New York Constitution of 1777, had been designed to end the "spiritual oppression and intolerance wherewith the bigotry and ambition of weak and wicked priests" had "scourged mankind."[24]

Although it was the proliferation of different religious groups that made possible this religious freedom, Americans generally did not celebrate their religious diversity; indeed, the fragmentation of religion in America appalled most people. Most Americans accepted differences of religion only in so far as these differences made toleration and freedom of conscience possible. Even an enlightened reformer like Jefferson hoped that eventually everyone would become a Unitarian.

Since refugees from the tyrannies of Britain and Europe were entering the United States in increasing numbers in the 1790s, Americans had every reason to believe that their country had become the special asylum of liberty. In the spring of 1794 the United Irishmen of Dublin sent the renowned scientist Joseph Priestley their best wishes as he fled from persecution in England to the New World. "You are going to a happier world—the world of Washington and Franklin . . . You are going to a country where science is turned to better uses."

All of this immigration meant that all the peoples of Europe were present in America, which in turn helped to fulfill the fraternal dream of the Enlightenment, as Benjamin Rush described it, of "men of various countries and languages . . . conversing with each other like children of one father."[25] Not that American leaders celebrated the ethnic diversity of America in any modern sense. Far from it. What impressed the Revolutionary leaders was not the multicultural diversity of these immigrants but rather their remarkable acculturation and assimilation into one people. John Jay lived in New York City, the most ethnically and religiously diverse place in all America, and was himself three-eighths French and five-eighths Dutch, without any English ancestry. Nevertheless, Jay could declare with a straight face in the *Federalist*, No. 2, that "Providence has been pleased to give this one connected country to one united people—a people descended from the same ancestors, speaking the same language, professing the same religion, attached to the same principles of government, very similar in their manners and customs and who, by their joint counsels, arms, and efforts . . . have nobly established general liberty and independence."[26]

The Revolutionary leaders' idea of a modern state, shared by enlightened British, French, and German eighteenth-century reformers as well, was one that was homogeneous, not one that was fractured by differences of language, ethnicity, and religion. Much of Europe in the eighteenth century was still a patchwork of small duchies, principalities, and city-states—nearly 350 of them. Even those nation-states that had begun consolidating were not yet very secure or homogeneous. England had struggled for centuries to bring Wales, Scotland, and Ireland under its control. Only in the Act of Union in 1707 had it created the entity known as Great Britain; and as events showed its struggle to create a single nation was far from over. France was even worse off. Its eighteenth-century ancien régime was a still a hodgepodge of provinces and diverse peoples and by modern standards scarcely a single nation at all. Spain had just recently begun assimilating the kingdoms of Castile and Aragon into a single state, but the Basque provinces and Navarre still maintained an extraordinary degree of independence from the central monarchy.

European reformers everywhere wanted to eliminate these differences within their national boundaries and bind the people of their state together in a common culture. The American Revolutionary leaders were no different. They thought that Americans had become the most enlightened nation in the world precisely because they were a more rational and homogeneous society. They had done away with the various peasant customs, craft holidays, and primitive peculiarities—the morris dances, the charavaries, the bearbaiting, and other folk practices—that characterized the societies of the Old World. The New England Puritans had banned many of these popular festivals and customs, and elsewhere the mixing and settling of different peoples had worn most of them away. In New England all that remained of Old World holidays was Pope's Day, November 5—the colonists' version of Guy Fawkes Day. Since enlightened elites everywhere regarded most of these different plebeian customs and holidays as remnants of superstition and barbarism, their relative absence in America seemed to be another sign of the new nation's enlightenment and oneness.[27]

In various ways Americans appeared to be more of a single people than the nations of Europe. Nothing made enlightened eighteenth-century Americans prouder than the fact that most people in America spoke the same language and could understand one another everywhere. That this was not true in the European nations was one of the great laments of enlightened reformers in the Old World. Europeans, even those within the same country, were cut off from one another by their regional and local dialects. A Yorkshireman could not be understood in Somerset and vice versa. On the eve of the French Revolution the majority of people in France did not speak French.

Americans by contrast could understand each other from Maine to Georgia. It was very obvious why this should be so, said John Witherspoon, president of Princeton. Since Americans were "much more unsettled, and mov[ed] frequently from place to place, they are not as liable to local peculiarities, either in accent or phraseology."[28]

In England, said Noah Webster, language was what divided the English people from one another. The court and the upper ranks of the aristocracy set the standards of usage and thus put themselves at odds with the language spoken by the rest of the country. America was different, said Webster. Its standard was fixed by the general practice of the nation, and therefore Americans had "the fairest opportunity of establishing a national language, and of giving it [more] uniformity and perspicuity . . . [than] ever [before] presented itself to mankind."

Indeed, Webster was convinced that Americans already "speak the most *pure English* now known in the world." Within a century and a half, he predicted, North America would be peopled with a hundred million citizens, "all speaking the same language." Nowhere else in the world would such large numbers of people "be able to associate and converse together like children of the same family."[29]

Others had even more grandiose visions for the spread of America's language. John Adams was among those who suggested that American English would eventually become "the next universal language." In 1789 even a French official agreed; in a moment of giddiness he actually predicted that American English was destined to replace diplomatic French as the language of the world. Americans, he said, "tempered by misfortune," were "more human, more generous, more tolerant, all qualities that make one want to share the opinions, adopt the customs, and speak the language of such a people."[30] We can only assume that this Frenchman's official career was short-lived.

It was understandable that American English might conquer the world because Americans were the only true citizens of the world. To be enlightened was to be, as Washington said, "a citizen of the great republic of humanity at large." The Revolutionary generation was more eager to demonstrate its cosmopolitanism than any subsequent generation in American history. Intense local attachments were common to peasants and backward people, but educated and enlightened persons were supposed to be at home anywhere in the world. Indeed, to be free of local prejudices and parochial ties was what defined an enlightened gentleman. One's humanity was measured by one's ability to relate to strangers, to enter into the hearts of even those who were different. Americans prided themselves on their hospitality and their treatment of strangers. In America, as Crèvecoeur pointed out, the concept of "stranger" scarcely seemed to exist. "A traveller in Europe becomes a stranger as soon as he quits his own kingdom; but it is otherwise here. We know, properly speaking, no strangers; this is every person's country; the variety of our soils, situations, climates, governments, and produce hath something which must please everyone."[31]

The truth, declared Thomas Paine in *Common Sense*, was that Americans were the most cosmopolitan people in the world. They surmounted all local prejudices. They regarded everyone from different nations as their countrymen and ignored neighborhoods, towns, and counties as "distinctions too limited for continental minds."[32] Because they were free men, they were brothers to all the world.

These were the enlightened dreams of Americans 200 years ago. Looking back from our all-knowing postmodern perspective we can only marvel at the hubris and hypocrisy involved in the building of their enlightened empire of liberty. Precisely because the United States today has become the greatest and richest empire the world has ever known, we can see only the limits of their achievement and the failures of their imaginations. All their talk of enlightenment and the promise of America seems hypocritical in light of their unwillingness to abolish slavery, promote racial equality, and treat the native peoples fairly. But in fact it was the Americans' commitment to being enlightened that for the first time on a large scale gave them both the incentive and the moral capacity to condemn their own treatment of the Indians and Africans in their midst. However brutally white Americans in fact treated Indians and Africans in the decades following the Revolution, and no one can deny the brutality, that treatment was denounced as a moral evil by more and more enlightened Americans in ways that had not been done in premodern pre-Enlightenment times.

Since these Enlightenment ideals still constitute the source of American nationhood, we need to understand them and their origins. Despite all our present talk of diversity and multiculturalism, because of these Enlightenment ideals we are still in the best position among the advanced democracies for dealing with the massive demographic changes and movements taking place throughout the world. All the advanced democracies of Europe are finding it very difficult to assimilate foreign immigrants and are experiencing serious crises of national identity. Whatever problems we have in this respect pale into insignificance compared to those of the European nations. We, of course, are not the only country to base its nationhood on Enlightenment values. France also claims to be grounded in universal Enlightenment principles. But ironically the French have taken the Enlightenment desire for a single homogeneous nation so seriously that that their collective sense of national oneness leaves little room for the existence of Arab and other ethnic minorities. Precisely because America ultimately came to conceive of itself not as a single entity but as a nation of individuals, in our better moments open to anyone in the world, it is better able to handle this explosive demographic future. The coming decades will test just how much of an enlightened nation of immigrants we Americans are willing to be.

Notes

1. Rush to Elias Boudinot?, Observations on the Federal Procession in Philadelphia, July 9, 1788, in *Letters of Benjamin Rush*, ed. L. H. Butterfield, 2 vols. (Princeton: Princeton University Press, 1951), 1: 470–475.

2. John Adams, "Dissertation on the Feudal and Canon Law" (1765), in *The Rising Glory of America, 1760–1820*, ed. Gordon S. Wood (New York: Braziller, 1971), 29.
3. Charles S. Hyneman and George W. Carey, eds., *A Second Federalist: Congress Creates a Government* (Columbia, SC: University of South Carolina Press, 1967), 24.
4. "Centinel" [Samuel Bryan], in *The Debate on the Constitution*, ed. Bernard Bailyn, 2 vols. (New York: Library of America, 1993), 1: 686.
5. Allen R. Pred, *Urban Growth and the Circulation of Information: The United States System of Cities, 1790–1840* (Cambridge, MA: Harvard University Press, 1973), 26.
6. Evarts B. Greene, *The Revolutionary Generation, 1763–1790* (New York: Macmillan, 1943), 418; Colin Bonwick, *English Radicals and the American Revolution* (Chapel Hill: University of North Carolina Press, 1977), 13–14; Alan D. McKillop, "Local Attachment and Cosmopolitanism—The Eighteenth-Century Pattern," in *From Sensibility to Romanticism: Essays Presented to Frederick A. Pottle*, ed. Frederick W. Hilles and Harold Bloom (New York: Oxford University Press, 1965), 197; David Ramsay to John Eliot, August 11, 1792, in *David Ramsay . . . Selections From His Writings*, ed. Robert L. Burnhouse, trans. American Philosophical Society (Philadelphia: American Philosophical Society, 1965), 133.
7. Richard Price to Benjamin Franklin, September 17, 1787, in Papers of Benjamin Franklin, unpublished.
8. Julie Richter, "The Impact of the Death of Governor Francis Fauquier on His Slaves and Their Families," *The Colonial Williamsburg Interpreter* 18 (1997): 1–7, 2.
9. Joel Barlow, *Advice to the Privileged Orders in the Several States of Europe* (Ithaca: Cornell University Press, 1956; republished from the original 1792 edition), 17; Harry C. Payne, *The Philosophes and the People* (New Haven: Yale University Press, 1976), 7–17.
10. Virginia Ratifying Convention, in *The Documentary History of the Constitution*, ed. John P. Kaminski and Gaspare J. Saladino (Madison: States Historical Society of Wisconsin, 1999), 9: 1044–1045.
11. Hector St. John Crèvecoeur, *Letters from an American Farmer* (New York: Penguin, 1981), letter III, 67.
12. Jefferson to Martha Jefferson, March 28, 1787, in *Papers of Jefferson*, ed. Julian P. Boyd et al. (Princeton: Princeton University Press, 1950–), 11: 251.
13. Jefferson to Lafayette, April 11, 1787, in Boyd et al., eds., *Papers of Jefferson*, 11: 285.
14. David Ramsay, *The History of the American Revolution*, ed. Lester H. Cohen, 2 vols. (Indianapolis: Liberty Classics, 1989; republished from the original edition of 1789), 2: 630.
15. Edward T. Martin, *Thomas Jefferson: Scientist* (New York: Henry Schuman, 1952), 54.

16. Benjamin Rush, "Of the Mode of Education Proper in a Republic," in *The Selected Writings of Benjamin Rush*, ed. Dagobert D. Runes (New York: Philosophical Library, 1947), 90, 88.

17. Frank L. Mott, *A History of American Journalism in the United States . . . 1690–1940* (New York: Macmillan, 1941), 159, 167; Merle Curti, *The Growth of American Thought*, 3rd ed. (New York: Harper and Row, 1964), 209; Donald H. Stewart, *The Opposition Press of the Federalist Period* (Albany: State University of New York Press, 1969), 15, 624.

18. Jefferson to Maria Cosway, October 12, 1786, in Boyd et al., eds., *Papers of Jefferson*, 10: 447–448.

19. Thomas Paine, "The Rights of Man" (1791), in *The Complete Writings of Thomas Paine*, ed. Philip S. Foner (New York: Citadel Press, 1969), 1: 265–266.

20. Louis P. Masur, *Rites of Execution: Capital Punishment and the Transformation of American Culture, 1776–1865* (New York: Oxford University Press, 1989), 37.

21. Ibid., 77; *American Museum*, March 1970, 137.

22. Masur, *Rites of Execution*, 82.

23. Michael Meranze, *Laboratories of Virtue: Punishment, Revolution, and Authority in Philadelphia, 1760–1835* (Chapel Hill: University of North Carolina Press, 1996), 71; ibid., 65, 71, 80–82, 88, 87; Adam J. Hirsch, "From Pillory to Penitentiary: The Rise of the Criminal Incarceration in Early Massachusetts," *Michigan Law Review* 80 (1982): 1179–1269; Linda Kealey, "Patterns of Punishment: Massachusetts in the Eighteenth Century," *American Journal of Legal History* 30 (1986): 163–176; Michael Meranze, "The Penitential Ideal in Late Eighteenth-Century Philadelphia," *Pennsylvania Magazine of History and Biography* 108 (1984): 419–450; Bradley Chapin, "Felony Law Reform in the Early Republic," *Pennsylvania Magazine of History and Biography* 113 (1989): 163–183.

24. Greene, *Revolutionary Generation*, 80.

25. *Letters of Benjamin Rush*, 278–284.

26. Jacob Cooke, ed., *The Federalist* (Middletown, CT: Wesleyan University Press, 1961), no. 2.

27. Richard L. Bushman, "American High Style," in *Colonial British America: Essays in the New History of the Early Modern Era*, ed. Jack P. Greene and J. R. Pole (Baltimore: Johns Hopkins University Press, 1984), 371–372.

28. John Witherspoon, "The Druid, No. V," in *The Works of John Witherspoon*, 2nd ed., 4 vols. (Philadelphia: William W. Woodward, 1802), 4: 417.

29. Noah Webster, *Dissertations on the English Language* (Boston: Isaiah Thomas and Company, 1789), 36, 288. See Michael P. Kramer, *Imagining Language in America: From the Revolution to the Civil War* (Princeton: Princeton University Press, 1992).

30. Andrew Burstein, *Sentimental Democracy: The Evolution of America's Romantic Self-Image* (New York: Hill and Wang, 1999), 152.
31. Crèvecoeur, *Letters from an American Farmer*, letter III, 80.
32. Ramsay to Benjamin Rush, April 8, 1777, in *Ramsay . . . Selections From His Writings*, 54; Arthur L. Ford, *Joel Barlow* (New York: Twayne Publishers, 1971), 31; Paine, "Common Sense," in Foner, ed., *Complete Writings of Thomas Paine*, 1: 20.

Chapter 7

Enlightenment and Experience: The Virginia Constitution of 1776

Colin Bonwick

People during the second half of the eighteenth century commonly remarked that they lived in an enlightened age. This was as true in Revolutionary America as in western Europe. Yet in seeking to be universal in their scope, ranging from grand cosmology to political action and human behavior, perhaps they attempted too much, particularly as far as the United States was concerned. The Enlightenment, once so dominant as an organizing system within which to examine the intellectual character of early American constitutionalism, has come to seem diffuse and has fallen into neglect. In recent years it has been supplanted by two other competing rival theories, republicanism and liberalism.[1] Each has contributed substantially to our understanding of the Revolution, but both are limited in scope. It is time now to reexamine the Enlightened thesis. The argument that U.S. constitutionalism has (or does not have) at least some basis in the Enlightenment is a proposition that can and should be tested by historical analysis.

This chapter will explore one important component since it is impractical to assess the entire founding era, let alone the full gamut of American practice. Analysis of the intellectual context of the Enlightenment will be conducted within the two-dimensional framework of a particular time, the Revolutionary era, and a specific location, the Commonwealth of Virginia. The questions to be addressed are first, whether the concept of enlightenment has any remaining utility as an organizing principle for illuminating the ideological character of Virginian constitutionalism during the Revolution, and second, to examine its role for any value it may have. At this point it is necessary to enter a caveat. The analysis will explore enlightenment as a possible component of Virginian constitutionalism during the Revolution, but will not claim exclusive authority for it. The Constitution's theoretical origins had many strands. Its character was also shaped in part by the state's particular social structure and the various interests of the controlling elite, and also by their experience in domestic politics and memories of subordinate membership of the British Empire, which conditioned its authors' outlook. But if social structure and political experience formed the warp of constitutional cloth, philosophical principles in all their diversity were important components of the weft that created its pattern. In short, the fabric of Virginian constitutionalism can be better described as a tartan than as plain cloth. A simple answer to the question "what was enlightened about the Virginia Constitution?" will be that the Enlightenment remains a useful but not unique concept for illuminating it.

The choice of Virginia as a case study requires some explanation. It is tempting to focus predominantly on the U.S. Constitution of 1787 since it has long since come to dominate national politics. But development of the Union will not be discussed here. For many early decades the federal Constitution treated only two aspects of American government—albeit profoundly important ones. The central government dealt only with foreign affairs and matters of general concern to the Union as a whole; its almost total dominance lay far in the future. Moreover, the philosophical foundations of American constitutionalism had been laid down by the states acting individually well before the Philadelphia Convention met in 1787. Throughout the first decade of independence the states were substantively as well as nominally the sovereign powers within the Union. The Articles of Confederation (drafted in 1777 and ratified long after the states had established themselves) explicitly acknowledged their claims to sovereignty, and the question of the "true" nature of the Union was only definitively settled on the battlefields of the Civil War. Well into the nineteenth century (and arguably beyond) the states did most of the governing in domestic affairs.

Perhaps surprisingly, since the Revolution was a joint venture, each state constructed an individual frame of government. For a time in 1776 Congress thought of drafting a standard constitution that could be applied uniformly in every state, but this proposal was quickly rejected on the grounds that circumstances differed too much from one state to another for this to be practical.[2] Its decision was prudent. The constitutions ranged from relatively democratic in Pennsylvania to conservative in Maryland, the variations being heavily influenced by differences in the social and political contexts within which they were drafted. But what was also evident was the extent to which they shared common principles. Most obviously, all of them drafted written constitutions, but there were other similarities: thus all but Pennsylvania and Georgia constructed bicameral legislatures and most incorporated a declaration of rights. Some states can be ruled out as candidates for close analysis on particular grounds. Rhode Island and Connecticut did no more than tinker with their colonial charters, and although New Hampshire and South Carolina drafted their constitutions earlier than did Virginia, each intended its document to be only temporary. All other states followed Virginia in time and fullness of constitutional construction. This being so, the Commonwealth of Massachusetts might be thought to be the most appropriate model for testing. It shared the principles of the other states and completed the procedure for constructing a constitution by introducing what immediately became the distinctive American device of a specially elected constitutional convention followed by public ratification. However, the delay in completing the process (in 1780) rules it out; by that time the main philosophical principles had already been laid down.

In contrast, Virginia is the most appropriate state to test, even though its process of constitution-making was in some respects defective by later standards. It was the largest state by area, the most heavily populated, and the richest; moreover, it was preeminent throughout the Revolutionary era. Also, the gentlemen who effectively controlled the state and led it to independence were able to draft a constitution in relative tranquility compared with the social turbulence of Pennsylvania and Maryland, the upheavals of the Carolinas, and the nuisance of British occupation in New York; their debates were only briefly interrupted by the presence of British forces downstream from Williamsburg. But there are more significant reasons than these for selecting Virginia as the most appropriate test bed for enlightened ideas and behavior in the development of Revolutionary constitutionalism. Virginia was the first state to publish a Declaration of Rights (on June 12, 1776) and to approve a complete constitution (on June 29). To a degree both became examples for other states; as such they exercised a disproportionate influence over contemporary thinking. They preceded the Declaration of Independence, and there is ample evidence that the Virginia principles influenced Thomas Jefferson's drafting of it.[3] Moreover, other states modeled their Declarations of Rights on the Virginia example—and thirteen years later the French National Assembly used it as the basis for its Declaration of the Rights of Man.[4] And crucially in the context of this discussion, the format of Virginian constitutionalism was shaped by political philosophy as well as the experience of colonial government and the particular circumstances of separation from the British Empire. Unfortunately, the Constitution contained defects that proved extremely difficult to correct, but that is a matter that must be set aside here.

One thing was clear during the summer of 1776. Since Virginia's colonial structure of government was contained within its governor's commission of office, independence and repudiation of the Crown meant that Virginia needed some form of new constitutional framework to replace the previous imperial system. To some extent it was a matter of tinkering with the colonial system and preventing future repetitions of unacceptable government behavior. Thus all escheats, penalties, and forfeitures that had previously gone to the king would in future go to the Commonwealth.[5] Similarly, the Declaration of Rights condemned general warrants, just as the English Bill of Rights of 1689 had outlawed the unacceptable practices of James II.[6] The British practice of dividing government into legislature, executive, and judiciary (so different from the practice of the great continental European powers) was continued, though on terms very different from those of the Empire. But these modifications were insufficient, if only because it was necessary to find a source of legitimate authority different from the Crown, which had been the fount of legitimacy in colonial America. The need to do this demonstrated explicitly the importance of ideology as well as experience; under the circumstances of 1776, authority derived solely from coercive power was never likely to convince free Americans to support the new regime. Hence the search by contemporaries and modern scholars alike for an intellectual system to legitimate it.

Approaches by scholars to this problem have varied considerably. Forty or so years ago, historians such as Merle Curti, Winton U. Solberg, and Charles A. Barker rested their political analyses firmly on the intellectual system of the Enlightenment. Adrienne Koch subtitled her collection *Power, Morals and the Founding Fathers* as *Essays in the Interpretation of the American Enlightenment*, and she published a collection of the writings of leading revolutionaries as *The American Enlightenment*.[7] To some extent this approach has been continued by Henry F. May, Henry Steele Commager, and Robert A. Ferguson, but all approach the concept of American Enlightenment in rather general terms. The preeminent modern constitutional history of the United States bypasses the Enlightenment as an organizing principle for Revolutionary government.[8] More recently, scholars concerned with the ideological character of the Revolution (both as the achievement of independence and construction of domestic government) have offered markedly different approaches. Thus the great debate currently rages between the advocates of "republicanism" as the driving force behind American political behavior during the Revolution and proponents of "liberalism" as the ideological imperative. The first thesis stresses the importance of citizenship and argues that society took precedence over the individual. Thus it became the duty of the citizen to be virtuous and to place the public welfare above private interests. The second virtually inverted republican philosophy by stressing the centrality of economic behavior and insisting on the supremacy of individuals' pursuit of their private interests: it was the sum of individual activities that led to the public welfare. The formation of government was no more than a contract, the purpose of which was to enable the process to take place. Republicanism had a long intellectual ancestry but was arguably too optimistic in its demands on human nature. Liberalism, more recent in its origins, was arguably too pessimistic and cynical. Evidence for both psychologies is amply present throughout the Revolutionary era—the self-sacrifice of service in the war, and the rampant economic development afterward, for example—but both were rather narrow in range and neither provides a fully satisfying explanation for certain aspects of Virginian constitutionalism. Neither, for instance, provides a satisfying justification for the egalitarianism that, however defective in application, was a major component of public rhetoric.

At this point we can return to the Enlightenment. First, it is necessary to point out that Enlightenment included philosophical systems but was strongest on grand cosmology; it did not in itself provide a single systematic, self-justifying, and usable political system. Also, most of its practitioners regarded themselves as "philosophes" rather than systematic philosophers; this was especially true of Americans. People considered themselves to be "enlightened," but seldom if ever used the substantive term "Enlightenment" to identify their work and age. Rather, Enlightenment was a way of approaching the issues that particularly concerned eighteenth-century men and women. To use the German term, the Aufklärung was a letting in of light. As Immanuel Kant argued, it was an age of Enlightenment, not an enlightened age; Enlightenment meant process, not result.[9] It incorporated a spirit of enquiry, and arguably a method of testing structures, values, and behavior; as such it promoted debate and argument, and permitted—and even encouraged—contradiction. Such flexibility was highly advantageous when the American states came to drafting constitutions. Beyond this, American practice diverged from its European counterpart. Leading European intellectuals such as Voltaire, Rousseau, and Diderot were not directly active in government, though they often advised monarchs such as Frederick the Great of Prussia and Catherine the Great of Russia. Even in England, men like Richard Price and Joseph Priestley were only publicists in the outer circles of the political world; they depended on others to apply their theories. The circumstances confronting the United States in 1776 were very different. Enlightened men were at the heart of political activity. They had an obligation as well as an opportunity to implement enlightened principles—or repudiate them entirely.

No more than the briefest analysis of the Enlightenment is necessary in this context. Three concerns recurred with great frequency among enlightened people: nature, reason, and progress. Enlightened people saw nature as a logical system constructed by a benign God within which Mankind and human society were incorporated and Man was endowed with certain natural rights. By reason they meant that Man possessed the necessary intellectual faculty that enabled him to discover the rules by which the universe, human society, and his own position within it operated—and then apply them to political systems and practice. Furthermore, and most importantly, Enlightenment demanded that people should think for themselves rather than accept the dictates of authority.[10] Lastly, they shared a belief in the possibility of progress. They argued that for the first time Mankind possessed the capacity to direct its future and that the world could be emancipated from ignorance and corruption. At last, they believed, there was a serious possibility of long-term improvement—though not the certainty of it. Human beings could easily make matters worse. All three elements were clearly visible in the structure of American Revolutionary constitutionalism, particularly in Virginia.

Enlightened cosmology and social theory were explicitly universal in character. By comparison, republicanism, liberalism, and traditional English constitutionalism were more limited in range, thus permitting Enlightenment to incorporate certain elements of each. Three things directly relevant to the American experience flowed from this universalism. First, intellectual universality could be extended to political universality: theoretically it applied to all people in all places at all times. Second, the doctrine of natural rights implied equality, though there was much dispute over the nature of that equality. And third, Enlightenment encouraged—and even required—the people to think for themselves. Put differently, it possessed the capacity to develop into the modern idealized model of democracy and equality.[11]

Educated Americans shared these philosophical concerns among their many interests. Benjamin Franklin enquired into the natural world with his electrical experiments. Thomas Jefferson profoundly admired David Rittenhouse's orrery, which modeled the solar system, and constantly observed and recorded the behavior of nature closer to home. They possessed a strong sense of belonging to a worldwide intellectual movement—a conviction exemplified by their participation in observation of the transit of Venus in 1769. Along with James Cook and Sir Joseph Banks, who traveled to observe it from Tahiti, Joseph Brown tracked it in Rhode Island and Rittenhouse took measurements in Pennsylvania. They also extended their interest to human society, particularly when the Revolution required them to consider and reconstruct American political institutions. In Virginia, James Madison, entering province-wide politics for the first time in 1776, had studied Scottish-Enlightened thought under the tutelage of John Witherspoon at Princeton. Later he followed the enlightened process of systematically gathering evidence on the operation of political systems elsewhere, analyzing it and proposing reforms for the improvement and development of American government. George Mason, primary author of both the Virginia Declaration of Rights and Constitution, was far from alone in being well read in the classical history that contributed to the enlightened outlook.

Rebellion against British authority gave the Revolutionary generation an almost unique opportunity to implement their theoretical principles by designing a form of government suited to the long-term needs of their societies. As John Adams of Massachusetts asked his friend Richard Henry Lee of Virginia "When, before the present epocha, had three millions of people full power and a fair opportunity to form and establish the wisest and happiest government that human wisdom can contrive?"[12] All hoped for improvement, but also feared the worst. Progress was possible but not certain. This was, of course, particularly the case with the Revolution in its double sense. Even if independence was achieved—and this was far from certain in 1776— the survival, integrity, and development of the American Union and its member states could not be guaranteed.

It is now necessary to look briefly at the circumstances and experience to which enlightened ideas might expect to be applied: the warp of the fabric to the weft of ideology from which Virginian constitutionalism was woven. Some threads, such as population growth and economic change contributed to the pattern but do not need to be considered. More to the point are the social structure of the province and the conflict with Britain that precipitated the Revolutionary reconstruction of government. By American—though not European—standards colonial Virginia was a stratified and socially differentiated society, even if black slaves are excluded on the grounds that they were no more than the property of their owners. Among whites there were many poor day laborers, tenant farmers, and marginal farmers who owned their land but did no more than eke out a living; only about 30 percent of farmers owned between 100 and 500 acres. More significant, especially in political life, were the richest farmers owning an average of 3,000 acres, some of whom held much more. These great planters and their families formed no more than about 5 percent of the white population, but they dominated society. Even if the British hierarchy of Crown, aristocracy, and gentry that controlled the British Empire are superimposed on this local society, they did not disturb the structure. Britannia might rule the waves before 1775, but the Randolphs and the other First Families always ruled Virginia. And since they led the rebellion against Britain, the state's gentlemen largely controlled its constitutional development. There were, of course, important political consequences flowing from this dominance. Some elements of the enlightened project were relatively easy to implement because they were compatible with the perceived interests of the elite—though perhaps it would be better to say that the elite failed to appreciate the possible long-term consequences of their actions. But in other respects their application of universal principles was modified by the imperatives of race, gender, and social standing. If they held advanced political principles, many of their social attitudes expressed more traditional eighteenth-century values. To oversimplify by putting it brutally, by the standards of the twenty-first century the gentlemen of Virginia were racist, sexist, and elitist. Also in one important respect (demands for an extended franchise) the political impetus for change came from outside their ranks. Nevertheless, it is suggested, there remains much that was enlightened in their constitutional revolution.

The act of claiming independence brought major changes in both the philosophical underpinnings and mechanics of Virginian government. Before the imperial crisis that began in 1765, Virginians were contented members of an empire within which lawful authority flowed from the Crown downward—if only because they had little need to think about it. Paradoxically, perhaps, the royal governors formally possessed more legal powers than the Crown in Britain, but the inescapable tension between the local interests of the legislature and the broader interests of the empire at large were only manageable given goodwill, prudence, and tact. As Jack P. Greene and Bernard Bailyn have in their different ways demonstrated, the practice of colonial politics differed from its formal theory.[13] Royal governors like Francis Fauquier and Lord Botetourt exercised their authority with discretion and were consequently accepted as friends to liberty, protectors of the colony's rights, and promoters of its welfare. This happy state of affairs did not last. Successive British governments from the mid-1760s onward attempted to recast the imperial relationship in an effort to extend their central control. Not all the legislation directly affected Virginia, but its implications certainly did. Above all, the Declaratory Act of 1766 baldly asserted that Parliament possessed the right to legislate for the colonies "in all cases whatsoever."[14] Political resistance to such provocative policy degenerated into rebellion in 1775 and the bid for independence fourteen months later.

Some changes were inevitable, but they went a lot further than they need have done. The circumstances of the summer of 1776 absolutely required no more than minor adjustments to the colonial system to account for the absence of a royal governor, but the opportunity was seized to make far more radical changes. The Virginia Convention, which directed the rebellion, established a special committee that drafted a Declaration of Rights and Constitution at speed. Symbolically the committee eventually included a quarter of the Convention's members, thus providing its actions with both theoretical and pragmatic support. By later standards their procedure was defective. The Convention continued to conduct normal business and made no attempt to secure the community's approval of its work. Instead it merely declared the Constitution to be in effect. Nevertheless, what is striking about Revolutionary Virginian constitutionalism is the extent to which it moved beyond the traditional practices of English and colonial government. All that was strictly essential was reconstruction of the executive, and reuse of most of the old materials, especially with local government—but far more changes were made. Moreover, the changes were placed firmly on new and enlightened foundations and then deployed in different ways. The nature of the change can be clearly seen in the mind of George Mason, principal author of both the Declaration and the Constitution. Ten years earlier he had applauded the wisdom of the British constitution and claimed "Nothing but the Liberty & Privileges of Englishmen."[15] By 1776 he rejected most of the central principles of that constitution in favor of a radically different approach to the exercise and regulation of political authority. The actions of the Virginia Convention make it clear that he was speaking for the great generality of Virginia's dominant elite— with all the advantages and evasions that that might entail.

To evaluate the extent of change it is worth looking briefly at the system being rejected. The eighteenth-century British constitution was still a largely medieval structure, though substantially modified by the growth of the power of the House of Commons during the previous hundred years or so. It consisted of not only the institutions of government but also a ragbag of propositions, statutes, and judicial decisions, together with numerous conventions that made it operational and the practices by which it slowly adjusted to changing circumstances. These components were so intermixed that no line was visible between the British constitution and normal legislation. Its operation rested not on carefully articulated philosophical principles but on custom and practice that over time had acquired prescriptive authority. Thus exposition of the English common law purported to identify principles permanently in existence and then apply them to particular legal circumstances. The checks and balances of powers, whether by estates (monarch, aristocracy, and people) or functions (executive, legislature, and judiciary) were largely nominal. Regardless of William Blackstone's inflated rhetoric about Parliament's absolute power, in reality the success of the parliamentary system depended on the ability of the executive to control the House of Commons.[16] If the House was, as some people claimed, the jury of the nation standing in judgment on the government of the day, it seldom delivered a guilty verdict. Moreover, the Crown retained large areas of royal prerogative, notably in the conduct of foreign policy, war, and, to the colonies' great annoyance, the administration of colonial affairs. Such powers would have been of immense value to state governors, especially in wartime, had they been retained after the Revolution. Ironically, the Virginia Convention drew the opposite conclusion from their experience of the British government. What its members particularly abhorred was what they regarded as excessive power in the executive: they were determined to curb it. In their eyes, contemporary royal political practice demonstrated what was wrong with the British constitution, and thus its unsuitability as a model for Virginia.

Absorbed as they were in administering public affairs, the Virginia elite partly depended on outside sources to interpret and supplement their political experience. They had no thought of finding a royal replacement for George III in the way that England had been obliged to invite William of Orange as well as Mary to take the throne during the Glorious Revolution of 1689. It was already certain that Virginia would become a republic, if only in the limited sense that it would lack a monarch. This assumption encouraged members of the Convention to go back to first principles. Mason had begun to think of the philosophical basis of society and power when defending the Non-importation Association: it was nature, he argued, that implanted principles in Man, and individuals had an overriding duty to society when its liberty and happiness was at stake.[17] In 1770, it was still possible to implement that principle within a continuing British imperial system; six years later it seemed impossible. In the summer of 1776 the Convention rejected the old prescriptive constitutional model and sought to locate the new republican regime on a modern enlightened platform. This new set of principles had been latent before the rebellion but became overt during it and fundamental to the process of forming new governments. It was very different from the contemporary British emphasis on custom, practice, and prescription, the concept of parliamentary sovereignty, and a restricted role for the mass of the people. In common with the other states Virginia felt that it was essential to place the authority of government on a much clearer and more explicit basis. Although much of the machinery of government was derived from the British constitutional inheritance, notably the tripartite separation of powers, its philosophical justification was altered. Many of the encrusted barnacles of British practice, such as the corruption of its electoral system, the hereditary membership of the upper house, and its brigades of sinecures, were swept away. In future not even George Washington would be permitted Lords of the Bedchamber even if he was often addressed as "Your Excellency." These accretions, so characteristic of British constitutionalism, were replaced by a rational and orderly system set out publicly (if not always unambiguously, as it turned out later) in the written Declaration of Rights and Constitution. Moreover, this process of composing a carefully considered statement of philosophical principles and then setting out the constitutional rules and machinery for their application was itself a classic example of the enlightened process. And the fact that this transformation took place so rapidly demonstrates the degree to which Enlightenment was already embedded in the American mind.

The opening clauses of the Declaration of Rights, which set out the new principles of American government, came from the heart of the enlightened political creed. Beneath their phraseology were a series of unarticulated cosmological premises quite different from the constitutional system from which Virginia was largely departing. They were recognizably the principles concerning the orderly structure of the universe and man's position within it, the possibility of identifying those principles through the exercise of human reason, and, of course, the possibility (but not certainty) of improvement, on which there was striking agreement among enlightened men. Debate probably revolved more around detail and particular procedural incorporations than philosophical principles, to judge by the similarity between the ideas Mason sketched out a year previously and the opening phrases of the

Declaration.[18] Nevertheless, as will be seen below, there was at least one important modification to the phraseology. Taking the theoretical underpinnings as read they baldly declared that "[a]ll men are by nature equally free and independent and have certain inherent rights"; these included the enjoyment of life and liberty, the means of acquiring and possessing property, and pursuing happiness and safety. It went on to insist "[t]hat all power is vested in, and consequently derived from, the people; that magistrates are their trustees and servants, and at all times amenable to them." Moreover, government was instituted for the benefit of the community and had a duty to promote their happiness and safety.[19]

These were noble theoretical principles. They set out grand objectives for the new republican government very different from the narrower, essentially pragmatic purposes that powered contemporary British constitutionalism, but at the same time they created a host of theoretical as well as practical problems. What, for example, did the term "people" actually mean? Did it incorporate the entire population, or only the male population, or the white male population, or the free population, or was it no more than a synonym for "community"? Enlightened principles no doubt provided a broad and universal theoretical answer but in one of the clearest instances of definitions being shaped by social values and experience, the ensuing Constitution provided a different one. Implicitly the gentlemen of Virginia interpreted the term "people" as synonymous with "community," thus enabling them to slide over the glaring social, racial, and gender inequalities of which they were the principal beneficiaries. Instead of extending the franchise beyond its admittedly broad colonial range, they continued to exclude up to half the white adult population as well as everyone else. However, their choice of language opened the gate to greater participation than they intended. Since the term "people" was capable of several meanings, it could be extended almost indefinitely. Those who were initially excluded could (and did) claim to be integral components of the community and thus entitled to the people's political rights, particularly since their contribution was literally vital to the achievement of independence. It took many generations for this process to work itself out, but there were no longer any grounds of principle on which exclusion could be based; quite the reverse. The door remained closed for some considerable time, but the bolts had been drawn back: further progress toward full implementation of the concept of popular sovereignty remained possible. The concepts of equal freedom and inherent rights raised similar difficulties and were treated in similar ways. The First Gentlemen of Virginia felt themselves to be members of a natural elite in a cultural as well as economic sense.[20] They believed that it was not in the general interest for them to share authority with their social inferiors. As for the concept of "happiness" as an objective, it was left undefined. Rather, much of the Declaration was concerned with institutionalizing protection against a recurrence of the political and legal offences of royal government. For example, no men were to be allowed exclusive privileges except as rewards for public service, men were entitled to free trials, general warrants were prohibited, and juries were preserved in civil suits.[21] These were, of course, principles that particularly protected the elite since they were most likely to be involved in legal disputes.

Nevertheless, and in spite of limits imposed by the obvious self-interest of its authors, the Declaration defined the legitimacy of government in relation to a people possessing equal natural rights. As Article 3 made clear, it was instituted for the common benefit, and the criterion of its success was the greatest happiness (whatever that might mean) and safety of the people (whatever that might mean).[22] Moreover, if the people were dissatisfied they were permitted to revise the frame of government. These terms on which the gentry claimed to represent their community were drastically different from those on which a small group of aristocrats had claimed to represent England when it dismissed James II in 1688 and offered the throne to William III. In a psychological and symbolical change of profound importance, the gentry had transformed subjects of a Crown into citizens of a republic. Furthermore, by transforming themselves they also transformed all citizens into persons entitled to equal consideration.

Much of the Constitution that derived from these principles was essentially organizational in character, but there was one respect in particular in which its drafters determinedly attempted to apply a principle contained in the Declaration. A feature of the British constitution that gave Blackstone great satisfaction was the separation of powers among legislature, executive, and judiciary, and between the two houses of Parliament. This political structure was greatly admired by continental European philosophes as an essential component of the English liberty that was so different from their own countries; unfortunately, as has been argued above, the separation was more apparent than real. In Virginia the principle of separation was applied only after it had been filtered and interpreted through the prism of enlightened analysis. Baron Montesquieu, one of the most influential thinkers of the French Enlightenment, misinterpreted the British system to mean a total separation of powers between legislature, executive, and judiciary and incorporated the misunderstanding into his exposition of enlightened government.[23] Nevertheless, it provided a logical and orderly model for regulating political power and had the added advantage of conforming closely to the practice of politics in colonial Virginia. Within this structure the legislature was made responsive to the will of the electorate by annual elections, and the governor was denied prerogative powers. However, the method of electing governors by joint ballot of the two houses of legislature proved unsatisfactory, for its effect was to make them subordinate to them, thus infringing the principle of separation in a manner opposite to that in Britain. Only New York and Massachusetts solved the problem by providing for separate popular election by the people.

Declaring rights and drafting a fairly short Constitution was insufficient to deal with every issue of potential constitutional significance. Other important matters were neglected, ignored, or evaded in 1776 but still required consideration. The enlightened principle of Aufklärung (the spirit of enquiry and the letting in of light) required close attention to the world of the intellect. In its political context this involved education and freedom of the press and religion. However, translation of general principles on these matters into constitutional practice was incomplete at this stage. It was generally agreed that an educated citizenry was essential if a republic was to flourish. Massachusetts explicitly provided for the government of Harvard College and the advancement of knowledge in its Constitution, but Virginia made no move in that direction either in the Declaration or Constitution, and later rejected Thomas Jefferson's draft bill for a state educational system. Freedom of the press, "one of the great bulwarks of liberty" was only protected in general terms in the Declaration; later experience was to demonstrate that its defenses needed to be laid out in much greater legal detail if they were to be effective. It also went no further than asserting that all men were entitled to the free exercise of religion, thus similarly leaving important consequential issues unresolved.[24] In these instances no particular social issues were involved.

In the others the social context of enlightened action becomes clear. Some states, notably Massachusetts, applied the principle of popular sovereignty to constitution-drafting, and others, notably Pennsylvania, extended the franchise almost to a universal male suffrage. Ironically, Maryland, whose 1776 constitution was very conservative, was the first state to concede universal white male franchise, although it did so in 1802 for strictly pragmatic, not principled, reasons. In Virginia the white franchise was held at the colonial level in the interests of the controlling elite; there was, of course, no question of considering the claims of women to participate in any aspect of the political process. Similarly, almost all inhabitants of African origin continued to be excluded on grounds of their enslavement.

In the event there was a lot of unfinished constitutional business when the Convention declared its work had come into effect. Ironically, in order to complete the enlightened project it was necessary to revert to the British process of accretional development. Since the Constitution failed to provide for a process of amendment, normal legislation had to be used for quasi-constitutional purposes until such time, in 1830, that a second constitution could be approved. It is also here that the social context of enlightened action becomes clearest. Three examples illustrate how the implementation of enlightened principles interacted with actual experience and circumstances. The first demonstrates how circumstances could override principle. In the second, principles partly triumphed and partly failed, and in the third, circumstances ran in concert with principles to produce what is the apotheosis of American enlightened action.

The treatment of slavery is, of course, the first example. The principle that "all men are by nature equally free and independent," so eloquently enlightened, was logically universal in scope and accepted as such. It included African Americans as well as whites, and the logic of equality surely demanded emancipation. Given the existence of slavery throughout the colonies, the drafting of state constitutions everywhere provided an opportunity to apply enlightened values and processes toward the advancement of social progress. Some progress was made, yet the Revolutionary record is at best patchy. None of the original thirteen states incorporated the central principle of freedom in its constitution. Vermont emancipated its handful of Africans in its 1777 Constitution—but was not admitted as a state until 1791. Massachusetts abolished slavery by constitutional interpretation, and Pennsylvania by statute, and some blacks were permitted to vote, but in neither state were there large numbers of slaves. The situation in Virginia was far more challenging. More than 40 percent of its population were enslaved, slavery lay at the heart of its labor system, and the racial division between white and black lay at the heart of its social relationships. Furthermore, the members of the Convention were themselves slaveholders. Tragically, but unsurprisingly, the enlightened moment of constitution-making to achieve a major enlightened goal was missed.

The first clause of George Mason's first draft of the Declaration of Rights was formulated in such a way as potentially to destroy the legal basis of slavery by affirming the equality at birth of all men, and their inalienable natural right to life, liberty, and property. Unfortunately, the implications of the phrasing clashed with another enlightened proposition, the right to property, though in this case the form of property under threat was the profoundly unenlightened one of human slavery. Some slaveholders, particularly Robert Carter Nicholas, resisted. In the end the weasel phrase "when they enter into a state of society" was inserted. Its effect was designed to exclude blacks from the rights protected in the Declaration: since they were property they were not considered to be members of society.[25] Thomas Jefferson incorporated antislavery clauses in his draft constitutions of 1776 and 1783, but to no effect.[26] Emancipation remained a private initiative, and in the meantime even enlightened Virginians failed to implement a principle that was central to the enlightened project. Slavery flourished. Only when circumstances were ripe during the closing stages of the Civil War did it become possible to apply such a revolutionary principle, even though it was implicit in Virginian—and American— constitutionalism.

The second instance, where enlightened reform was partly successful and partly not, was the revision of the laws. Republican Virginia had inherited a mishmash of English and local statutes, common law, customs, and practices. Consolidation and revision of the laws into a coherent system was clearly desirable. Jefferson secured authority from the Virginia Assembly to draft a revision of the law, and in the end a small committee produced 126 bills ranging from land law through inheritance law to criminal law and the structure of the court system. The normally conservative Edmund Pendleton proposed writing a full legal code, but Jefferson urged merely a revision on the strictly pragmatic ground that codification would take too long and be more demanding.[27] Some revisions, notably the repeal of primogeniture and entail, were quickly accepted because they benefited the ruling gentry, but others were slower and some failed. Jefferson attempted to reduce the criminal law and penalties to logical coherence along the lines recommended by the enlightened Italian criminologist, the Marquis Beccaria, but he was only partly successful. His criminal code included restriction of the death penalty to treason and murder. It failed by one vote—according to James Madison because the horse fanciers in the legislature abhorred the elimination of the death penalty for horse thieves.[28]

In one respect, however, enlightened ideas were triumphant. A central tenet of the Enlightenment was the imperative need for freedom of speculative thought. Only this would enable humankind to exercise its faculty of reason to understand the universe and apply the knowledge gained to human improvement and the reformation of society. And since religious belief and affiliation were central to eighteenth-century society this required elimination of religious tests for office and public preference in favor of particular sects. In England there was a close connection between the Church of England, to which about 90 percent of the population nominally belonged, and the secular state to which all owed allegiance. Among other things membership of the former was deemed to be evidence of loyalty to the latter; refusal to conform to the established church was deemed evidence of potentially seditious intent. The consequence was exclusory legislation directed against all dissenters, particularly Roman Catholics. In colonial America the law was not as discriminatory as in Britain but nevertheless was far from satisfactory by enlightened criteria.

All the states eased their religious criteria during the Revolution, but Virginia ultimately established a new principle. Before 1776 the colony had an established Anglican Church to which all tithables were required to contribute; as in England it was closely tied to both provincial and local power. At the same time the numbers of several Protestant sects were expanding rapidly, so that the religious life of Virginia became far more heterogeneous than in England. This situation created considerable difficulty. It was generally agreed that shared religious beliefs and membership of particular religious congregations contributed materially to a communal sense of cohesion, and that they were appropriate matters for constitutional consideration on both philosophical and pragmatic grounds. Thus even after independence the states commonly required some form of religious test as a requirement for holding office. At the same time it was conceded that religious liberty was a major component of a citizen's right to liberty, thus creating a tension between the duty to share the fundamental values of society and the right to individual freedom of thought.

During the course of the Revolution Virginia moved from one end of the spectrum of options to the other. The reasons for the dramatic constitutional shift were a conjunction between the application of enlightened principle and the imperatives of denominational rivalries. Together they inverted the English (and thus colonial) principle that religious harmony was essential as an instrument for promoting social and political stability to a new principle that public order was best served by replacing all forms of religious favoritism with total and unfettered competition among as many sects as emerged. In his first draft of the Declaration of Rights Mason acknowledged the enlightened principle that religion could "be governed only by Reason and Conviction, not by Force or Violence," but he proposed that men should only enjoy "the fullest Toleration in the Exercise of Religion."[29] His phrasing implied that religious freedom for dissenters from the established church was merely a privilege, and implicitly condoned the continuance of religious tests for office and maintenance of the Anglican establishment. As a constitutional principle that would allow governments to continue operating under its aegis it was superior to the practice prevailing in countries like France, but little better than the ecclesiastical arrangements that caused great dissatisfaction among Protestant dissenters in England. James Madison, who was educated at Princeton in the Scottish Enlightenment tradition and who had recently arrived in the Convention, tried to extend the meaning of the clause sufficiently to wipe out the Anglican establishment in effect by prohibiting any form of confessional favoritism. This was too far at the time, and in the end the Declaration merely established the constitutional principle that all men were equally entitled to the free exercise of religion, thus specifying that it was a right rather than a concession.[30] This was acceptable to Church interests but demonstrated the limit to which intellectual argument could promote reform.

Even this left open several alternatives, and from thereon the driving force behind change was much more the interest of powerful sects, than the persuasiveness of intellectual argument. Disestablishment of a Church made unpopular by its association with the British colonial regime was fairly straightforward, but distribution of religious taxes among the several denominations in place of the single previously favored Church had much to commend it as a method of satisfying competing social demands. Many prominent men, including George Washington, Patrick Henry, Edmund Pendleton, and Richard Henry Lee, believed that religious belief was essential to the health of secular society and that religion required state support. In other words, religion was a part of the Constitution that extended beyond the boundary of the written document; moreover, the distribution of religious taxes went with the grain of contemporary Virginian society. This compromise was unacceptable on intellectual grounds to both Jefferson and Madison. Jefferson included among his proposals for revised laws in 1779 a bill "For establishing Religious Freedom." The apotheosis of American Enlightenment, its argumentation was grounded entirely on principles rather than consideration of interest or pragmatism. God had created the mind free, and it was sinful and tyrannical to compel men to contribute to the promotion of opinions that they disbelieve, and the intrusion of civil magistrates into the field of opinion destroys that religious liberty to which all men have a natural right. Its brief clauses proposed to prohibit all forms of statutory religious favoritism, discrimination, and tests.[31] Yet neither Jefferson's limpid prose nor the powerful rhetoric of Madison's 1785 "Memorial and Remonstrance" against the bill to provide for Christian Teachers were sufficient to persuade the Virginia legislature. What turned the tide was a barrage of petitions against religious assessment from across the state, resentment against taxes at a time of postwar economic difficulty, the acquiescence of the Episcopal Church, and above all political pressure from Presbyterians and Baptists. It was these circumstances that enabled Madison to gather the votes to slip Jefferson's bill through the Virginia Assembly in 1786 with very little alteration, thus taking Virginia further along the path to total separation of church and state than even the Evangelicals had intended.[32] In constitutional terms, however, there was a problem. The Statute of Religious Freedom expressed principles fundamental to the fabric of Virginian society and politics, and was implicitly an amendment to the Declaration of Rights, but in law it was no more than normal legislation that could be amended or repealed by any succeeding Virginia Assembly. Recognizing this, Jefferson attached a second clause that applied moral pressure on future generations by declaring that repeal would be infringement of citizens' natural rights. The Virginia Assembly later introduced Sabbath day observance and other so called blue laws, but if did not repeal the Statute.[33]

Enactment of the Statute for Religious Freedom provides an appropriate point at which to assess the influence of the Enlightenment on Virginian constitutionalism. Much of its substance was taken from its English and colonial inheritance, but the material was often reassembled in different ways, and independence required additional elements, notably those necessary to replace the traditional structure of authority by a republican system. The outcome was a constitution drastically different from its predecessor. Particular circumstances and experience of life within the British Empire formed much of the matrix of Virginian constitutionalism, and there was a strong element of contingency in its development. But it was also shaped and given a distinctive character by the intellectual traditions and approaches that drove forward much of its interpretation and the construction of its institutions. Enlightenment was only one among several intellectual influences, including the ancient Anglo-Saxon constitution, the republican tradition that originated in the Renaissance, and the more recent influence of liberal individualism. Arguably, however, the Enlightenment was more influential than any one of them. It was fresher than they were, and to a degree subsumed elements of each into its capacious folds; many of the leading figures in the republican and liberal traditions also appear in the Enlightenment. The doctrine of the Anglo-Saxon constitution, manifestly so archaic, gave psychological comfort: change could be dressed up as conservative restoration. What Enlightenment provided was a method of approaching political structures through the medium of free enquiry, an implicit premise of natural order and thus social organization, and confidence in the possibility (though not certainty) of improvement. It offered a set of general but flexible principles different from previous practices and capable of substantial development: equality, natural rights, popular sovereignty as the fount of legitimate authority and an explicit duty on government to promote public safety and happiness. It also provided an improved structure of government, with its concern for regulating authority and separating the three components of government that derived their legitimacy from the same source.

Not that the Enlightened approach provided a detailed blueprint for future development and solution to every problem. The Revolutionary settlement in Virginia was far from perfect by whatever criterion might be selected. Thus Justice George Wythe might insist that he would defend the rigid separation of the branches of government come what may, but the reality was different.[34] As this case study demonstrates, it was impossible to make a clear distinction between a codified constitution and the legislation that was enacted under its aegis. The Statute for Religious Freedom was a matter of such central importance that it should have been incorporated in the Declaration of Rights and Constitution, but in the event the principle could only be established by means of normal legislation. Nevertheless, the principle, so fundamental to the Enlightenment, came to acquire hegemonic status and was never repealed. Nor did enlightened principles immediately lead, as the rhetoric of equal creation suggested they ought to have done, to democracy in a more recognizably modern form, even for white men. The continued subordination of women and continuance of black slavery defied the principle even more flagrantly. Since Virginia was a socially hierarchical society and the members of the Convention were slave owners this was hardly surprising. But progress was made where it went with the grain of the Virginia elite, as men in the other states clearly acknowledged when they adapted the Declaration of Rights to meet the requirements of their own circumstances. For all its limitations, Virginia constitutionalism was far in advance of any contemporary European system. In Prussia Frederick the Great justifiably considered himself to be an enlightened monarch, and as such the first servant of the state. He felt he was responsible for the people—but utterly repudiated any suggestion that he was responsible to them. The Virginia structure of written principles and governments that were accountable to the people through the medium of annual elections, however defective in operation, was radically different in philosophy. It also provided a platform on which future construction could take place in the interest of all white men, black slaves, and all women. How succeeding generations would interpret and apply the principles and develop the machinery was, of course, a matter for them.

Notes

1. There is now an extensive literature on liberalism and republicanism as intellectual bases for almost all aspects of the Revolution, especially its ideological elements. See, e.g., Joyce Appleby, *Liberalism and Republicanism in the Historical Imagination* (Cambridge: Harvard University Press, 1992), esp. 1–33 and 320–339; and Lance Banning, "The Republican Interpretation: Retrospect and Prospect," in *The Republican Synthesis Revisited*, ed. Milton M. Klein, Richard D. Brown, and John B. Hench (Worcester: American Antiquarian Society, 1992), 91–117.

2. Willi Paul Adams, *The First American Constitutions: Republican Ideology and the Making of the State Constitutions in the Revolutionary Era* (Chapel Hill: University of North Carolina Press for the Institute of Early American History and Culture, 1980), 55–56.

3. Pauline Maier, *American Scripture: Making the Declaration of Independence* (New York: Alfred A. Knopf, 1997), 104, 133–134.

4. For a side-by-side comparison of the two Declarations, see Robert R. Palmer, *The Age of the Democratic Revolution: A Political History of Europe and America, 1760–1800*, 2 vols. (1959; paperbound ed., Princeton: Princeton University Press, 1969), 518–520.

5. Virginia Constitution, Article 20, *Sources and Documents Illustrating the American Revolution 1764–1788 and the Formation of the Federal Constitution*, ed. Samuel Elliot Morison, 2nd ed. (Oxford: Oxford University Press, 1929), 156.

6. Virginia Declaration of Rights, Article 9, *Sources and Documents*, 150; The [English] Bill of Rights, 1689, 1 Will. and Mar., Sess. 2, c. 2. *The Law and Working of the Constitution: Documents 1660–1914*, ed. W. C. Costin and J. Steven Watson (London: Adam and Charles Black, 1952), 1: 68.

7. Merle Curti, *The Growth of American Thought*, 3rd ed. (1943; New York: Harper and Row, 1964), 98–114, 123; Winton U. Solberg, ed., *The Federal Convention and the Formation of the Union of the American States* (New York: Liberal Arts Press, 1958), xcix–ci; Charles A. Barker, *American Convictions: Cycles of Public Thought, 1600–1850* (Philadelphia:

J. B. Lippincott, 1970), 189–327; Adrienne Koch, *Power, Morals and the Founding Fathers: Essays in the Interpretation of the American Enlightenment* (Ithaca, NY: Cornell University Press, 1961), esp. 1–6; Adrienne Koch, ed., *The American Enlightenment* (New York: George Braziller, 1965). These titles are of course merely samples of a much wider literature.

8. Henry F. May, *The Enlightenment in America* (New York: Oxford University Press, 1976); Henry Steele Commager, *The Empire of Reason: How Europe Imagined and America Realized the Enlightenment* (New York: Doubleday, 1978); Robert A. Ferguson, *The American Enlightenment: 1750–1820* (Cambridge and London, England, 1997); Alfred H. Kelly, Winfred A. Harbison, and Herman Belz, *The American Constitution: Its Origins and Development*, 6th ed. (New York: W. W. Norton, 1983).

9. Immanuel Kant; cited in Ferguson, *American Enlightenment*, 25.

10. Alexander Broadie, *The Scottish Enlightenment: The Historical Age of the Historical Nation* (Edinburgh: Birlinn, 2001), 1.

11. Whether this goal was ever achieved in the long term is a contentious matter not considered here.

12. John Adams, "Thoughts on Government," in *The Political Writings of John Adams*, ed. George A. Peek, Jr. (Indianapolis: Bobbs-Merrill, 1954), 92.

13. Jack P. Greene, *The Quest for Power: The Lower Houses of Assembly in the Southern Royal Colonies, 1689–1776* (Chapel Hill: University of North Carolina Press, 1963); Bernard Bailyn, *The Origins of American Politics* (New York: Alfred A. Knopf, 1968).

14. The Declaratory Act, 1766, in *English Historical Documents, American Colonial Documents to 1776*, ed. Merrill Jensen (London: Eyre and Spottiswoode, 1955), 9: 695–696.

15. George Mason to The Committee of Merchants in London, June 6, 1766, in *The Papers of George Mason: 1725–92*, ed. Robert A. Rutland (Chapel Hill: University of North Carolina Press, 1970), 1: 71.

16. Cf. J. H. Plumb, *The Growth of Political Stability in England, 1675–1725* (London: Macmillan, 1967), xviii, 179; J. C. D. Clark, *Revolution and Rebellion: State and Society in England in the Seventeenth and Eighteenth Centuries* (Cambridge, UK: Cambridge University Press, 1986), 130.

17. Mason to Richard Henry Lee, June 7, 1770, in *Papers of George Mason*, 1: 117–118.

18. George Mason, "Remarks on Annual Elections for the Fairfax Independent Company," ca. April 17–26, 1775, in *Papers of George Mason*, 1: 229–230. The drafting and intellectual provenance of the Declaration are discussed in detail in ibid., 274–291.

19. "Virginia Declaration of Rights," *Sources and Documents*, 149.

20. Cf. Gordon S. Wood, *The Creation of the American Republic: 1776–1787* (Chapel Hill: University of North Carolina Press, 1969), 497.

21. The Virginia Declaration of Rights, Articles 4, 8, 10, and 11, *Sources and Documents*, 150.
22. Ibid., 149.
23. Cf. Charles de Secondat, baron de Montesquieu, "The Spirit of the Laws," in *The Portable Enlightenment Reader*, ed. Isaac Kramnick, (New York: Penguin Books, 1995), book XI, 411–414.
24. The Virginia Declaration of Rights, Articles 12 and 16, *Sources and Documents*, 150, 151.
25. John E. Selby, *The Revolution in Virginia: 1763–1783* (Williamsburg, VA: Colonial Williamsburg Foundation, 1988), 108.
26. Julian P. Boyd et al., eds., *The Papers of Thomas Jefferson*, 31 vols. to date (Princeton, NJ: Princeton University Press, 1950–), 1: 353, 363; 6: 298.
27. Noble E. Cunningham, Jr., *In Pursuit of Reason: The Life of Thomas Jefferson* (Baton Rouge: Louisiana State University Press, 1987), 57.
28. James Madison to Thomas Jefferson, February 15, 1787, in *The Republic of Letters: The Correspondence between Thomas Jefferson and James Madison, 1776–1826*, ed. James Morton Smith, 3 vols. (New York: W. W. Norton, 1995), 1: 466.
29. "First Draft of the Virginia Declaration of Rights," ca. May 20–26, 1776, *Papers of George Mason*, 1: 278.
30. Ralph Ketcham, *James Madison: A Biography* (Charlottesville: University Press of Virginia, 1990), 72–73.
31. "A Bill for Establishing Religious Freedom," *Papers of Thomas Jefferson*, II: 545–547.
32. Thomas E. Buckley, S. J., *Church and State in Revolutionary Virginia, 1776–1787* (Charlottesville: University Press of Virginia, 1977), 144–164, 180.
33. Ibid., 181–182.
34. J. Wythe, Commonwealth v. Caton et al., Virginia Reports, 4 Call, 5 (1782), *Documents of American History*, ed. Henry Steele Commager, 9th ed. (Englewood Cliffs, NJ: Prentice Hall, 1973), 116–117.

Chapter 8

Nation-Making and the American Constitutional Process

J. R. Pole

The great distinction and historic achievement of the American Constitution was to weld the disparate, shambling cluster of the self-interested original states into a national union. In other words, *to create* a nation of shared principles. The idea that a true political community was to be defined as a community of principle had advocates among the many differing thinkers whose names have been variously linked with the concept or the forerunners of the Enlightenment, notably Machiavelli, Harrington, Locke, Montesquieu, Burlamaqui, Hume, and Rousseau.[1] In the longest of long runs, as Abraham Lincoln was to insist when he warned Americans that "[a] house divided against itself cannot stand,"[2] that principle would determine whether the United States could survive as a nation.

American colonists in their defiance of Parliament insistently based their opposition on principles of legal right. Self-interest might be the driving force, but the thrust of self-interest was protected by the glittering armor of law. The Union formed by the Articles of Confederation, however, was a product of political necessity before it was an embodiment of republican principle. The empire from which the Americans had separated themselves did not work to the rules of a written constitution, either domestically or imperially; as colonial dissent turned to opposition and opposition to defiance, any community of principle uniting Britain and its colonies became increasingly difficult to discern. The states for their part had many differences and rivalries among themselves; but they also had the advantages of much common experience; they shared long established institutional habits of self-government through representative bodies, and they had agreed to the specified intentions embodied in the Articles of

Confederation and the principles that were knit into the procedures of the common law. A common legal language had the inestimable advantage of enabling them to agree without internal dissension in characterizing their grievances as violated rights and their expectations as legal entitlements. But permanent unity would require more than a sense of shared indignation; it meant shared principles.

The Articles proclaimed the aim of perpetual union, an aspiration that already carried a strong commitment to the idea of an American nation. But the Articles proved unequal to the needs and responsibilities of an intercolonial government. To mold the confederated states into a permanent union and the union into a nation, a written constitution was indispensable. This made it essential to develop a consensus on the basic principles to which such a union would subscribe. American national sentiments already sprang from shared history as well as the recent experience of war. But so had ominous elements of a centrifugal particularism. If unity was to be achieved it must now grow from acts of will. The formal foundations of national unity were laid when a shared understanding of the common law and a principled recognition of common interests were transmuted into a federal Constitution that declared itself, in words recalling Magna Carta, to be the Supreme Law of the Land. In appearance, however, the written Constitution that emerged from Philadelphia provided first and foremost a structural and procedural plan of government. Apart from a few grand words at the beginning, it still lacked agreement on vital political principles. But such a plan could not achieve operational unity without certain a measure of moral agreement, as was implied by the plan itself—representation, for a leading example, gave government what we may call the machinery of consent; and another prevailing principle was to be embodied in the supremacy of federal law. But where differences of principle threatened the prescribed procedures, the best hope that supporters could offer in advocating adoption of the Constitution was that the passage of time would work to unify rather than to divide.[3] Over time differences of principle have come to be addressed more frequently in the Supreme Court than in legislatures, and in the eyes of many this has created severe tensions with the constitutional settlement on which national unity originally rested.

Such concerns remain central to American politics because, in a sense that would have been difficult to understand in France or Britain, the very nation incorporated as the United States of America was a *creation* of its own Constitution. When George Washington was about to retire from the presidency, and delivered his Farewell Address to the American people, he emphasized this theme by reminding his fellow citizens that unity of government constituted them "one people."[4] In the same Address Washington twice referred to the Constitution as an "experiment," urging Americans to give it a fair trial.[5] No one could be sure that it would work; no one could be sure that republican government over extended territory could protect both individual freedom and territorial integrity. No one could be sure that federal power would preserve the integrity of the states. But Washington was not content to appeal only to a collectivity of self-interests. He extended his appeal to patriotic sentiment. Sympathy was joined to interest. "Citizens by birth, or choice, of a common country, that country has a right to concentrate your affections."[6] And he went on to ascribe to "the name of American" a cluster of common characteristics in descent and religion as well as in political experience that somewhat exceeded the facts of America's less than homogeneous population. There is a thread connecting this appeal of Washington's with Lincoln's repeated claim that the Civil War was a test of whether humankind was capable of self-government. The viability of the written Constitution was crucial to this test.

The intense party rivalry that sprang up in the period of Federalist government was in a sense animated by rival claims to genuine patriotism. This politics of what has recently been called "binary polarity" was fed by rapid growth of party newspapers, of political rhetoric, activity, and participation in elections.[7] By the time the ferment died down, in the aftermath of the War of 1812, the United States as a nation and a country had become heir to what we may call a more settled constitutional patriotism. Since assuming office as chief justice in 1801, no man did more than John Marshall to strengthen federal authority by imposing it on the jurisprudence of the states. In two of the most important cases, Marshall made use of the contract clause of the Constitution to get his result. *Fletcher v. Peck* arose from a corrupt grant by the Georgia legislature of lands by an act that the succeeding legislature repealed. In overriding the repeal, Marshall argued that the abrogation of the legislation making the land grants (by which all the legislators had made personal gains) violated the constitutional ban on impairing the obligation of contract. In defining contract, he cited Blackstone's distinction between contracts executory, which meant those contracts that were remaining to be completed, and contracts executed, those that had been fulfilled.[8] It seems possible that Marshall could have invalidated the repeal of a completed transaction, say through the Fifth Amendment, without evoking the contract clause. (This was long before Marshall was to declare that the Fifth Amendment did not reach into the states.) But from the point of view of Marshall's long-term agenda, the case provided an opportunity for intervening to keep the channels of contract out of the hands of state governments. This was an early and very clear case of imposing the national Constitution against the express will of the local electorate; but the judgment is interesting for Marshall's reliance on the venerable authority of Blackstone, and by the same token his omission to cite J. J. Powell's much more recent tract, which happened to be the first English treatise specifically devoted to the common law of contract.[9] Marshall knew where he wanted to go and he got there by the quickest route; whether he had even read Powell we are in no position to know. In *Dartmouth College v. New Hampshire*, a case in which the state legislature had altered the terms of a state-authorized college charter in order to serve the public interest better, Marshall again ruled that the state's action was a violation of the contract clause.[10] Contract had a long common law history, which Marshall could have searched had he wanted to justify other conclusions; but again he chose the most direct route to the most explicit result. Marshall's strategy was to apply a substantive clause of the Constitution to the situation, at the same time invoking a fundamental common law principle. Many of the Marshall Court's decisions aroused opposition that took the form of demands to restrict federal judicial power over the states; and even of demands for the repeal of he Judiciary Act of 1789 (one clause of which had occasioned the exercise of judicial review in *Marbury v. Madison*). Near the end of Marshall's life, when the nation faced insubordination in South Carolina over the tariff and the power claimed by the state to nullify federal laws, and in Georgia over the rights of the Cherokees, the aging chief justice grew increasingly gloomy about the survival of the Constitution itself. In September 1832 he wrote to Joseph Story, who had similar apprehensions, "I yield slowly and reluctantly to the conviction that our Constitution cannot last."[11] Without a Constitution, there would be no nation. Without a supreme judicial power over the states, he and Story were convinced—rightly, I think—that no centripetal power would exist to hold them together. It was not only the "republic" but the nation that was in danger.

In 1854, a young Georgian student at Harvard, sitting in the Boston court at the trial that would determine the escaped slave Burns's claim to freedom, wrote to his parents that his blood boiled at having to listen to "false Negro testimony." For the claimant, Colonel Suttle, the Georgian professed such an attachment "as only a Southerner can feel for his brother Southerner when he finds himself in a land of abolitionists." He added, "Do not be surprised if, when

I return home, you find me a *confirmed disunionist.*"[12] For the youthful Charles Jones, who was later elected mayor of Savannah and served in the Confederate army, the Constitution had failed in the task of creating a nation; two separate nations were forming and the Constitution could not hold them together much longer.

Jones had made what proved to be a correct diagnosis of sociological realities rather than constitutional rules. However, the official Southern view both in the slavery expansion crises of the 1850s and in the apologias written by Confederate leaders after the Civil War was that the Constitution did protect Southern property rights and that it was the abuse of these rights by abolitionists, Free-Soilers, and the Independent Democrats that threatened disunion. In this sense, Southern apologists did not admit that their states had willingly rejected their American nationality; they only took that step when popular conventions voted for secession. But there is an important aspect of the question of Southern nationality as expressed in the votes of the secession conventions that historians commonly overlook. The power of the Confederate states to make independent political decisions on a basis of majority votes was exclusively in the hands of a white population whose political order rested on the produce of a black labor force, and that labor force, being enslaved, was completely excluded from political life. If that section of the population, which was everywhere substantial and in some Southern areas nearing or reaching a majority, is given its hypothetical political weight, with the high probability that its votes would have gone to the Republican Party and against secession, the picture of Southern adherence to American nationhood is transformed. This hypothesis is by no means fanciful: once the freedmen had been enfranchised, it was exactly what came about very soon after the Civil War. Where the Constitution failed, however, the armies of Grant and Sherman, backed by the iron will and flexible tactics of Abraham Lincoln preserved the Union. By a sort of reversal of the earlier process, Northern military supremacy re-created the nation and preserved its Constitution. By the time the Fourteenth and Fifteenth amendments had been enacted, it was as though in this conflict the nation created—or *re*created—the Constitution.

The Reconstruction amendments were made possible by the Civil War and there is not the slightest reason to suppose that they could ever have otherwise been adopted (at least in the nineteenth century), but they were not an inevitable outcome; they were products of the fierce and bitter conflicts provoked by Andrew Johnson's highly personal Reconstruction policies. We cannot be sure that the Fourteenth

Amendment would have been engrafted into the Constitution if Lincoln had lived. If this conclusion has paradoxical implications it is because the Fourteenth Amendment's clauses protecting human rights actually elaborate fundamental principles implicit in the original language of the Constitution, transforming them from implied principles into concrete law. Such implied principles were already present in Article 4 Section 2—known as the Comity Clause—itself a simpler and better drafted version of a similar principle in the Articles of Confederation—which lays down that citizens of each state are entitled to the same privileges and protections in the other states as those states afford to their own citizens. The clause assures American citizens of equality in the rights afforded by the states, without conferring on interstate travelers benefits that they would not enjoy at home. But South Carolina objected to the presence of free black mariners who were citizens of New England states and who, when their ships docked in Charleston, enjoyed liberties not available to the state's own black population. The result was a law passed in 1819 confining black sailors from other states to their ships while in harbor. The failure of federal authorities to enforce the Constitution against this violation was a small (and distant) but ominous sign, that of the dangers to the unity of the constitutional fabric from the growth in different sections of social mores embodying fundamentally divergent principles.

Equality of civic and political rights and privileges under federal authority among all American citizens regardless of the laws of individual states was implicit in the language of the Constitution. The power to define federal citizenship was expressly conferred on the Congress; although the matter was subjected to certain qualifications by state governments, it is hard to discern any constitutional authority by which a state could lawfully curtail the rights of citizenship.[13] Although the language of the first eight amendments was more susceptible to variable interpretation than that of the formal Constitution, the general character of the Bill of Rights reinforced the principle of equality in those rights that pertained to citizenship: and through the Comity Clause, to state as well as federal citizenship. In these respects, the Fourteenth Amendment may be said to have completed business left unfinished when the Constitution was ratified and the Bill of Rights adopted. If the United States was to be a nation of equals, then the Constitution was again proving itself to be the central instrument in the cause of making the nation. The Fourteenth Amendment implemented one of the doctrines of Enlightenment constitutionalism derived from Machiavelli: that a republic must restore its purity by periodically returning to first principles.[14]

Even first principles, however, could be open to disagreement. The Constitution was not chiseled in marble, and its most eloquent defenders knew that its language would be subject to changing interpretations in the light of changing needs, conditions, and demands. James Madison warned American electors in *Federalist* 37 that language, even when used by the Deity, was a cloudy and imprecise means of conveying meaning.[15]

Marshall himself ultimately failed to maintain a consistent focus on the centrality of federal jurisprudence. Late in his life, the opportunity to redress some of his encroachments into state autonomy arose in *Barron v. Baltimore*. The case, which involved conflict between the rights of private property and the supremacy of public interest, turned on the "takings" clause of the Fifth Amendment forbidding government to take private property for public purposes without just compensation. Barron, who operated a Baltimore wharf, alleged that civic improvements undertaken by the City of Baltimore had adversely affected the water supply on which his business depended.

It seems, for want of controversy on the subject, to have been assumed before Barron's challenge raised the issue, that "the supreme law of the land" carried the "takings" clause into the states, and that a conflict of jurisdictions would resolve in the federal government's favor. But two styles of prohibition are employed in these amendments: general and specific. The Fifth Amendment belongs to the group in which the prohibition is stated in the most general terms: "No warrant shall issue"; "No person shall be held to answer . . ." By contrast, where the restriction is specific to the Congress, the words are specific: "Congress shall make no law . . ." The literal inference appears to be that in the first instance, in which the terms are open, no authority, federal, state, or municipal, shall encroach on the rights so protected, from which it would follow that the prohibition restrained state as well as federal governments. Marshall did not think so, and, making short work of the carefully prepared arguments of Barron's distinguished counsel, declined to enter into the merits of the case on the ground that the Fifth Amendment could not have been intended to apply to the states.[16] The history of the amendment up to that date was inconclusive, having yielded differing inferences, but it hardly warranted such peremptory dismissal. Marshall himself, in earlier cases, had pressed the contract clause to its limits in order to reverse state actions;[17] William Rawle, whose textbook on the Constitution was widely used and regularly assigned by Joseph Story to his students at Harvard, was clear that the open-worded amendments *did* apply to the states; moreover, before 1833, at least six state appellate courts had regarded it as self-evident that "the supreme law of the land" was superior to state laws.[18] It might have been argued that in case of conflicting opinions, this self-assertion of federal supremacy would settle the question. Marshall, however, was clear, confident, and positive in his own opinion, was strikingly lacking in respect for alternative views, and carried a unanimous Court. This, however, did not conclude the matter, for state supreme courts—notably Georgia's—frankly disagreed with and ignored the *Barron* judgment on several occasions before the Civil War.

Other interpretations were available, plausible, and in fact were widely held. Marshall had a powerful argument but it was an argument, not a rule of law; had he chosen to find otherwise, he could have found other reasons. It is not unreasonable to ask whether Marshall might have had motives in the era of the Nullification Crisis that had not influenced him in the past. A plausible alternative view would attribute his decision to political expediency.[19] Times were changing in threatening ways, as Marshall and Story were painfully aware. Expediency might have suggested that it would be timely to avoid provocation by leaving to the individual states more latitude in providing for their internal affairs in a period, for other reasons than Barron's, of increasing tension in federal relations. If so, this was policy rather than jurisprudence, and policy of dubious long-term wisdom. The exclusion of the Fifth Amendment from the states had no inherent tendency to encourage the growth of an organic national unity.

The generation of state judges who differed from Marshall on the issue was equally close in time to the actual creation of the Bill of Rights. Marshall's confident language seems a shade opportunistic. If a poll could have been taken among contemporary state and federal judges, it would be difficult to be as sure of the outcome as Marshall made it appear. Whichever the intention, the states' rights standpoint could take more comfort from the decision than from many of its predecessors as handed down by Marshall's Court.

The *Barron* case did not involve judicial review of congressional legislation, which had been exercised only once, in 1803, was not anticipated as a normal event, and did not at that period involve the Court in controversy. Chief Justice Taney's attempt to lay the slavery issue to rest in the notorious *Dred Scott* case in 1857, in which the Supreme Court declared that the act of Congress constituting the Missouri Compromise of 1820 had been unconstitutional throughout the thirty-four years of its existence (it had been superseded in 1854) not only failed in its objective but involved the Court in charges of illegitimate exercise of judicial power. The fallacies in Taney's reasoning were devastatingly exposed in the dissenting opinion of Justice Curtis and need not detain us now; but from the point of view that looks to the Constitution's contribution to the making of the nation, Taney's logic has a certain anthropological interest. Taney tried to construct a picture of American citizenship as the formal embodiment of a homogeneous, organic relationship among Americans, based as much on descent as on values; this association he designated a "political family." This postulate enabled him to argue that the African population had never been members of "the political family" to which the Constitution applied, and therefore had no rights that a white man need respect. This reasoning was specious. It failed to acknowledge that its premise of the family was merely an unexamined metaphor. It failed to explain why immigrants whose ancestors had not even been present at the formation of the Constitution had any better claim to "family" membership, especially since black Americans were among the earliest of immigrants, and they exercised the right to vote and enjoyed the protections of citizenship in several states.[20]

Citizenship was the issue in the first major case to arise under the Fourteenth Amendment. The Louisiana legislature had granted a monopoly over the butchering business in New Orleans. Rival firms complained that this deprived them of the equal protection promised by the amendment. In *The Slaughterhouse Cases*[21] the Supreme Court ruled, first, that the Fourteenth Amendment was designed exclusively for the protection of the Negro race and therefore had no general application; and second, that its application was restricted to the rights appertaining to federal citizenship. This was never likely to be more than a small class of complaints. By this decision, the vast majority of civil rights cases—the real substance of the complaints, and the reason for the Fourteenth Amendment—were remitted to the care of the states and thus excluded from the Fourteenth Amendment's protection. Justice Stephen Field, in dissent, caustically observed that if this were the case, the Fourteenth Amendment was "a vain and idle enactment, which achieved nothing, and most unnecessarily excited Congress and the people on its passage." The Court by a five-to-four majority had indulged in a conscious act of judicial lawmaking.[22]

This decision began a process by which the federal judiciary steadily undermined the Fourteenth Amendment and by separating American citizens into discrete, racially defined blocs, corroded the fundamental principle that the Constitution bore equally on Americans as individuals. The *Slaughterhouse Cases* involved state legislation, not an act of Congress. But in 1875 Congress enacted a comprehensive Civil Rights Act. Showing no reticence about moving from jurisdiction over state to federal legislation, the Supreme Court collected a series of challenges to that act, which it invalidated in *The Civil Rights Cases* in 1883.[23] The process culminated in the Louisiana railroad accommodation case of *Plessy v. Ferguson*,[24] which authorized the spurious doctrine of "separate but equal."

By these and many other rulings, which have taken their place in the mainstream of American constitutional history, and without encountering significant contemporary protest, the Supreme Court entered into the process of declaring, which has effectively meant making, substantive law, frequently in matters that were regarded as subject to normal and historic processes of political policy. The Court has come to be commonly if informally referred to as "the unelected branch of the legislature." This adoption of a quasi-legislative role probably represents the greatest of all deviations from the founders' intentions in the history of the Constitution.

The practice has rested on two foundations: first, that since legislation can be challenged only after it has been passed by the Congress and signed by the president, the judiciary necessarily has the last word. But this is merely a result of procedure, not of constitutional reasoning. The order of events does not determine the merits of the argument. The last word is not by definition the best policy; nor does it follow that the Supreme Court is the only judge of what is and what is not constitutional. Both the legislative and executive arms operate under the Constitution and are equally entitled to their own interpretations. A second and more persuasive argument begins with the Constitution's self-description as "the supreme law of the land"; and since judges determine questions of law, it would appear to follow that judges must uphold the supreme law against any inferior law. While it may be true that judges are trained to interpret law, nominations to the bench are seldom made exclusively for reasons of legal preeminence, and the frequency with which Supreme Court justices disagree among themselves would alone be enough grounds on which to raise doubts as to the finality of their judgment. The supreme law doctrine, however, is the essence of Hamilton's argument in *The Federalist* 78, which is generally recognized as the principal contemporary statement of the case.

That case, however, can be correctly understood only in its historical context. Madison had observed in *Federalist* 51 that "[i]n republican government, the legislative authority, necessarily, predominates." For defense against legislative excesses, of which Madison in particular had seen all too much in Virginia, a judicial arm was essential. But on the other hand, Hamilton's tactical purpose in essay number 78 was to give a convincing reassurance against the forceful arguments advanced by the Anti-Federalist pamphleteer "Brutus," who had warned of an excess of quasi-legislative power by the federal courts. The balance was delicate. Might not a judiciary strong enough to check the legislative power subvert the basis of representation? Hamilton's answer sought to convey reassurance by explaining that, having no executive arm of its own, the judiciary would be "the least dangerous branch" of the tripartite constitutional system. The issues had been somewhat cursorily debated in the Constitutional Convention, probably because the case was already broadly understood and occasions for judicial review of legislation seemed likely to be very rare.

Yet Madison was not so sure. In *Federalist* 39 he anticipated the argument that Hamilton was later to elaborate; but he also recognized the danger of permitting the judiciary to become predominant, and a few months later he cautioned against making the Judiciary Department paramount, "which was never intended and can never be proper."[25] In June 1789 with the Bill of Rights in place, he again changed emphasis, anticipating that the courts would become its guardians.[26] Although Madison had much more than Hamilton to do with the drafting of the Constitution, he could find no stable solution for the problem of conflict between the legislature and the judiciary, and his comments can hardly be regarded as a definitive guide to whatever intentions may be attributed to the founders. Hamilton, meanwhile, had reinforced his case in *Federalist* 78 by exalting the Constitution as the will of the people. This thesis, when viewed from the twenty-first century, assumes that the people have remained an unchanging entity with an unchanging will over more than two centuries. In its own time it failed to explain why the will of the people expressed once, at the founding, should be considered superior to the will of the people as expressed through their elected legislators two centuries later.

Nothing in the language of the Constitution mandates the power of judicial review of congressional legislation. If a congressional majority, resolved to place public policy in the hands of the people's elected representatives, were to seek a means, they would find a remedy not only available but also with the force of historical precedent. It can be stated simply: in the event—by no means infrequent—of a judicial veto, both houses could repass the same bill, which on being resigned by the president, would become law. It is reasonable to presume that members of Congress are capable of reading and understanding the Constitution; but presumably a judicial decision of unconstitutionality would not be lightly overridden. If this procedure were adopted, it would be desirable that it should enter into the conventions of unwritten law; but if the Supreme Court persisted in its veto, the Congress could exercise its authority under Article 3 Section 2, which gives it power to make "exceptions and regulations" to the appellate jurisdiction of the Supreme Court.[27]

The principle that Supreme Court judgments should be definitive was not clear at the time of the *Dred Scott* decision. Lincoln confronted the problem in his debates with Douglas in 1858 by declaring that, although he would accept the Court's decisions in the specific cases to which they applied, he would not feel obliged to accept them as a general rule of policy. Although he held the Supreme Court in high respect, if he were a member of Congress he would vote to reverse the *Dred Scott* decision.[28] At that time, Lincoln evidently believed that Congress could override the Court. When he returned to the issue in his first Inaugural Address, he seemed somewhat to modify his position, explaining that he would accept the decision as it stood but would work to get it judicially reversed in a future case involving the same issue. Precedents were not conclusive; an obnoxious particular decision instead of becoming fixed precedent might be overruled by a subsequent decision. He was aware of the dilemma, which remained unresolved, since the principle at stake was self-government. "At the same time, the candid citizen must confess that if the policy of the Government upon vital questions affecting the whole people is to be irrevocably fixed by the Supreme Court . . . the people will have ceased to be their own rulers, having to that extent practically resigned their Government into the hands of that eminent tribunal."[29] Thirty years as chief justice had not chastened Taney's conviction of judicial prerogative. His last act was to write a memorandum declaring that the Supreme Court's decisions on constitutional questions were to be considered as definitive. But Taney died before he could pronounce it from the bench.[30] This gesture may well have been provoked by the action of Congress in an act of 1862 banning slavery from the territories, which clearly contradicted the *Dred Scott* decision.[31] In 1866, hardly a year from the Civil War, the Congress enacted the first federal Civil Rights Act.[32] This historic measure, which in part anticipated the Fourteenth Amendment, was the first federal law to enact that all persons born or naturalized in the United States were to be citizens of the United States. In both these acts the Congress *reversed* an existing Supreme Court decision.

Congress could now return to these precedents if it wished to establish itself as the embodiment of the full legislative power with which it began its existence. In doing so it could recall that the abolition of slavery and the elevation of all Americans to equal citizenship in principle completed the work of creating a nation.

Barely twenty years had elapsed since the adoption of the Fourteenth Amendment when James Bryce famously distinguished for purposes of comparison between "rigid" and flexible constitutions, meaning the written American and the unwritten British constitutions.[33] The constitution of England, he observed, was constantly changing; that was its character and the key to its survival. But he promptly proceeded to undermine this distinction by noting the numerous ways in which the American Constitution had itself been adapted to changing circumstances. It had stood the test of time, he observed, "because it has submitted to a process of constant, though scarcely perceptible, change which has adapted it to conditions of a new age." The word *process*, which appears in the title of this paper, therefore claims some historical authority. "Habit," Bryce also remarked "fixes some things, time remoulds them."[34]

This at last brings me to the Argonauts, a bunch of rough seafaring men not much given to philosophical speculation. But one speculative problem did engage their attention and that was whether their ship, which had been repaired and its fabric restored every time they put into port, was the same ship in which they had first embarked. They concluded that it was indeed the same ship. The same question and the analogy of a much repaired ship occurred to John Selden, from whom it was picked up in the 1660s by Sir Matthew Hale, chief justice of the Common Pleas, both of them referring to the common law of England.[35] And both reached the same conclusion. I reckoned myself in good company when the analogy occurred to me with reference to the Constitution of the United States.

Is it the same Constitution? I think it is. But whether the founders would have agreed is another question, which, perhaps happily, must remain unresolved.

Notes

The author wishes to acknowledge support from Slaughter and May of London and Getty, Meyer and Mayo of Lexington, Kentucky.

1. David A. J. Richards, *Foundations of American Constitutionalism* (New York: Oxford University Press, 1989), 294–295.
2. Paul M. Angle, ed., *Created Equal? The Complete Lincoln-Douglas Debates* (Chicago: University of Chicago Press, 1958), 1–9.
3. Which is the underlying theme of Jacob E. Cooke, ed., *The Federalist* (Middletown, CT: Wesleyan University Press, 1961).
4. John Marshall, *Life of George Washington.*,5 vols. (New York, 1925) 5: 279–306 for the full text, 283.
5. Ibid., 285.
6. Ibid., 284–285.

7. Andrew W. Robertson, " 'Look on this picture . . . And on this!':
   Nationalism, Localism and Partisan Images of Otherness in the
   United States, 1787–1820," *American Historical Review* 106 (2001):
   1263–1280.
8. 6 Cranch 87 (1810).
9. J. J. Powell, *Essay Upon the Law of Contracts and Agreements*, 2 vols.
   (London: For J. Johnson and T. Whieldon, 1790).
10. 4 Wheat. 518 (1819).
11. Walker P. Mayo, "The Federal Bill of Rights and the States before the
    Fourteenth Amendment," DPhil thesis, Oxford University, 1993,
    223–227.
12. Charles C. Jones, Jr., to the Rev. C. C. Jones, May 30, 1854, in *The
    Children of Pride: a True Story of Georgia and the Civil War*, ed.
    Robert Manson Myers (New Haven and London: Yale University
    Press, 1972), 37–38.
13. The leading work is James H. Kettner, *The Development of American
    Citizenship, 1608–1870* (Chapel Hill: University of North Carolina
    Press, 1978), esp. 213–246. The right to citizenship and related
    duties were matters of heated party debate.
14. J. G. A. Pocock, *The Machiavellian Moment: Florentine Political
    Thought and the Atlantic Republican Tradition* (Princeton: Princeton
    University Press, 1975), 204–205.
15. Cooke, *Federalist*, no. 37.
16. Mayo, "Federal Bill of Rights," 1–26, appendix D; William W.
    Crosskey, *Politics and the Constitution in the History of the United
    States*, 2 vols. (Chicago: University of Chicago Press, 1953), 2: 1070;
    attacked by Charles Fairman, "The Supreme Court and the
    Constitutional Limitations on State Governmental Authority,"
    University of Chicago Law Review 21 (1953): 40–78; Crosskey's reply,
    William Winslow Crosskey, "Charle's Fairman, 'Legislative History,' and
    the Constitutional Limitations on the State Authority," *University of
    Chicago Law Review* 22 (1954): 1–143; Fairman's rejoinder, Charles
    Fairman, "A Reply to Professor Crosskey," *University of Chicago Law
    Review* 22 (1954): 144–156; J. R. Pole, "The Individualist
    Foundations of American Constitutionalism," in *"To Form a More
    Perfect Union": Critical Ideas of the Constitution*, ed. Herman Belz,
    Ronald Hoffman, and Peter J. Albert (Charlottesville: University of
    Virginia Press, 1992), 98–101.
17. The contract clause did restrain the states but hardly on the grounds
    applied in *Fletcher v. Peck* (1810) or *Dartmouth College v. Woodward*
    (1817).
18. Mayo, "Federal Bill of Rights," 155.
19. William Rawle, *A View of the Constitution of the United States of
    America* (Philadelphia: H. C. Carey and I. Lea, 1825); Mayo, "Federal
    Bill of Rights," 256–257. These remarks represent an attempt to rec-
    oncile the dissenting views expressed in my essay, "The Individualist

Foundations," above, with the persuasive Marshallian argument of Akhil Reed Amar, *The Bill of Rights* (New Haven: Yale University Press, 1998), 140–171.

20. The issues are analyzed in J. R. Pole, *The Pursuit of Equality in American History* (Berkeley: University of California Press, 1993), 180–185; Don E. Fehrenbacher, *The Dred Scott Case: Its Significance in American Law and Politics* (New York: Oxford University Press, 1978) for comprehensive cover.

21. 83 Wall. 16 (1873).

22. William E. Nelson, *The Fourteenth Amendment: From Political Principle to Judicial Doctrine* (Cambridge, MA: Harvard University Press, 1988), 156–159. Pole, *Pursuit of Equality*, 224–226.

23. *The Civil Rights Cases*, 109 U.S. 3 (1883).

24. *Plessy v. Ferguson*, 163 U.S. 357 (1896).

25. *The Writings of James Madison*, ed. Gaillard Hunt, 9 vols. (New York: Putnam's Sons, 1910), 5: 294.

26. Ibid., 565.

27. The practice of reversal is in fact known in Congress and among certain special interest lobbies, but not in connection with such constitutional or public policy issues as we are concerned with.

28. Angle, *Created Equal?*, 306.

29. Noel T. Dowling and Gerald Gunther, *Constitutional Law: Cases and Materials*, 7th ed. (Brooklyn: Foundation Press, 1965), 49–50.

30. *Constitution of the United States, Analysis and Interpretation*, 82nd Cong., 2nd sess., S. Doc 170, 513 (1951).

31. United States, *Statutes at Large of the United States of America, 1789–1873* (Boston, 1863), 12: 432.

32. United States, *Statutes at Large of the United States of America, 1789–1873* (Boston, 1866), 14: 27.

33. James Bryce, *The American Commonwealth* (London and New York: Macmillan, 1891) I: 27.

34. Ibid, I: 390.

35. Alan Cromartie, *Sir Matthew Hale: Law, Religion and Natural Philosophy* (Cambridge: Cambridge University Press, 1995) 36, 107.

Chapter 9

Ticklish Experiments: The Paradox of American Constitutionalism

Jack N. Rakove

The United States entered the twenty-first century with the structural features of its eighteenth-century Constitution still largely intact. In celebration, the political fates conspired to produce one of the strangest elections in its history. In the presidential election of 2000, the remarkably narrow division in the national electorate was replicated in six states where a swing of a few hundred or thousand voters would have moved the electors into the opposing column; and the outcome of the national election came to depend on the final disposition of ballots in Florida. Five weeks of political and legal maneuvering over the balloting in Florida ended when the Supreme Court of the United States effectively halted any further recount of the vote in that state. Although this decision falls short of the "self-inflicted wound" label ritually pinned on its ruling in *Dred Scott v. Sandford* (1857), or the moral obloquy associated with the "separate but equal" implications of *Plessy v. Ferguson*, the *per curiam* opinion in *Bush v. Gore* seems destined to sustain searching criticism for years to come.[1] Perhaps the best defense of the ruling came from the celebrated jurist-academic Richard A. Posner, who essentially argued that the Court had to act as it did to avoid the greater constitutional crisis that would occur should the final evaluation of the Florida vote fall to Congress, as both the Constitution and the relevant statute strongly indicated it should.[2] Why the Constitution would be better preserved by an imperious assertion of judicial authority than by requiring Congress to live up to its own duty was not explained. The clear implication appeared to be that a Constitution entering its twenty-second decade of operation remained too delicate or frail a mechanism to withstand this sort of challenge.

The furor in Florida eclipsed a second constitutional aspect of the 2000 election. For the first time since 1888, the candidate with the greatest number of popular votes lost the election after his opponent carried the electoral college by a margin of four votes (excluding a "faithless" elector who voided her ballot in protest of the denial of congressional representation to the District of Columbia). For a few days after the nation went to the polls, this disparity between the popular and electoral votes attracted a modicum of interest. Occasional calls were heard for the abolition of the electoral college. But within a week, the subject vanished from the national agenda, even as the counting of absentee ballots widened the popular plurality of the candidate destined for electoral defeat. As everyone knows, even to discuss elimination of the electoral college would be an exercise in futility. Because its system of allocating electoral votes favors less populous states, and because Article 5 of the Constitution requires that amendments be ratified by three quarters of the states, the least populous states can veto any amendment that would presumably reduce their electoral weight. Former president Jimmy Carter only summarized the conventional political wisdom when, at the first meeting of the National Commission of Federal Election Reform, he rebutted the earnest pleadings of a naive academic with this forthright statement: "I think it is a waste of time to talk about changing the Electoral College. I would predict that 200 years from now, we will still have the Electoral College."[3]

Exactly two centuries earlier, the original version of the electoral college had also misfired, producing a tie vote between the two candidates of the opposition Democratic-Republican party, Thomas Jefferson and Aaron Burr, thereby throwing the election into the House of Representatives. That "constitutional crisis" led to the adoption of the Twelfth Amendment, requiring electors to cast separate votes for president and vice president (rather than casting two undifferentiated votes).[4] The authors of that amendment had evidently believed that errors of institutional design exposed by experience should be subject to correction via amendment. Two centuries later, that attitude would be dismissed as either heretical or grossly impractical.

There is something dispiriting about having to acknowledge that the expected opposition of the least populous states of the Union provides a sufficient reason against even discussing, much less advancing the idea of reforming an archaic institution that violates fundamental democratic norms by making the votes of some citizens superior to those of others simply because of the accident of residence in one state or another. It would be one thing if the conventional arguments in favor of the electoral college were persuasive: that a state-based system of presidential elections advances the cause of federalism, or prevents campaigns from being narrowly targeted at particular clusters of voters. But the first of these defenses rests on a confused notion of federalism, while the second was itself conveniently disproved by the election of 2000 as well.[5] Yet again, none of this undercuts the conventional wisdom that says that it is foolish to discuss constitutional amendments in general and this one in particular.

Herein lies a paradox of American constitutionalism—or if not a paradox, at least a puzzle worth pondering. In its revolutionary origins, American constitutionalism displayed a remarkable confidence in the capacity of human reason to create new institutions of government organized on republican principles. In this exercise, the Americans were neither utopians nor forerunners of the radical visionaries who came to the fore with the French Revolution and the distinct revolutionary tradition that it founded. But they did believe that the science of politics was a body of knowledge capable of "improvement" and that lessons drawn from experience could be applied to the task of designing institutions of constitutional government. Today, however, most Americans shrink in horror from the idea that later generations could ever improve upon the wisdom of the Founders. Even in the abstract, one could barely contemplate the idea of holding a constitutional convention, for fear of the terrible mess such a project might produce. Better to err on the side of inertia than to risk relying on our collective capacity to reason constitutionally.

There is, of course, another argument to be made in favor of preferring the virtues of inertia over the risk of experimentation. Constitutional stability is advantageous in itself. No one can readily calculate the "transaction costs" of implementing significant constitutional change, and the doctrine of unintended consequences warns us that unforeseen costs would doubtless arise. A more perfect union can never become a perfect union in this vale of tears. Better to let the people believe that the system is still working well, than to risk "interesting too strongly the public passions" in constitutional questions. Better to hope, therefore, that the disparity between popular and electoral votes in the 2000 election was the equivalent of a random political error, rather than evidence of a fundamental flaw in the constitutional system.

The tension between the openness to constitutional experimentation and the fondness for constitutional stability was also manifested during the founding era of American constitutionalism. It lies at the heart of the fascinating digression on which Madison embarked in

Federalist 49 and 50 when, amid his attempt to reformulate the doctrine of separated powers, he went out of his way to criticize Thomas Jefferson's proposal for resolving constitutional disputes between the branches of government by "periodical" or "occasional" appeals to the sovereign authority of the people. The basic point was reprised a year later, when Jefferson asked Madison to consider "[t]he question Whether one generation of men has a right to bind another." This eventually led him to observe "that no society can make a perpetual constitution, or even a perpetual law," and that as a matter of right, "Every constitution, then, & every law, naturally expires at the end of 19 years"—the point at which he calculated that a declining senior generation no longer represented the living majority of society.[6] Madison's response to this query was consistent with the anxiousness about constitutional ferment that he had expressed as Publius a year earlier. But before we explore the sources of that anxiety about the "ticklish experiments" of constitutional politics, it would be useful to ask why the first generation of American constitutionalists had cause to rejoice in their labors.

Scholars who write about the content and substance of American constitutionalism typically emphasize the doubts about the potential excesses of popular government that gave rise to the distinctive American conceptions of checks and balances, separated powers, and especially the counter-majoritarian animus of judicial review. But those who are concerned primarily with the *origins* of American constitutionalism can hardly escape its self-conscious awareness of its own historical novelty and possibility and its underlying confidence. In the opening paragraph of *The Federalist*, Alexander Hamilton sounded much the same note that John Adams had struck a decade earlier in closing his important pamphlet, *Thoughts on Government*. Hamilton seized the moment not to inform but rather to remind his readers of the remarkable opportunity that now awaited them:

> It has been frequently remarked that it seems to have been reserved to the people of this country, by their conduct and example, to decide the important question, whether societies of men are really capable or not of establishing good government from reflection and choice, or whether they are forever destined to depend for their political constitutions on accident and force.[7]

So too Adams had exulted in 1776 at the prospect of being

> sent into life at a time when the greatest lawgivers of antiquity would have wished to live. How few of the human race have ever enjoyed an opportunity of making an election of government, more than of air,

soil, or climate, for themselves or their children! When, before the present epocha, had three millions of people full power and a fair opportunity to form and establish the wisest and happiest government that human wisdom can contrive?[8]

Whatever else had changed between 1776 and 1787, these declarations suggest a striking continuity in the sense of historical possibility and innovation that the revolutionary experience created. Nothing better expressed the Enlightenment's deeper confidence in its project than the belief that government itself could be designed and remodeled in the light of human reason and experience.

For both Adams and Hamilton, participation in this process was not limited to the heroic figure of "the lawgiver" whom Adams also evoked. In the political science of the Enlightenment, the lawgiver was a solitary individual whose philosophical wisdom and charisma would somehow conspire to establish a new code of laws and the institutions to preserve them. As the historian Harry C. Payne has observed, the "half-mythical, half-historical . . . figure of the legislator who shapes and unifies his society dominates the political and historical writings of the philosophes." The idea that such a lawgiver could indeed operate in historical time was not a historical fiction: Montesquieu, after all, had praised the visionary William Penn as "a true Lycurgus."[9] But neither did the image of the lawmaker offer the first American constitutionalists a useful model to emulate. From the start, they assumed that constitution-making required at least one and possibly two forms of collective deliberation. The first and necessary one would be devoted to the drafting of constitutions; the second, perhaps optional, one would require some form of popular assent to make this exercise valid. That assent might require nothing more than a prior expression of approval authorizing an appropriate body to frame and promulgate a constitution. But read more expansively, it required would-be lawgivers to subject their work to the subsequent approval of the community. "Reflection and choice" were to be exercised twice, not once: first in framing, then in ratifying a constitution.

Most discussions of the origins of the Constitution focus on the bargains and decisions that gave the institutions of the new government their particular form. But understanding the origins of the American form of constitutionalism, and the distinctive constitutional traditions to which it gave rise, requires stepping back from the drama of decision-making to reflect on structural aspects of the larger enterprise of constitution-making. Viewing that enterprise in these terms entails considering at least four distinct substantive problems. First, what conditions and circumstances of deliberation are most conducive to the framing of constitutions? Second, how is the consent of the people to the proposed constitution to be registered and measured? Third, how does one regulate the process of constitutional adoption so that it simultaneously accommodates the interests of those constituencies whose support and assent are necessary while preventing them from securing lasting advantages that may be inimical to maintaining the constitutional order and equilibrium over the long run? Fourth, what mechanisms will be established for dealing with constitutional silences, unanticipated problems, or the lessons of experience?

On the first two of these problems, the Americans clearly made remarkable progress in the decade after independence. In 1776, the first Revolutionary constitutions of the states were drafted by bodies that were simultaneously engaged in the conduct of the war. This circumstance was not only an urgent distraction from the enterprise of constitution-writing; it also rendered these constitutions vulnerable to the charge that their legal authority was merely statutory. Under the common law maxim of statutory construction, *quod leges posteriores priores, contrarias abrogant*, a subsequent legislative enactment of doubtful constitutionality would in fact enjoy superior legal authority over a constitution previously promulgated by a merely legislative body. By 1787, however, emerging doctrine held that constitutions had to be drafted by specially appointed conventions that would discharge no other duties, and that these charters would operate as fundamental law, superior to ordinary legislative enactments.

In 1776 too the idea that a constitution had to be ratified through some subsequent act of popular sovereignty was barely a glimmer in the eye of the most advanced thinkers. Popular assent was to be expressed in the election of delegates to the next session of the provincial conventions that would undertake the work. In effect, the people were understood to be authorizing their delegates to write a constitution, but not reserving a right to approve or reject whatever text the convention drafted. By 1787, however, it was well understood that a constitution had to be ratified and not merely promulgated. This too deepened the definition and understanding of a constitution as a distinct form of higher or fundamental law.

Finally, in 1776 there was no clear or detailed understanding of the idea of constitutional revision, amendment, or interpretation. The first constitutions marked a transition from the condition of dissolution of government in which the collapse of imperial authority after 1774 had placed the colonies, to the restored legal governments that gave these communities their new political identities as autonomous, quasi-sovereign states, or commonwealths. Given the political exigencies of the time, it is not surprising that the question of constitutional revision was neglected. By 1787, however, the framers of the U.S. Constitution understood that rules of amendment had to be laid down in advance. And even though the procedures of Article 5 now appear impossibly restrictive—as the discussion of the electoral college confirms—at the time they seemed far less onerous than the unanimous consent of the states required for revisions to the Articles of Confederation.

But if a constitution could be amended, then agreements reached in its formation might be undone. That possibility in turn implicated a more vexing development in the American conception of a constitution. The enterprise of crafting such a document involved something more than agreeing upon the design of institutions or the allocation of particular powers and duties. All the parties to the compact could be expected to act upon calculations of interest and advantage. Those calculations could obviously affect decisions relating to the prospective allocation of political influence within the government (as through procedures for election or the apportionment of seats within the legislature). Or they might relate to the exercise of particular powers that promised to affect the essential interests of particular constituencies.

In 1776, it had not been easy to conceive how the adoption of a written constitution could be used for such ends. But by 1787, Americans were beginning to recognize that constitutions could be an extension of politics by other means. That is, once a constitution was recognized as supreme law, the advantages to be gained by protecting some cherished interest constitutionally, rather than entrusting its fate to the ordinary vicissitudes of politics, would prove difficult to resist. Long after the original rationale for this entrenchment had been disproved or become outmoded, the advantage gained would still be secure. In the abstract, a constitution might be regarded as a neutral set of rules and procedures for establishing institutions and structuring decisions. But if the bargaining over its adoption made it possible to gain permanent protection for some essential interest—say, the ownership of property in other men, or the rights of less populous states to be overrepresented in the Senate or the electoral college—one would be foolish not to seize the opportunity.

There was, finally, one other fundamental problem of constitutionalism to which no clear answers could be available prior to the actual implementation. How would ambiguities in the meaning of the constitutional text be resolved? Given the novelty of the entire enterprise of governing under a written constitution conceived as fundamental law, it is hardly surprising that this was a question that could hardly be asked, much less answered. Was the true intent of the Constitution to be discovered or "liquidated" (as Madison might say) only through a course of precedent-setting decisions or adjudications? Was its meaning something that later interpreters could recover from the records of the ratification debates, as Madison came to argue by 1796? Was each branch of the national government equally empowered to discharge the task of constitutional interpretation? Or, inadvertently or by design, was it the peculiar province of the judiciary to say what the law of the Constitution finally was? Could the process of interpretation be insulated from the vicissitudes of ordinary politics, or was it likely to become an extension or even escalation of politics by other means? To these possibilities, the first generation of American constitutionalists could devise answers only as they went along.

Because American constitutional scholarship is preeminently a study of the theory and practice of constitutional adjudication, it is difficult to view the interpretative problem in nonlegal terms—that is, to imagine any alternative to judicial review as the dominant mechanism for resolving constitutional ambiguities.[10] That might not have been the case, had the amendment procedures of Article 5 proved easier to invoke. But following the adoption of the initial ten amendments (the Bill of Rights), the amendment process has been little used, with of course the noteworthy exception of the three Civil War amendments approved between 1864 and 1870. Both literally and figuratively, those were amendments with a vengeance, but the very fact that they emerged from the cataclysm of the Civil War suggests that they constituted as much of a post-upheaval political settlement as a considered use of the amending power. Indeed, had it not been for the crises of the 1860s, it is conceivable that Article 5 would have remained in the desuetude into which it had fallen since the adoption of the Twelfth Amendment in 1803.[11] Only twelve amendments have been adopted since Reconstruction, and of these one repealed another (the prohibition amendments), one was proposed as long ago as 1789 (the original Second Amendment, now the Twenty-seventh), and three prohibit the right of suffrage from being "denied or abridged" on the basis of gender, the nonpayment of poll taxes, or youth. Precisely because the formal amendment process is so unwieldy, some scholars have begun to suggest that numerous other substantive "amendments" have taken place outside the formal parameters of Article 5.[12]

When constitutional change thus occurs, as it inevitably does, it does so either through judicial interpretation or an accretion of political decisions that effectively alter the working constitution while leaving the formal text intact. Academics and committed citizens alike often fault the constitutional jurisprudence of the Supreme Court, and one can plausibly argue that its decisions are, at bottom, hardly less political than those of the political branches of government (which is hardly surprising, given the increasing politicization of the appointments process[13]). Yet the alternative possibility, that constitutional change can, could, or should occur through the amendment process, seems more frightening to Americans than the frequently voiced complaint that an imperious Supreme Court simply decides what the Constitution means on the basis of the justices' preferences. The latter fear often takes the form of railing against an "activist judiciary," but judgments of activism are notoriously subjective and inconsistent. Notwithstanding all the criticism that the Court receives from across the political spectrum, its role in finally determining what the Constitution means appears so settled as to be beyond dispute.

Article 5, by contrast, is difficult to take seriously. The problem is not only that its super-majoritarian requirements are so onerous as to be unworkable, but it is also that American political and constitutional culture lacks the confidence to think it could ever improve upon the wisdom of 1787. This diffidence may be perfectly reasonable in itself, but it stands in contrast to the confidence of the 1780s. Or perhaps that confidence has all along been more tempered than Hamilton's commonplace in *Federalist* 1 or Adams's exultation in 1776 might suggest. That at least is the conclusion to be drawn from James Madison's reflections in *Federalist* 49 and 50, to which we now turn.

At first glance, no one could have felt greater confidence about the capacity of human reason to make improvements to the science of politics than James Madison, arguably the leading constitutionalist of his era on either side of the Atlantic. Madison doubtless learned a great deal from his deep reading in history, philosophy, political theory, and the emerging social sciences of the eighteenth century, but he was also acutely aware and proud of the pioneering contributions that Americans had made to the science of politics on the basis of their own Revolutionary experience and the course of innovation on which it had launched them. This attitude is clearly expressed, for example, in his first Helvidius letter of 1793, written to rebut Hamilton's claim (as Pacificus) that the framing and conduct of foreign policy were inherently executive functions. Pacificus must have been influenced, Madison surmised, by the writings of such authorities as Locke and Montesquieu; but both those authors labored "under the same disadvantage, of having written before these subjects were illuminated by the events and discussions which distinguish a very recent period"—that is, the American Revolutionary era itself. The ensuing paragraph pursuing the difficulties of bringing these two authorities— the Founders' "teachers," as they are sometimes known—to bear on the American case ends abruptly with the injunction: "But let us quit a field of research which is more likely to perplex than to decide."[14]

Madison had sounded a similar note five years earlier. In *Federalist* 14, his second essay as Publius, he laid the reigning imprecision in distinguishing republican and democratic forms of governments to "the artifice of some celebrated authors, whose writings have had a great share in forming the modern standard of political opinion," but whose status as "subjects either of an absolute, or limited monarchy" had skewed their judgment. Madison closed this essay on a strikingly florid note. Rebutting the Anti-Federalist call to reject the Constitution for its very novelty, he urges his countrymen to "shut your ears against this unhallowed language" and "shut your hearts against the poison which it conveys." The conclusion is a celebration of political innovation. "But why is the experiment of an extended republic to be rejected merely because it may comprise what is new?" Madison asked.

> Is it not the glory of the people of America, that whilst they have paid a decent regard to the opinions of former times and other nations, they have not suffered a blind veneration for antiquity, for custom, or for names, to overrule the suggestions of their own good sense, the knowledge of their own situation, and the lessons of their own experience? To this manly spirit, posterity will be indebted for the possession, and the world for the example of the numerous innovations displayed on the American theatre, in favor of private rights and public happiness.

The concluding paragraph of this essay continues in the same rhapsodic vein, so atypical of the sobriety and fondness for drawing careful distinction that characterizes Madison's writings. The Americans had "accomplished a revolution which has no parallel in the annals of human society," Madison concluded. "They reared the fabrics of governments which have no model on the face of the globe. They formed the design of a great Confederacy, which it is incumbent on their successors to improve and perpetuate."[15]

Of course, *The Federalist* and Federalists more generally had no choice but to defend the necessity of innovation and the reasonableness of reasoning about improvements in the science of politics. As in so much political debate—including most contemporary constitutional debate—the structure of argument and the innate preferences of the parties dictated many of the rhetorical and polemical moves that partisans on either side had to make. Yet if we recognize that these preferences were not solely determined by calculation of immediate interest, but also reflected substantively divergent understandings of politics, openness to constitutional innovation can no longer be reduced to mere rhetorical strategy. It instead represents authentic attitudes that not only describe but also explain underlying political beliefs. Much of the scholarly literature analyzing the constitutional debates of the late 1780s has accordingly sought to explain the reigning political divisions in terms of distinct modes of reasoning about politics.

Probing Madison's views of constitutional innovation, however, reveals a more complicated and prudent position than the rhetorical enthusiasm of *Federalist* 14 would suggest. For when he returned to this question in later essays as Publius, he repeatedly stressed the inherent difficulties and even dangers of constitutional politics. In part, these later passages were designed to persuade the moderate Anti-Federalists and wavering citizens who were his targeted audience why they could not expect any constitution to be immune to all possible objections or free of deviations from abstract principles. But in more subtle ways, his reflections address a deeper problem: whether or not it is a good idea for ordinary citizens, or even their elected representatives, ever again to engage in debates that implicate the fundamental arrangements laid down in a written constitution.

A useful point of departure for these deeper concerns can be found in the private letter that Madison sent to his friend and sometime political ally, Edmund Randolph, in January 1788. Randolph was one of the three delegates still in attendance who balked at signing the Constitution when the Federal Convention adjourned in mid-September 1787. Randolph eventually trimmed his way back to the Federalist cause and played a major role at the Virginia ratification convention, but in the winter of 1788 he still favored holding a second constitutional convention, the better to answer and hopefully remove the objections voiced since September. Madison thought this was political madness. The problem was not only that Anti-Federalists were so divided and expansive in their own criticisms of the Constitution as to make agreement with its supporters impossible. It was also that the space for maneuvering and compromising left open for the 1787 convention by the absence of binding instructions from the state legislatures might well be closed in a second meeting. Once leaders back in the states knew what the stakes really were, they could bind their delegations with instructions that would serve as effective ultimata. The results, he concluded, would be "infinitely precarious."[16]

Beyond these expedient calculations, however, Madison challenged the case for a second convention on deeper grounds. "Whatever respect may be due to the rights of private judgment, and no man feels more of it than I do," he wrote

> there can be no doubt that there are subjects to which the capacities of the bulk of mankind are unequal, and on which they must and will be governed by those with whom they happen to have acquaintance and confidence. The proposed Constitution is of this description. The great body of those who are both for & against it, must follow the judgment of others not their own.

Madison meant this, in part, as a personal rebuke. Had Randolph, Richard Henry Lee, George Mason, and Patrick Henry not fomented popular opposition to the Constitution in Virginia, he noted, the state would almost unanimously favor ratification, and not find itself narrowly divided over its merits. But again, Madison drew a more general conclusion: "[I]f a Government be ever adopted in America, it must result from a fortunate coincidence of leading opinions, and a general confidence of the people in those who may recommend it." If Randolph's proposal for a second convention was accepted, Madison observed, it would destroy popular confidence in the original meeting at Philadelphia, while the ensuing contrast between the first and second versions of a national constitution would "give a loose to human opinions, which must be as various and irreconcilable concerning theories of Government, as doctrines of Religion; and give opportunities to designing men which it might be impossible to counteract."[17]

The doubts expressed in this letter comport with Madison's other comments from this period on the subject of public opinion, but here they are voiced with a candor rarely found in his other writings. In 1787 and 1788, the framers and their Federalist supporters *had* to appeal to public opinion in order to place the mandate of popular sovereignty behind the new Constitution. Only by appealing directly to the people could they attain the dual objectives of making the Constitution the supreme law of the land while circumventing the legalistic but entirely trenchant objection that the Convention had acted illegitimately by defying the amendment rules of the Articles of Confederation. This refinement of the vague concept of popular sovereignty into a workable doctrine sustaining the new constitutional order was another of the great achievements of revolutionary American constitutionalism. But the utility of that doctrine depended on its being carefully confined to powerful but limited ends. Federalists took special care to assure that when the people's delegates assembled in convention, they could express their judgment only by accepting or rejecting the Constitution in toto, not by voting separately on its individual articles and clauses, nor by making a state's ratification contingent on the adoption of some preferred amendment or a declaration of rights. The appeal to popular sovereignty and the public opinion on which it rested was one of the most powerful weapons in the Federalist armory, but it was also one of the most dangerous. Madison was intent on seeing that this explosive force was directed only against its intended target and not deployed for casual use.[18]

A day after Madison wrote to Randolph, *Federalist* 37 appeared in the New York *Independent Journal*. Here and in the next three essays, Madison reflected anew on the inherent difficulties in constitution-making, in the process occasionally touching upon the problems of involving public opinion in the process. In this series of essays, the timbre of Madison's rhetoric often varies. *Federalist* 37, for example, contains an extended meditation, unique in the literature of ratification, on the epistemology of the science of politics, while *Federalist* 39 patiently applies these reflections to the task of determining whether the proposed Constitution will create a government more national than federal in character. This is Madison at his labored best, carefully drawing distinctions in the name of identifying true difficulties and sources of uncertainty. By contrast, passages of *Federalist* 38 and 40 match the impassioned polemical fervor of *Federalist* 14.

In these essays Madison repeatedly reminds readers what a difficult exercise constitution-making must be, and how few (if any) successful examples could be found in the recorded annals of history. Thus the closing paragraph of *Federalist* 37 notes that "[t]he history of almost all the great councils and consultations held among mankind for reconciling their discordant opinions, assuaging their mutual jealousies, and adjusting their respective interests, is a history of factions, contentions, and disappointments, and may be classed among the most dark and degraded pictures which display the infirmities and depravities of the human character." *Federalist* 38 opens with the observation that "[i]t is not a little remarkable that in every case reported by ancient history, in which government has been established with deliberation and consent, the task of framing it has not been committed to an assembly of men, but has been performed by some individual citizen of preeminent wisdom and approved integrity." Madison then reviews the efforts of the famous lawgivers of antiquity, noting that even when they enjoyed the apparent confidence of their countrymen, they had to resort to various "expedients . . . in order to carry their reforms into effect." Thus Solon "confessed that he had not given to his country-men the government best suited to their happiness, but most tolerable to their prejudices," while Lycurgus "was under the necessity of mix-ing a portion of violence with the authority of superstition, and of securing his final success by a voluntary renunciation, first of his coun-try, and then of his life." The moral seemed clear. "If these lessons teach us, on one hand, to admire the improvement made by America on the ancient mode of preparing and establishing regular plans of government, they serve not less, on the other, to admonish us of the hazards and difficulties incident to such experiments, and of the great imprudence of unnecessarily multiplying them."[19]

Statements like these served an obvious rhetorical function within the structure of the debate over ratification. Any court-day critic or tavern philosopher could grumble over the consolidationist tendencies of the Constitution or the dangers lurking in any of a number of its provisions. To remind readers how inherently difficult the enterprise of constitution-making must be, or of the inevitable conflicts that must have arisen among delegations representing the vested interests of their states, was a natural response to Anti-Federalist carping. But as the concurrent letter to Randolph confirms, there was nothing contrived or disingenuous or propagandistic about Madison's obser-vations on this score. What he wrote in private and in public were of a piece and consistent. Constitution-making was hard work, and the chances for its succeeding, on the scale of reform that the Convention had attempted, depended on the general inability of Americans prior to May 1787 to anticipate how far the delegates might be induced to go, if they displayed the "manly confidence" that Madison celebrated in *Federalist* 40.[20] All of this is consistent too with his blunt refutation of Randolph's proposal for a second convention.

"Is it an unreasonable conjecture," *Federalist* 38 accordingly asked, "that the errors which may be contained in the plan of the convention are such as have resulted rather from the defect of antecedent experi-ence on this complicated and difficult subject, than from a want of accuracy or care in the investigation of it; and, consequently such as will not be ascertained until an actual trial shall have pointed them out?"[21] But what course of action should be followed once "errors" were indeed "ascertained"? That was the question that Madison took up in *Federalist* 49 and 50, two essays lodged within the general discussion of separated powers that began in *Federalist* 47 and concluded with the famous *Federalist* 51.

These two essays have not received quite the attention they merit. In part that is because they are overshadowed by the better known essays that sandwich them: *Federalist* 48, which explains why the legislature, that "impetuous vortex," is the most dangerous branch of republican government; and *Federalist* 51, where the ambitions of non-angelic men must be made to counteract each other for the equilibrium of government to be preserved. Their lesser importance also reflects the fact that they appear as something of a digression. Their ostensible subject is Jefferson's proposal, included in the draft constitution appended to his *Notes on the State of Virginia*, to enable any two branches of government, whenever they "shall concur in opinion . . . that a convention is necessary for altering the constitution or *correcting breaches of it*," to summon popularly elected conventions "for the purpose." This proposal, whatever its abstract merits, did not figure in the proposed federal Constitution. Nor is there any evidence that it had garnered much interest or attention since its publication, notwithstanding the fact that Jefferson's "plan, like every thing from the same pen, marks a turn of thinking original, comprehensive and accurate," as well as displaying "a fervent attachment to republican government."[22] For Madison to go out of way, in effect, to write two additional essays to discuss a proposal *not* before the American public suggests that he attached particular importance to the position Jefferson espoused and the assumptions on which it rested.

Those assumptions may have been more representative of American constitutional thinking, around 1787, than much constitutional scholarship has recognized. As Larry Kramer has recently argued, prevailing conceptions of "popular constitutionalism" left the sovereign people themselves, not any particular arrangement of institutions, or any one institution—such as an omnicompetent Supreme Court—as the ultimate guarantor of constitutional equilibrium and final source of interpretative authority.[23] Some of that authority might be exercised through the routine process of elections, but in a regime of written constitutions, it could also presumably take the form of an exercise of popular sovereignty in ways not bound by the constraints placed on the ratification conventions of 1787–1788. In calling attention to Jefferson's obscure proposal, Madison was challenging a central assumption of republican constitutionalism. He must have written these two seemingly digressive essays so because he felt there was a critical point to be established.

Madison opens his discussion of Jefferson's proposal by conceding one major point in its favor: If the people are indeed "the only legitimate fountain of power," as they must be in a republican government, then it is entirely consistent with that theory "to recur to the same original authority," not only whenever the powers they have delegated to government require revision, but also to resolve the fundamental problem of "encroachments"—the buzzword invariably evoked to describe the problem of one institution of government exceeding its just authority and interfering with another.[24] Against this concession, however, Madison offers his objections, in ascending order of importance.

Madison first observes that "frequent appeals" to the people to resolve constitutional disputes would risk "depriv[ing] the government of that veneration which time bestows on every thing, and without which perhaps the wisest and freest governments would not possess the requisite stability." Once that "prejudice" in favor of government has been established among a citizenry who will lack the temperament of philosophers, it would act as an independent source of equilibrium for the regime as a whole.[25]

Where this first objection is concerned with maintaining the respect of individual citizens for the Constitution, Madison's second major criticism addresses the problems of collective deliberation that will arise from "a frequent reference of constitutional questions to the whole society." Here, again, the enthusiasm and confidence he had elsewhere expressed for the cause of constitutional reform are muted by a powerful reminder of how difficult and precarious an enterprise constitution-making is. "Notwithstanding the success" that Americans have enjoyed thus far, Madison remarks,

> [I]t must be confessed, that the experiments are of too ticklish a nature to be unnecessarily multiplied. We are to recollect that all the existing constitutions were formed in the midst of a danger which repressed the passions most unfriendly to order and concord; of an enthusiastic confidence of the people in their patriotic leaders, which stifled the ordinary diversity of opinions on great national questions; of a universal ardor for new and opposite forms, produced by a universal resentment and indignation against the ancient government; and whilst no spirit of party connected with the changes to be made, or the abuses to be reformed, could mingle its leaven in the operation.

Americans could hardly expect such exceptional conditions to favor them again.[26]

What conditions, then, would govern a future recourse to popular constitutionalism, should Jefferson's proposal or something like it be adopted as a mechanism for correcting violations of the constitutional equilibrium? Madison's third and "greatest objection" reflected his underlying conviction that all the real political forces would usually operate to the advantage of the dominant legislative party that, consistent with his general analysis of the problem of separated powers, would also be the most likely source of encroachment in the first place. They would exert by far the greater influence over the electorate, and retain a higher share of the people's confidence; and in the event of a convention being held, they would be most likely either to gain seats themselves or influence those elected. "The convention, in short, would be composed chiefly of men who had been, who actually were, or who expected to be, members of the department whose conduct was arraigned," Madison predicted. "They would consequently be parties to the very question to be decided by them."[27]

Here as elsewhere, Madison directed his quizzical analysis of the perils of constitutionalism toward identifying the real forces that will control the workings of institutions and the resulting competition for political influence and advantage. That concern had been manifest in his discussion of the comparable resources available to the Union and the states in *Federalist* 45 and 46. It also recurred in the key letter to Jefferson where Madison explained his reservations about the efficacy of bills of rights by noting that "the real power" in a republican polity "lies in the majority of the Community, and the invasion of private rights is cheifly [*sic*] to be apprehended, not from acts of Government contrary to the sense of its constituents, but from acts in which the Government is the mere instrument of the major number of the constituents."[28] A simple extension of that analysis to the problem of maintaining the separation of power would support the inference that appeals to the people to resolve constitutional disputes would be problematic because the people themselves were more likely to be the ultimate source of legislative overstepping than the vulnerable objects of self-serving legislative manipulation.[29]

There is, however, one further element to Madison's analysis that militates against virtually *any* conceivable appeal to the people as constitutional arbiters. It might well be the case, Madison hypothesized, that "the usurpations of the legislature might be so flagrant and so sudden, as to admit of no specious colouring" (or spinning, we might say). Then "the public decision might be less swayed by prepossessions in favor of the legislative party." Yet the underlying analysis still held.

> But still it could never be expected to turn on the true merits of the
> question. It would inevitably be connected with the spirit of pre-existing
> parties, or of parties springing out of the question itself. It would be
> connected with persons of distinguished character and extensive influence
> in the community. It would be pronounced by the very men who had
> been agents in, or opponents of, the measures to which the decision
> would relate. The *passions* therefore not the *reason*, of the public, would
> sit in judgment. But it is the reason, alone, of the public, that ought to
> control and regulate the government. The passions ought to be con-
> trolled and regulated by the government.

Read literally, or taken to its logical conclusion, Madison's analysis virtually presupposes that the American people will never again be in a
position where they can engage in reasoned debate and decision about
constitutional subjects. Any question serious enough to require popular
consideration would come so freighted with political commitments,
influences, and prejudices as to defy rational deliberation—"the public
decision," it merits repeating, "could *never* be expected to turn on the
true merits of the question." Not only does Madison suppose that
there must be some proper ("true") answer for every constitutional
question; he would seemingly deny the community the capacity to
think afresh about such questions, even though to have reached this
point they must have been exposed to experiences superseding the
original intentions or understandings of the framers and ratifiers.
Madison did concede "that a constitutional road to the decision of the
people, ought to be marked out, and kept open, for certain great and
extraordinary occasions," and perhaps sensing that he had gone too
far in his challenge to popular constitutionalism, he inserted a similar
qualifying sentence in the opening lines of *Federalist* 50. "It will be
attended to, that in the examination of these expedients, I confine
myself to their aptitude for *enforcing* the constitution by keeping the
several departments of power within their due bounds, without particularly considering them, as provisions for *altering* the constitution
itself."[30] While one is reluctant to read this disclaimer skeptically, it
must be asked, what are the circumstances under which Madison
could contemplate allowing the amendment power to operate? The
threshold would presumably be crossed only after the need or desire
for constitutional change had become so manifest as to preclude
serious division within the polity over the merits and substance of
the proposed change. Such a situation arguably arose, for example, in
the aftermath of the Jefferson-Burr electoral tie in 1800, leading to

the adoption of the Twelfth Amendment requiring electors to cast two distinct votes, one for president, the other for vice president, thereby correcting an obvious constitutional glitch that the framers had simply not anticipated. But if constitutional controversy already divided the public, the last thing Madison could contemplate was allowing that controversy to inflame the popular passions even further.

To corroborate this argument, Madison used *Federalist* 50 to review the experience of the one state that had instituted a mechanism of constitutional review akin to Jefferson's proposal. The radical Pennsylvania Constitution of 1776 included a provision for a council of censors to meet at periodic intervals "to enquire 'whether the constitution had been violated, and whether the legislative and executive departments had encroached on each other." That body had met in 1783–1784, and Madison found ample evidence that its deliberations had replicated the political divisions that had formed around this constitution from the moment of its adoption. Nor would Madison accept the excuse that Pennsylvania, with its deep partisanship, was an exceptional case from which useful generalizations could not be drawn. "Is it to be presumed that any other state, at the same or any other given period, will be exempt" from "the rage of party," Madison asked?[31]

Soon enough, Madison would learn the bitter lesson that "the rage of party" could beat so strongly as to overcome the theory of constitutional equilibrium that, having completed the digression of *Federalist* 49 and 50, he proceeded to sketch in the next, far more closely studied essay. That theory held that the Constitution would rely on the "ambition-counteracting-ambition" commitment that officeholders would form to their particular institutions, with the special bond between the president and Senate forming the key mechanism.[32] In one critical test—the controversy over the Jay Treaty in 1796—that prediction worked quite well, when the president and Senate resisted the constitutionally dubious call of Madison's House of Representatives to review papers relevant to John Jay's mission to Britain. But that episode was, in a sense, the exception that proved the rule. In most constitutionally charged controversies, the political loyalties and policy preferences of elected officials would trump the sense of institutional attachment on which Madison's theory of constitutional equilibrium rested.

In another sense, however, this constitutionalization of politics in the 1790s—that is, the escalation of disputes over policy into controversies about the appropriate decisional responsibilities of particular institutions—only confirmed Madison's underlying fears. In the abstract, we would like to agree with Madison that there should be a true answer to every constitutional quarrel. And we would similarly like to regard a constitution, optimally, as a set of more or less neutral rules for determining which responsibilities are allocated to which institution and therefore for revealing how decisions are to be reached. If consensus exists on these points, then the inevitable disagreements that are the stuff of ordinary politics should be managed at a level that falls short of calling the Constitution itself into question. But this hopeful scenario overlooks the extent to which inevitable ambiguities in the constitutional text and unforeseen contingencies create incentives for partisans to escalate disputes over policy into constitutional controversies, in effect raising the stakes by adding a new dimension of seemingly principled conflict to the existing quarrel over mere preferences. It is one thing to charge opponents with supporting the wrong policy, another to suspect that their willingness to play fast and loose with the Constitution in order to achieve the desired outcome reveals the desperate lengths to which they are willing to go. Seen in this light, constitutional interpretation simply becomes a continuation of partisan conflict by other means. To judge from the evidence of the 1790s and other tumultuous decades in American history, Madison was right to fear the consequences of exactly this sort of escalation, "of interesting too strongly the public passions" in the resolution of constitutionally charged disputes. The fact that he proved no more immune to its pull than his colleagues only demonstrates how great the danger was.

But why did Madison originally feel this concern more deeply than most of his colleagues and contemporaries? There are two essential answers to the question. One is that his own unparalleled involvement in the politics of constitutional reform in the 1780s left him uniquely aware of just how dicey and "ticklish" the whole experiment had been and remained. As confident as Madison was in the improvements that he and his closest collaborators were capable of making to the science of politics, his experience in Congress and the Virginia legislature and his chariness about popular politics were constant reminders that the outcomes of collective deliberation were never a sure thing. Madison professed to be optimistic about the superior level of deliberation that might be obtained in a national Congress (or convention), but he knew that was only a hypothesis to be tested.

The second answer returns us to the reasons why Madison opposed Edmund Randolph's idea of holding a second convention in 1788 to improve upon the wisdom of 1787. In April 1787, Madison had carefully calculated the reasons why he thought that his insistence on applying the principle of proportional representation to *both* houses of the new Congress could overcome the anticipated adhesion of the small states to the rule giving each state an equal vote in the national assembly. Although the logic on which that principle rested was faultless, the strategic calculation of its success was not, and the small states retained their cherished equality in the Senate while gaining a marginal advantage in the allocation of presidential electors.[33] In the course of that grueling debate, Madison had tried to use the palpable reality of the persisting *regional* differences between slave and free states to explain why the Convention need take no account of the meaningless distinction between small and large states—meaningless because the size of a state's population would never determine the interests or political behavior of its citizens. But the net effect of this appeal, and of the Convention's concurrent discussion of the formula for apportioning seats in the House of Representatives, was to legitimate the claim that both classes of "minority" interests—slave states and small states—deserved special protection through the mechanisms of the Three Fifths Clause in the House and the equal state vote in the Senate.[34]

Could either of those two compromises over representation be replicated if a second convention were to be held? Or was it more likely that delegates from different blocs of states would arrive encumbered by instructions stipulating the positions they were obliged both to affirm and oppose? These "compromises" had been sources of sharp dispute and mutual recriminations during the weeks of June and July 1787 when the issues of representation were agitated, and in fact, the key decision over the Senate was far more of a defeat for the large states than a compromise in the true sense of the term. But by early September, when the key decisions over the presidency were taken, the delegates' collective investment in their joint labors over the preceding three months made it easier for them to recognize that compromise had indeed taken place—so much so that the formula for allocating presidential electors among the states was clearly conceived to replicate and reinforce the bargains over representation. There could be no assurance, however, that constituents judging these results from afar, and knowing little of the considerations that had made them persuasive, would be inclined to be so indulgent. Open up the possibility of reviewing the decisions over representation, or other key matters, and state legislatures would be foolish not to seek to lock their delegations into fixed positions, or to insist that a subsequent ratification of a revised constitution be given in some form other than the straight up-or-down vote that the framers and Federalists were bent on requiring. If bargaining at the first convention had been ticklish enough, the process of reaching agreement at a second could become a downright howler.

So at least Madison probably reasoned, with reason, during the ratification winter of 1787–1788. The experiment *was* ticklish; its multiplication might produce less favorable results; one could not count upon optimal conditions of deliberation driven by a sense of urgency to prevail on other occasions; and the more Americans understood what was at stake in such deliberations, the more tempted they would be to impose constraints that might not be conducive to reaching the desired consensus. And if one were especially sensitive to the dangers of sectional suspicions, as Madison assuredly was, it would make much more sense to adhere to the agreements already reached than to take a second chance that compromise would prevail again.

That understanding would hold true for the next seven decades of American history, helping to give the Constitution the unamendable status that it enjoyed after the adoption of the Twelfth Amendment in 1803. The mounting fragility of the Union during these decades provided ample warrant for treating the agreements of 1787 as a perpetual treaty, not to be altered for fear of the consequences that might await. Two centuries later, the sources of that original fragility are matters of merely historical concern, and the same fears need no longer make the prospect of constitutional review so ominous. Yet Madison's notion of the ticklish nature of the constitutional experiment seems more persuasive than ever. It may not be a paradox, but it is certainly a puzzle. Is it too early to start planning for the tricentennial of the Constitution in 2087?

Notes

1. For early examples, see the essays collected in Cass Sunstein and Richard Epstein, eds., *The Vote: Bush, Gore, and the Supreme Court* (Chicago: University of Chicago Press, 2001); Howard Gillman, *The Votes That Counted: How the Court Decided the 2000 Presidential Election* (Chicago: University of Chicago Press, 2001); Larry D. Kramer, "The Supreme Court in Politics," and Pamela S. Karlan, "Equal Protection: *Bush v. Gore* and the Making of a Precedent," in *The Unfinished Election of 2000*, ed. Jack N. Rakove (New York: Basic Books, 2001), 105–200; Michael V. Klarman, "*Bush v. Gore* through the Lens of Constitutional History," *California Law Review* 89 (2001): 1721–1765.

2. Richard A. Posner, *Breaking the Deadlock: The 2000 Election, the Constitution, and the Courts* (Princeton: Princeton University Press, 2001).

3. For a transcript of the hearing, see http://www.reformelections.org/data/transcripts. I was the academic in question.

4. Tadahisa Kuroda, *The Origins of the Twelfth Amendment: The Electoral College in the Early Republic, 1787–1804* (Westport, CT: Greenwood Press, 1994).

5. For an elaboration of these arguments, see Jack N. Rakove, "The E-College in the E-Age," in Rakove, *Unfinished Election*, 201–234.

6. Jefferson to Madison, September 6, 1789, in *The Papers of James Madison*, ed. Robert A. Rutland et al. (Charlottesville: University Press of Virginia, 1979), 12: 382–387. The best analysis of this letter can be found in Herbert Sloan, *Principle and Interest: Thomas Jefferson and the Problem of Debt* (New York: Oxford University Press, 1979). On Jefferson's calculation of the life span of generations, see Daniel Scott Smith, "Population and Political Ethics: Thomas Jefferson's Demography of Generations," *William and Mary Quarterly* 56 (1999): 591–612.

7. Benjamin Wright, ed., *The Federalist* (Cambridge, MA: Harvard University Press, 1961), 89.

8. John Adams, *Thoughts on Government* (Philadelphia, 1776), in *The Founders Constitution*, ed. Philip Kurland and Ralph Lerner (Chicago: University of Chicago Press, 1987), I: 110.

9. Harry C. Payne, *The Philosophes and the People* (New Haven and London: Yale University Press, 1976), 61–62; for Montesquieu's comment on Penn, see *The Spirit of the Laws*, book IV, chap. 6.

10. For one valiant effort to do so, see Larry D. Kramer, "Foreword: We the Court," *Harvard Law Review* 115 (2001): 5–169.

11. On this point, see especially Michael Vorenberg, *Final Freedom: The Civil War, the Abolition of Slavery, and the Thirteenth Amendment* (Cambridge: Cambridge University Press, 2001), 5–6, 10–22.

12. The leading provocateur here is Bruce Ackerman, *We the People*, vol. 1, *Foundations*, and vol. 2, *Transformations* (Cambridge, MA: Harvard University Press, 1991, 1998); and see Sanford Levinson, ed., *Responding to Imperfection: The Theory and Practice of Constitutional Amendment* (Princeton: Princeton University Press, 1995). The best survey of the formal use of Article V is David E. Kyvig, *Explicit and Authentic Acts: Amending the U. S. Constitution, 1776–1795* (Lawrence: University Press of Kansas, 1996).

13. See Michael J. Gerhardt, *The Federal Appointments Process: A Constitutional and Historical Analysis* (Durham, NC: Duke University Press, 2000).

14. Madison, Helvidius No. 1, in *James Madison: Writings*, ed. Jack N. Rakove (New York: Library of America, 1999), 540.

15. *Federalist*, no. 14, in *Madison: Writings*, 172–173.

16. Madison to Edmund Randolph, January 10, 1788, in *Madison: Writings*, 190–191.

17. Ibid., 191–192.

18. Jack N. Rakove, *Original Meanings: Politics and Ideas in the Making of the Constitution* (New York: Alfred A. Knopf, 1996), 94–130.
19. *Madison: Writings*, 200–203.
20. Ibid., 224.
21. Ibid., 203. This echoes the observation in *Federalist* 37 that "All new laws, though penned with the greatest technical skill, and passed on the fullest and most mature deliberation, are considered as more or less obscure and equivocal, until their meaning be liquidated and ascertained by a series of particular discussions and adjudications." Ibid., 198.
22. Ibid., 286. For Jefferson's proposed constitution, see Julian Boyd, ed., *The Papers of Thomas Jefferson* (Princeton: Princeton University Press, 1950–), 6: 294–305; the convention proposal is at 304.
23. Kramer, "We the Court."
24. *Madison: Writings*, 286.
25. Ibid., 287–288. I omit the preliminary objection that Jefferson's scheme, requiring two departments to rally together against the third, encroaching party, does not deal with the problem of two departments banding against one.
26. Ibid., 288.
27. Ibid., 288–289. This echoes the passage in *Federalist* 10 where Madison portrays legislators as parties to the very issues they are to decide. Ibid., 162–163.
28. Madison to Jefferson, October 17, 1788, in ibid., 421.
29. In this context, it can hardly be coincidental that Madison used the phrase "parchment barriers" to disparage both bills of rights in general and the formulaic affirmation of separated power that many of the state constitutions and declarations of rights contained. Thus in the letter to Jefferson just quoted, Madison observes that "[r]epeated violations of these parchment barriers have been committed by overbearing majorities in every State." In *Federalist* 48, Madison asks whether it will "be sufficient to mark with precision the boundaries of these departments in the constitution of the government, and to trust to these parchment barriers against the encroaching spirit of power." Ibid., 420, 281.
30. Ibid., 287, 291.
31. Ibid., 292–293.
32. This is the proper meaning of the sentence in *Federalist* 51 that asks whether "this defect of an absolute negative [in the president may] be supplied by some qualified connection between this weaker department [the executive], and the weaker branch [the Senate] of the stronger department [the legislature], by which the latter may be led to support the constitutional rights of the former, without being too much detached from the rights of its own department." This is a clear reference to the tie between the president and Senate formed by their joint exercise of the treaty and appointment powers, but it leaves open

the question, why would Madison call the Senate, with its longer term and additional powers beyond those exercised by the House, the weaker house of Congress? The answer, of course, is that the House will be *politically* more powerful because it is the popularly elected institution. *Madison: Writings*, 296.

33. Madison to Washington, April 16, 1787, in *Madison: Writings*, 80–81. For further discussion, see Rakove, *Original Meanings*, 54–55, 58–83.

34. See especially Madison's speech of June 30, 1787, in *Madison: Writings*, 117–119.

Chapter 10

James Madison and the Idea of Fundamental Law

C. Bradley Thompson

The framing of the American Constitution was not the work of any one man. It was drafted by a group of fifty-five men and ratified by hundreds. Still, we reserve a special place of honor for James Madison, the man we most often refer to as the "Father of the Constitution." The title is not undeserved.

It was Madison, after all, who played a central role in organizing the federal convention; he was largely responsible for drafting the Virginia Resolutions, which became the Philadelphia Convention's working plan; he played, arguably, the leading role in the Convention's deliberations; he transcribed its debates for posterity; he coauthored the best and most enduring commentary on the Convention's plan; he led Virginia's ratifying convention to support the new plan; and he was the man most responsible for completing the Constitution through his successful advocacy for amending the Bill of Rights to the document. The Constitution's genetic code bears a remarkable resemblance to that of James Madison.

It should not surprise us, then, that Madison's political thought has attracted the attention of some of the best scholars working in the field of early American history. And yet, despite the exciting new work being done on Madison, scholars have not, in my view, penetrated to the deepest level of his thought. Thus our approbation is often premature and incomplete because we praise the man as if his act of procreative statesmanship were the beginning and end of his constitutional paternity.

But the simple act of procreation does not make one a good father. Fatherhood, properly understood, carries with it the responsibility of nurturing, protecting, and guiding one's progeny. Madison not only thought longer and harder than any other framer about the problems associated with political foundings, but he also thought deeply about the need and requirements for perpetuating our political institutions. He took seriously the role of constitutional guardian, which points us to the architectonic principle of his political thought: the idea of a written constitution as fundamental law.

This idea, however, is not simply one piece—or even the last and biggest piece—in a larger constitutional framework. All the principles and institutions associated with his new science of politics—for example, republicanism, separation of powers, checks and balances, and federalism—lead ultimately to the idea of a written constitution as a higher law.

Since a full presentation of Madison's science of politics is impossible here, we must content ourselves with an introductory account of his reflections in *The Federalist* on the difficulties associated with founding and constitutional preservation. To that end, I shall explore three issues in particular: first, his understanding of America's founding act; second, the modes of reasoning that he used when designing and framing the Constitution; and, finally, his attempt to preserve the Constitution from the decay and degeneration associated with the exigencies of time.

Madison on Founding

In the thirty-eighth essay of *The Federalist*, Madison introduces the subject of political foundings. His purpose is twofold: first, to demonstrate the theoretical and practical superiority of America's founding act, and second, to bolster the proposed Constitution's credentials in order to prevent the calling of a second convention.

In order to demonstrate the remarkable achievement of the Philadelphia Convention, Madison contrasts the American founding with those ancient and modern regimes that had been similarly established on the basis of "deliberation and consent" (*The Federalist*, no. 38, p. 239).[1] As we shall see, Madison regarded America's founding act to be fundamentally different from, and ultimately superior to, all past experiments in republican constitution-making. His own contribution to this new and improved mode of political founding self-consciously sought to synthesize the virtues of the ancient and modern approaches to political foundings and to overcome the vices inherent in each.

How and why was the American Convention able to succeed when all others had failed? Madison begins his examination of ancient and modern political foundings with the assumption that governments founded on the basis of "reflection and choice" are superior to those founded on "accident and force" (no. 1, p. 3). But he also recognized a difficulty, an inherent tension in those governments founded on the basis of "reflection and choice" and "deliberation and consent." On the one hand, reflection and deliberation point toward inequality, that is, toward the wise few; on the other hand, choice and consent point toward political equality, that is, toward the right of the many for self-government. At the heart of the modern liberal problem is this tension between the absolute standard of consent (i.e., equality) on the one hand, and the need for wisdom (i.e., inequality) on the other.

The modern doctrine of consent, which Madison saw as embodied in the Revolution of 1776, was the irreducible moral foundation on which all legitimate governments, and republican governments in particular, must rest. In this sense, he was strictly a modern in outlook. In *Federalist* 37, for instance, he writes that the "genius of Republican liberty" demands "that all power should be derived from the people" (p. 234). In fact, the relationship between the principle of popular sovereignty and republican government can be, he claims, strictly identified with the "genius of the American people," with the "fundamental principles of the revolution," and with "that honorable determination, which animates every votary of freedom, to rest all our political experiments on the capacity of mankind for self-government" (no. 39, p. 250). The legitimacy and authority of all constitutional charters, Madison notes explicitly in *Federalist* 49, derives strictly from the will of the people; they are the "only legitimate fountain of power" (p. 339). Since it is obvious that the people themselves could not design and build a constitution, it was necessary that they commission a body of constitutional architects to do the work for them.

The great question was whether 3 million people were up to the task of selecting a small body of representatives to design and construct a constitution. In fact, establishing a mechanism or process to accomplish this posed overwhelming theoretical and practical difficulties. One obvious difficulty was the fact that a federal government already existed under the Articles of Confederation. Was that government to be reformed and remodeled or should it be torn down and a new one established in its place? And on what foundation would a new government be established? Another difficulty seemed to be that it was difficult if not impossible for a deliberative assembly to be particularly deliberative.

Madison saw modern history—particularly the histories of the Florentine, Swiss, Dutch, and English republics—as a graveyard of failed republican experiments. His pre-Convention studies of confederacies in 1786 taught him that virtually all attempts in the modern era to establish new republican governments or to reform old ones on the basis of deliberation and consent had ended badly. At the end of *Federalist* 37, Madison notes that the history of all "the great councils and consultations, held among mankind for reconciling their discordant opinions, assuaging their mutual jealousies, and adjusting their respective interests" had resulted in "factions, contentions, and disappointments." The failure and disgrace of these modern constitutional assemblies, he lamented, "may be classed among the most dark and degrading pictures which display the infirmities and depravities of the human character" (p. 238). It would seem, then, that while the consent of the people is necessary to establish just and legitimate government it is not sufficient for founding a wise and good government. In fact, it may actually be a barrier to this task. Because Madison saw the modern project as defective or incomplete in its understanding of political creation, he turned to another source to complete and perfect the idea of founding a new nation on the basis of "reflection and choice."

Madison begins *Federalist* 38 by explicitly contrasting the failed modern experiments in constitution-making with the more successful ancient foundings. While it is true, he notes, that the ancient foundings resemble their modern counterparts in that they were "established with deliberation and consent," they are nonetheless different in one important respect: the "task of framing [them] has not been committed to an assembly of men; but has been performed by some individual citizen of pre-eminent wisdom and approved integrity." As Madison begins to discuss the particular circumstances surrounding the actions of the ancient Lawgivers (e.g., Minos of Crete, Zaleucus of the Locrians, Theseus, Draco and Solon of Athens, Lycurgus of Sparta, Romulus, Numa and Tullus Hostilius of Rome), he reveals that their authority would not have met the modern standard of consent. It turns out that it is not actually known in every case precisely "how far they might be cloathed with the legitimate authority of the people." In the case of Sparta, for example, the "proceedings under Lycurgus were less regular." Even Spartan reformers were willing to put their trust in the "efforts of that celebrated patriot and sage, instead of seeking to bring about a revolution, by the intervention of a deliberative body of citizens" (pp. 239–240).

Madison feigns astonishment at the ancient mode of constitution-making and asks rhetorically how it is "that a people as jealous as the Greeks were of their liberty, should so far abandon the rules of caution, as to place their destiny in the hands of a single citizen?" How was it possible, he asks, "that the Athenians . . . should consider one illustrious citizen as a more eligible depository of the fortunes of themselves and their posterity, than a select body of citizens, from whose common deliberations more wisdom, as well as more safety, might have been expected?" Quick to answer his own question, Madison notes that the citizens of ancient Greece were more fearful of "the discord and disunion" that would result from a deliberative assembly than they were of the "treachery or incapacity in a single individual" (no. 38, pp. 240–241). At the very least, then, the Greeks recognized the difficulties associated with collective decision-making, ultimately deferring to the superior wisdom of one man.

In the end, what lessons does Madison draw from the history of political foundings? Most importantly, he learned that the ancient foundings relied on the superior wisdom of one man and succeeded, whereas the modern foundings relied on deliberative assemblies and failed. Madison seems to suggest that the ancients were more successful at constitution-making precisely because they ranked wisdom higher than consent, or, at the very least, because they made room for wisdom. In other words, the ancients might have something to teach modern constitution-makers.

Over the course of the preceding twenty years or so, Madison had come to believe that constitution-makers of America had devised a superior method of governmental design and construction—one that combined the strengths of the ancients (i.e., the need for wisdom) with that of the moderns (i.e., the need for consent). He is quite explicit in complimenting his American audience for their admirable improvement over the "ancient mode of preparing and establishing regular plans of government" (no. 38, p. 241). Madison is here referring to the extraordinary American invention in the years after 1776 of constitutional conventions established for the sole purpose of drafting constitutions that would then be sent to special ratifying conventions of the people's representatives.[2] These supra-legal bodies stood above ordinary legislatures; they became the means by which the people's will was captured, filtered and sanctified in the form of a written constitution that would in turn create and give life to governments. But, as we shall see, this distinctly American approach faced several challenges.

The immediate rhetorical purpose of Madison's digression on the ancient foundings was to confront the Anti-Federalist charge that the actions of the Philadelphia Convention were "irregular," illegal, revolutionary, and an usurpation. The "official" purpose of the Convention, they argued, was to revise the Articles of Confederation and not to radically alter the government of the Union. The proposed constitution had the effect of not only revising and reforming the Articles of Confederation but also of destroying them and of establishing a new government on an entirely different foundation. At the Virginia ratifying convention, Patrick Henry lent a powerful voice to the Anti-Federalist position: "My political curiosity, exclusive of my anxious solicitude for the public welfare, leads me to ask who authorised them to speak the language of, *We, the People*, instead of *We, the States?* . . . The people gave them no power to use their name. That they exceeded their power is perfectly clear."[3] Furthermore, the process by which the new Constitution was to be ratified was in contravention of Article 13, which said that no alteration could be made to the Confederation "unless such alteration be agreed to in a Congress of the United States, and be afterwards confirmed by the Legislatures of every State." The proposed constitution, however, was to be ratified by special conventions of the people in the states—and only nine state conventions at that. The Anti-Federalists stood on solid legal ground, then, when they argued that the Convention's proposals violated Congress's commission and the method of amendment required by the Articles of Confederation. These were powerful arguments that had to be met. Madison wrote therefore to defend the legality of the Constitutional Convention and, more particularly, to prevent the calling of a second convention. The question that Madison first raises in *Federalist* 38 and then attempts to answer in 40 and 43 is whether the proceedings of the Constitutional Convention were strictly "regular" or legal.

In *Federalist* 40 and later in 43, Madison begins to examine the legal authority and handiwork of the Constitutional Convention. His first task was to determine if the Convention had exceeded its commission. At its February 1787 session, the Continental Congress authorized the meeting of a convention to revise the Articles of Confederation. According to its congressional charge, the proposed Convention was created for the "sole and express purpose of *revising the articles of confederation*" such that it would "render the Federal Constitution *adequate to the exigencies of government and the preservation of the Union.*" Madison's ingenious and latitudinarian interpretation of the charge given to the Convention by the Congress recapitulated its purpose in these terms: "They were to frame a *national government*, adequate to the *exigencies of government* and *of the Union*, and to reduce the articles of confederation into such form as to accomplish these purposes." According to Madison, the

Convention had the authority to establish a national government "adequate to the *exigencies of government* and *of the Union*" because the "rules of construction dictated by plain reason, as well as founded on legal axioms" say that the "means should be sacrificed to the end" (no. 40, p. 259–260).

The key legal question, Madison wrote in *Federalist* 43, comes down to this: "On what principle the confederation, which stands in the solemn form of a compact among the States, can be superceded without the unanimous consent of the parties to it?" (p. 297). On one level, he writes, it is possible that an answer "may be found without searching beyond the principles of the compact itself." Madison reveals that the Confederation itself had not in all cases been ratified by special ratifying conventions and that it "had received no higher sanction than a mere legislative ratification." In other words, the process by which the Articles of Confederation was established and ratified was defective. The consequences of this forgotten fact are devastating. Madison brought into doubt the legitimacy and authority of the Articles themselves:

> A compact between independent sovereigns, founded on ordinary acts of legislative authority, can pretend to no higher validity than a league or treaty between the parties. It is an established doctrine on the subject of treaties, that all the articles are mutually conditions of each other; that a breach of any one article is a breach of the whole treaty; and that a breach committed by either of the parties absolves the others; and authorizes them, if they please, to pronounce the treaty violated and void. (no. 43, p. 297)

Because the Articles of Confederation was "founded on ordinary acts of legislative authority," it does not have the status of fundamental law—indeed, he seems to be suggesting that the authority and legal status of the Confederation is dubious. This means of course that the legal authority of the proposed constitution cannot be measured against the Articles of Confederation. Only the "express authority of the people alone" (no. 43, p. 296) can legitimize a constitution. By emphasizing the difference between founding a new political system on the basis of legislative ratification and ratification by constitutional convention, Madison was establishing the groundwork on which the new Constitution would be elevated to the status of fundamental law.

Furthermore, Madison argues that because the Articles have no more authority than an alliance, that is, a "league or treaty between parties," the obligation to adhere to its forms and formalities is absolved when any one article of the treaty is breached by any one party. No one, Federalist or Anti-Federalist, doubted that the Articles had been violated repeatedly over the years. Madison's argument serves two interrelated purposes: first, to discredit the authority of the Articles and, second, to elevate the moral and legal authority of the Convention. The obvious inference to be drawn is that the Articles of Confederation does not have the status of a proper constitution, which further means that it does not have to be annulled by a formal act of the people. This leaves open the possibility and justifies the somewhat irregular process undertaken by the Convention.

More importantly, though, Madison argues that "considerations of duty arising out of the case itself, could have supplied any defect of regular authority." He justifies the extraordinary actions of the Convention on the moral grounds that its members had a duty to the nation that transcended the obligations to their commission. It is important that his audience keep in mind the critical problems and the "ground on which the Convention stood" in 1787. The members of the Convention "were deeply and unanimously impressed with the crisis which had led their country almost with one voice to make so singular and solemn an experiment" (no. 40, pp. 263–264). They were also impressed with the "absolute necessity" of the situation. They were justified in appealing therefore

> to the great principle of self-preservation; to the transcendent law of nature and of nature's God, which declares that the safety and happiness of society are the objects at which all political institutions aim, and to which all such institutions must be sacrificed. (no. 43, p. 297)

According to Madison, the Articles had failed so miserably that the protection of the natural rights for which civil societies are established in the first place was insecure. The internal and external affairs of the nation were now at a critical juncture—indeed, the very existence of the Union was at stake. The force of necessity caused by the mortal diseases of the Confederation drove the Convention to recur to the Revolutionary principles of the Declaration of Independence: the transcendent law of nature must take precedence over positive law. The Philadelphia delegates

> must have reflected, that in all great changes of established governments, forms ought to give way to substance; that a rigid adherence in such cases to the former, would render nominal and nugatory, the

transcendent and precious right of the people to "abolish or alter their governments as to them shall seem most likely to effect their safety and happiness." (no. 40, pp. 263–265)

The Anti-Federalists were right in one sense: the proposed constitution represents a radical innovation. Madison and the Federalists were not reforming the Articles of Confederation; they were beginning de novo; they were invoking the Revolutionary right of the people to "abolish or alter their governments." Ratification of the Constitution by special ratifying conventions in just nine states circumvented entirely the authority of both Congress and the states. This was not a revision but a revolution.

It is important to recall, however, that Madison did not faithfully reproduce the full passage from the Declaration, which goes on to say that it is also the right of the people "to institute new Government."[4] This is the point at which Madison breaks with or modifies Lockean social contract theory. The principles on which a people might "alter or abolish" government were fixed, well defined, and self-evident to even the most common people, but the forms of government that a people might institute are unlimited and the knowledge required to design and construct them is complex and well beyond the capacities of ordinary citizens. This is not a task for which they are particularly well suited. Madison did not think that the people themselves had the capacity to construct constitutions, but he did regard them as having the "virtue and intelligence to select men of virtue and wisdom" for tasks they themselves were incapable of completing.[5] He also thought that it is inconvenient, if not impossible, for the people "spontaneously and universally, to move in concert" in order to frame a government on their own. Madison therefore thought it "essential, that such changes be instituted by some *informal and unauthorized propositions*, made by some patriotic and respectable citizen or number of citizens" (no. 40, pp. 263–265). That Madison would leave open the possibility that a single "patriotic and respectable citizen" should assume responsibility is as remarkable as it is revealing.

At the Convention, Madison had urged his fellow delegates to liberate themselves from the instructions of their constituents. Rather than serving simply as a mirror to the people's passions, opinions, and interests, he encouraged the delegates to transcend their constituents and to reflect upon the permanent needs of the nation. "If the opinions of the people were to be our guide," he remarked, it would be "difficult" to know "what course we ought to take." He thought it impossible for any delegate to really know "what the opinions of his

Constituents were at this time; much less could he say what they would think if possessed of the information & lights possessed by the members here; & still less what would be their way of thinking 6 or 12 months hence." Madison therefore encouraged his fellow delegates "to consider what was right & necessary in itself for the attainment of a proper government."[6] In other words, he was challenging them to think and act philosophically.

Madison was even more explicit in identifying the need for a Lawgiver in an extraordinary letter that he sent to John Randolph in 1788. There were many subjects on which the "private judgment" of most men was sufficient, he wrote, but there were other "subjects to which the capacities of the bulk of mankind are unequal and on which they must and will be governed by those with whom they happen to have acquaintance and confidence." This was particularly true, he said, of the "proposed constitution":

> The great body of those who are both for & against it, must follow the judgment of others not their own. Had the Constitution been framed & recommended by an obscure individual, instead of the body possessing public respect & confidence, there can not be a doubt, that altho' it would have stood in the identical words, it would have commanded little attention from those who now admire its wisdom.[7]

The distance that separated the American and ancient foundings described by Madison in *Federalist* 38 seems somewhat closer now. In fact, by turning over their constitution-making authority to "some patriotic and respectable citizen or number of citizens" (no. 40), Madison believed that the Americans had successfully reconciled ancient aristocratic modes of founding with the modern democratic teaching on consent.[8] The Convention's patriotic few were commissioned by the people to deliberate, construct, and present back to the people for ratification a constitution and new form of government.

In the end, Madison writes, the whole question of the Convention's authority and the legality of the Constitution amounts to nothing. He then plays his trump card. The Convention's powers, Madison notes, "were merely advisory and recommendatory." The Convention "planned and proposed a Constitution, which is to be of no more consequence than the paper on which it is written, unless it be stamped with the approbation of those to whom it is addressed" (no. 40, pp. 263–264). The matter is quite simple: the people can either accept or reject the proposed Constitution. The Convention, it is true, sidestepped Congress and the state legislatures in seeking ratification for the proposed Constitution, but it did so in order to take the proposed Constitution directly to the people for ratification. In other words, the Convention used "irregular" forms in order to establish a national government on a proper or strictly regular foundation. In a dazzling display of logical and rhetorical power, Madison turned the Anti-Federalist argument against itself.

Madison's rhetorical purpose in writing was to explain why it is important that the proposed Constitution be ratified immediately. The specter that most haunted him was the Anti-Federalist call for a second convention to either amend or completely redesign the proposed Constitution. But Madison was, if nothing else, a prudent man, who thought a perfect constitution impossible and the constant attempt to revise the fundamental law would in the end destroy it. Frequent revision would subject the nation to all the discordant opinions and factions that plagued all other modern constitutional assemblies. Madison understood all too well that experiments in political creation are necessarily fraught with "hazards and difficulties," which means that it would be an act of "great imprudence" to unnecessarily multiply them (no. 38, p. 241).

Constitution-making is a delicate business that owes a good deal to *fortuna* and good timing. Remarkably, the Philadelphia Convention had been largely exempt from the turbulence and factions associated with virtually all other founding acts. Still united and harmonious in the shadow of the War of Independence, the Convention, Madison notes, "must have enjoyed . . . an exemption from the pestilential influence of party animosities; the diseases most incident to deliberative bodies, and most apt to contaminate their proceedings" (no. 37, p. 239). The men who came to Philadelphia held many competing theories of the best form of government, and they certainly came with a variety of competing interests; nonetheless, in the end, they all united to support the Constitution, held together "by a deep conviction of the necessity of sacrificing private opinions and partial interests to the public good, and by a despair of seeing this necessity diminished by delays or by new experiments" (no. 37, p. 239). So extraordinary was this act of political founding that Madison found it "impossible for the man of pious reflection not to perceive in it, a finger of that Almighty hand which has been so frequently and signally extended to our relief in the critical stages of the revolution" (no. 37, p. 238). It was indeed a miraculous event.

Ironically, Madison's portrait of the actions and legality of the Constitutional Convention bears a striking resemblance to Lycurgus's founding act. The constitutional handiwork of the Philadelphia

Convention stands, he wrote, "as fair a chance for immortality, as Lycurgus gave to that of Sparta, by making its change to depend on his own return from exile and death, if it were to be immediately adopted, and were to continue in force, not until a BETTER, but until ANOTHER should be agreed upon by this new assembly of Lawgivers" (no. 38, p. 246). In other words, by disbanding and in effect committing suicide, the Philadelphia Convention mirrored Lycurgus's self-exile and suicide in order to achieve Lycurgan-like immortality for its republican constitution.

The Constitution, now framed and soon to be ratified, was the culmination of a twenty-year intellectual and political movement. As American Revolutionaries struggled intellectually to make sense out of the arbitrariness of the Declaratory Act (which gave Parliament the authority to pass laws for the colonies "in all cases whatsoever") and the doctrine of unlimited parliamentary sovereignty, they began—slowly and haltingly at first—to develop the idea of a constitution that was very different from the traditional English conception, which equated statutory law with the unwritten English constitution. During the years of the Imperial Crisis and the revolutionary period of state constitution-making, the Americans discovered a fundamental distinction "between a constitution established by the people, and unalterable by the government; and a law established by the government, and alterable by the government." Their great invention, of course, was the idea of a written constitution as a higher and fundamental law grounded in the sovereignty of the people. Madison's attempt to establish the Constitution of 1787 as a "fixed," "paramount," and permanent law—one that would stand above the ordinary powers of government and that could withstand the exigencies of time—was the final act in this extraordinary drama (no. 53, pp. 360–362).

Madison's Political Epistemology

In the first essay of *The Federalist*, Alexander Hamilton wrote that it had been reserved to the American people to decide the most important of all political questions: whether political societies could establish good government on the basis of "reflection and choice," or whether "they are forever destined to depend, for their political constitutions, on accident and force." But what exactly does it mean to establish government on the basis of "reflection and choice"? We have just examined the process by which the Framers and the American people exercised their "choice"; we turn now to an examination of the nature of their "reflection." Madison takes up this difficult issue in *Federalist* 37.

The thirty-seventh *Federalist* essay is a pivotal essay in the work as a whole. It marks the transition from a discussion of the vices of the confederacy to an examination of the Constitution's virtues. The essay serves a threefold purpose: first, to give the reader an insight into James Madison's own thinking processes and modes of political reasoning; second, to reveal the difficult intellectual and practical problems confronted by the Convention in dissolving and refounding the regime; and third, to explain how Madison wanted the American public to deliberate about the Constitution. It offers a succinct statement of the complex questions associated with political founding and the nature of deliberative statesmanship. The essay's ultimate purpose is to educate the American public—particularly those who are to sit in judgment of the Constitution—on how to *think* about and to judge the proposed Constitution by introducing them to the modes of reasoning employed by those who framed it. In other words, it opens a window onto what might be called the Framers' political epistemology.

While it is true that Madison thought the people lacking in a comprehensive knowledge of the political sciences and intellectually incapable of designing a new constitutional structure, he did think it necessary—as we have already seen—that they formally give their consent to the new constitution. When the proposed constitution was made public by the Convention, a firestorm of debate swept the country. In the "great national discussion" (no. 1, p. 5) that followed, the Constitution's merits and demerits were discussed openly in countless newspapers, pubs, clubs, parlors, and ratifying conventions. But a debate of this sort was fraught with extraordinary dangers. The Convention had the advantage of meeting behind closed doors and in secret, thereby increasing the likelihood of dispassionate and disinterested deliberations. But now that the proposed constitution had been moved "out-of-doors" and brought into the light for public examination, a Pandora's box of fears and doubts, passions and interests had been opened. Federalists and Anti-Federalists alike scrambled to shape public opinion.

Publius's challenge was to educate and elevate, to recreate for ordinary citizens the experience and intellectual complexities of constitution-making. He hoped that the Framers' wisdom might be shared with the people. He wanted their consent to be enlightened. Because the proposed Constitution instituted new modes and orders, because it could be interpreted in different ways, and because it "touches the springs of so many passions and interests," Madison knew that it would have friends and enemies, neither of which was inclined to a "fair discussion and accurate judgment of its merits" (no. 37, pp. 231–232). He therefore encouraged that "candid and judicious part of the community," those with a "temper favorable to a just estimate" to pursue a calm, reasoned, deliberative assessment of the Constitution (nos. 36 and 37, pp. 230, 232), and he castigated those partisans who read the Constitution superficially and with a predisposition to either praise or censure it. In other words, Madison is suggesting that a national deliberation of such importance must rise above factional or party politics. But this can only be achieved by men and women willing to temper and overcome their partisan passions and interests.

In order to evaluate fairly the merits and demerits of the proposed Constitution, Madison advised his readers to examine critically, dispassionately, and thoroughly the "work of the Convention." Recalling Montesquieu's advice to philosophic and reforming Legislators in book XXIX of *The Spirit of the Laws*, Madison explicitly invoked the "spirit of moderation" as the necessary condition on which to attain "to a just estimate of their real tendency to advance or obstruct the public good." The problem of course is that reasoned deliberation of the public good is rarely ever possible. This was somewhat true of the Convention itself and it was particularly true of the public debates over ratification. Human nature and the tried course of human affairs are such that inflamed passions and interests will interfere with a rational deliberation of justice and the public good. In order to effect a "just and fair result," Madison felt compelled to help establish the intellectual and rhetorical grounds on which a more genuinely reflective national deliberation might take place. He hoped to foster in the people themselves the same "spirit of moderation" and sobriety that guided the Convention much of the time and that was Madison's particular virtue.

Madison was particularly sensitive to the claims of those theoretical perfectionists who thought a better constitution could have been designed. He sought to temper and moderate the claims of those who would pursue "that artificial structure and regular symmetry, which an abstract view of the subject might lead an ingenious theorist to bestow on a Constitution planned in his closet or in his imagination" (no. 37, p. 238). Moderation for Madison meant recognizing the limitations of human reason and abstract theory, and it meant judiciously measuring new principles against experience, history, and circumstances. "Theoretic reasoning," he warned, must always be "qualified by the lessons of experience" (no. 43, p. 293). The spirit of moderation is, moreover, a precondition for that other important political virtue: prudence. Prudence is a companion to moderation; it is the virtue that reconciles theory and practice, ideas and interests, principles and circumstances. *Federalist*, no. 37 is a brief for philosophic moderation and prudence.

What modes of reasoning, then, did the Framers employ in designing the proposed Constitution? How should the Constitution be studied by those who were to judge its worth? What intellectual and practical difficulties did the Framers have to resolve or overcome?

The Convention, according to Madison, confronted five major problems: first, the very "novelty" of their task; second, reconciling the "requisite stability and energy in Government, with the inviolable attention due to liberty, and to the Republican form"; third, "marking the proper line of partition, between the authority of the general, and that of the State Governments"; fourth, resolving the competing claims of large and small states; and fifth, resolving the conflict between northern and southern states. Madison lists these difficulties in descending order from the most theoretical to the most practical. They are all characterized by the need to make and reconcile theoretical and practical distinctions—distinctions between old and new, stability and liberty, nation and states, large and small states, free and slave regions. Reconciling this general dichotomy between theory and practice represented the great political task for Madison and the Convention's other constitutional architects.

But Madison understood that any attempt to address and resolve these difficulties is compounded by an even deeper problem: the character of human reason itself and the limits of human knowledge. The nature of this acutely philosophical problem, Madison wrote, is known to anyone who is accustomed to contemplating and discriminating between objects "extensive and complicated in their nature." At a certain level, man's knowledge of nature, human nature, and things man-made must remain uncertain. The difficulty, he says, is in forming clear and distinct ideas of the objects of human cognition and then communicating that conceptual knowledge to others. Madison lists three factors that limit our ability to properly identify, define, and discriminate between objects natural and man-made: (1) the indistinctness of the object; (2) the imperfection of the organ of conception; (3) the inadequateness of the vehicle of ideas.

The great objects of human inquiry are, according to Madison, often shrouded in mystery. The wisest "metaphysical philosophers" have not been able to distinguish and define the "faculties of mind" (i.e., "sense, perception, judgment, desire, volition, memory, imagination"); "natural philosophers" have not been able to adequately identify and distinguish the "boundaries between the great kingdoms of nature" (i.e., "the lines which separate unorganized matter from vegetable life and both from the animal kingdom"); the "greatest adepts in political science" have still not been able to define and distinguish between the "three great provinces" of political power (i.e., "the Legislative, Executive and Judiciary; or even the privileges and powers of the different legislative branches"); and the most "enlightened Legislators and jurists" have been unable to delineate the precise nature and limits of different legal codes (i.e., common, statute, maritime, ecclesiastical, corporations, and other local laws and customs), the jurisdiction of different and competing courts (i.e., general and local, law, equity, admiralty, etc.), not to mention an inability to make clear the meaning of new laws.

Madison concedes that it is possible, though difficult, to know with certainty and to accurately distinguish between the "various faculties of the mind" or the "great kingdoms of nature" precisely because they are natural—that is, because every natural entity has a particular identity. In Aristotelian terminology, a thing is what it is. The dilemma is compounded, however, when one turns to the study of "human institutions." Establishing boundaries between political things is even more difficult because the things in themselves are imperfect, they are imperfectly known, and their identity is imperfectly communicated to others. The real source of man's inability to attain true knowledge has more to do with the imperfection of human cognition and man's inability to clearly articulate his conceptual knowledge. Not only must an idea be clearly formed, but to be understood its definition in language must be objectively precise. The problem, however, is that there are no languages "so copious as to supply words and phrases for every complex idea, or so correct as not to include many equivocally denoting different ideas." Even if men accurately discriminate between objects as they truly are in nature, they can nonetheless be misunderstood and misrepresented by the "inaccuracy of terms" in which they are delivered.

Madisonian constitution-makers must therefore begin with a degree of intellectual modesty and patience. *Federalist* 37 is itself an exercise in moderation. As we shall see, this extraordinarily difficult essay forces the reader to give pause, to slow down, and to think long and hard about the complex problems confronted by the Convention. The Discussion in the thirty-seventh essay of the limits of human reason and knowledge is meant to moderate the expectations of those who wanted something much better by highlighting the enormous difficulties inherent in constitution-making. In doing so, Madison also elevated the opinions of those who are unable to fully understand the Convention's enormous intellectual achievement.

Madison on Preserving the
Constitution as Fundamental Law

We turn now, briefly, to Madison's efforts at constitutional preservation. History taught the Virginian that the romance associated with the founding of ancient and modern republics was always followed by the tragedy of their decline and fall. The history of republican governments was an endless cycle of political conception and political death. In a nutshell, the question confronted by all republican constitution-makers was this: how can a nation founded on the people's right to revolution establish constitutional order?

Among all the founders, Madison thought most deeply about the difficulties of framing a constitution that could withstand the exigencies of time. In the forty-first *Federalist* essay, in a passage rarely analyzed by scholars, he framed the problem this way: "A system of Government, meant for duration, ought to contemplate these revolutions, and be able to accommodate itself to them" (p. 276–277). The revolutions that Madison refers to included the ceaseless conflict between the few wealthy and the many poor, the evolution of American society from an agricultural to a commercial and urban society, and the unknown designs of hostile foreign nations. But Madison did not think of republican politics and statesmanship as a sufficient guarantor of republican rights. He thought it "vain" to assume that "enlightened statesmen will be able to adjust these clashing interests, and render them all subservient to the public good." The difficulty of course is that "[e]nlightened statesmen will not always be at the helm" (no. 10, p. 60). Something greater, higher, more permanent was needed. At the most theoretical level, building a constitutional order that replaces the need for "enlightened statesmen" and which provides permanent constitutional dikes and barriers against the cycle of "revolutions" became the great intellectual dilemma for Madison. His solution was to conceptualize and establish a constitutional regime that is "fixed" or permanent, one that could withstand the exigencies of time. Madison sought to achieve a kind of constitutional stasis that would de-politicize American politics by placing constitutional issues beyond the reach of particular legislators and popular whims. It was his most important contribution to American constitutionalism.

The Constitution of 1787 stands as a monument to Madison's political genius and founding prudence. Its creation required that the whole of society—with its contending social, economic, and religious differences—be seen at once and reconciled in a harmonious whole, that a variety of political institutions, forms, and structures be established, separated, and balanced in a working system, that the government be given enough power to fulfill its purposes without becoming tyrannical, that preexisting political communities be incorporated into a new federal system, and, finally, that all this be done with a view to anticipating future changes in American society. The Constitution must be somehow preserved, sanctified, and made permanent; it must somehow stand outside the exigencies of time. But Madison also realized that a constitution constructed in part through compromise and accommodation to present opinions and interests could never be perfect, and that it must have some means by which to perfect itself over time and adapt to change.

In 1783 Thomas Jefferson appended to his "Notes on the State of Virginia" a draft constitution for Virginia that included a proposal requiring the calling of popular conventions "for altering the constitution or *correcting breaches of it.*" Jefferson's proposal—his attempt to institutionalize revolutionary consent—challenged Madison to think through and resolve the necessary tension between constitutional change and stability. More than any other founder, Madison was determined to design and frame a constitution that would endure for ages. But a constitution cannot be long-lasting if it is too easily changed, nor can it endure if it cannot change at all. If the constitution is too rigid it will encourage usurpations; if it is too loose it will be subject to frequent changes. In either case, the people will loose the veneration for it that is necessary to maintaining its authority. In order to make the Constitution the permanent, fundamental law of the land, Madison understood that it was necessary to strike a delicate balance between change and stability.

Federalist 49 contains Madison's most sophisticated argument for establishing the Constitution as fundamental law and his most explicit criticism of the argument for frequent constitutional revision. In responding to Jefferson's proposal, Madison concedes that the people "are the only legitimate fountain of power" and that their consent is required "whenever it may be necessary to enlarge, diminish, or new-model the powers of government." He fully supported the idea that a "constitutional road" should be "marked out" that would provide the people with an avenue for amending their constitution when necessary. Unlike Jefferson, though, Madison thought there were "insuperable objections against the proposed recurrence to the people"; he thought that revision of the fundamental law should be reserved only for "certain great and extraordinary occasions." Madison rejects Jefferson's proposal on two major counts.

First, he argues that frequent appeals to the people to alter the Constitution would bring into doubt the Constitution's wisdom and status as higher law; they would imply that the Constitution is defective and thereby "deprive the government of that veneration, which time bestows on every thing, and without which perhaps the wisest and freest governments would not possess the requisite stability." All governments—and free governments in particular—depend upon public opinion, and public opinion gains force and authority, indeed, a "double effect," when it is held by a large number of people for a long period of time. Political stability, according to Madison, is grounded on the people having a "reverence for the laws." To venerate the Constitution is to look up to it and hold it as an object of loyalty, and to look up to it is to elevate and sanctify it as a higher law above the will of the people. Reverence of this sort is a kind of passion but a moderating, decent, elevating passion—the thinking man's prejudice we might say. It is true of course that in "a nation of philosophers," an enlightened voice of reason would inculcate a love of the laws, but a "nation of philosophers is as little to be expected as the philosophical race of kings wished for by Plato." Even the most rational government must be supported by "the prejudices of the community" to preserve it. But such prejudices need not be blind or ignorant; instead, they should imitate and reflect the Framers' reason. Reverence represents for Madison an enlightened prejudice or patriotism that venerates the Constitution not because it is old but because it is good. Ultimately, it serves as a kind of constitutional gold standard, one that elevates the Constitution to the status of higher law and that stands above the immediate and inflationary pressures of the people's passions and interests. The effect of constitutional reverence, then, is to induce in the people a form of constitutional fortitude.[9]

A second objection to a "frequent reference of constitutional questions, to the decision of the whole society" was that public tranquility would too often be disturbed "by interesting too strongly the public passions." Such experiments, he warned, "are of too ticklish a nature to be unnecessarily multiplied"; they reopen the question of the nation's fundamental principles and purposes; they ignite party passions and inflame individual ambition; and they serve to alienate citizens from the one bond that unites them in a free and liberal society. Madison believed that revolutionary foundings should be rare and extraordinary acts, and that "*reason*" and not the "*passions*" should "sit in judgment" (no. 49, p. 343). He knew that the framing of the Constitution of 1787 was a unique event that occurred at a special moment in American history. The simultaneous convergence of four

critical conditions in 1787 made the framing of the proposed constitution possible: first, the people were united against a common enemy
and therefore "repressed the passions most unfriendly to order and
concord"; second, the people had an enthusiastic confidence in their
"patriotic leaders, which stifled the ordinary diversity of opinions on
great national questions"; third, there was a "universal ardor for new
and opposite forms, produced by a universal resentment and indignation against the antient government"; finally, there was no "spirit of
party" to inflame public passions against any of the changes to be
made. America's founding moment was unique, but Madison thought
it highly unlikely that these conditions could ever be replicated.

The wisdom that was necessary to create the Constitution and the
reverence that is necessary to sustain it would both be undercut by frequent change. Madison thought that the continual second-guessing
associated with periodic conventions would eat away at the law-abiding
habits that are necessary to sustain a constitutional order based on the
rule of law. He did not think that a constitution founded in doubt
could sustain itself. The Constitution, indeed, the regime itself, would
eventually be destroyed from within by chronic nay-saying.

In the end, Madison did not think that periodic conventions to
revise the Constitution were necessary because he thought that the
Constitution was self-perpetuating and self-perfecting. The Constitution's *internal* principles and mechanisms rendered the *external*
changes associated with frequent revision unnecessary. It goes without saying that to fully understand Madison's attempt to establish the
Constitution as fundamental law, one would also have to take into
account his new science of politics—that is, his views on republicanism, representation, separation of powers, federalism, the amending
process, and bills of rights. These are subjects, though, that we must
leave for another day.

Notes

1. Jacob E. Cooke, ed., *The Federalist* (New York: Meridian Books,
   1961), 39. The parenthetical citations in the text are to this edition.
2. The best discussion of the development of the idea of special constitutional and ratifying conventions is Gordon S. Wood, *The Creation of the
   American Republic* (New York: W. W. Norton, 1969), 306–43. See
   also Robert R. Palmer, *Age of the Democratic Revolution: A Political
   History of Europe and America, 1760–1800*, 2 vols. (Princeton:
   Princeton University Press, 1969), 1: 214.
3. Patrick Henry, "Speech in the Virginia Ratifying Convention" [June 4
   1788], in *The Anti-Federalist: Writings by Opponents of the*

Constitution, ed. Herbert J. Storing (Chicago: University of Chicago Pres, 1981), 297.

4. See Gary Rosen, *American Compact: James Madison and the Problem of Founding* (Lawrence: University Press of Kansas, 1999), 123.

5. James Madison, "Speech in the Virginia Convention" (June 20, 1788), in *The Debates in the Several State Conventions, on the Adoption of the Federal Constitution . . .*, ed. Jonathan Elliot, 2nd ed., 5 vols. (Washington: Taylor and Maury, 1836), 3: 536–537.

6. Madison, "Speech in the Federal Convention," June 12, 1787 in *Notes of Debates in the Federal Convention of 1787, Reported by James Madison,* with an introduction by Adrienne Koch (Athens, OH: Ohio University Press, 1966), 107.

7. Madison to John Randolph, January 10, 1788, in *The Papers of James Madison,* ed. William T. Hutchinson, William M. E. Rachal, Robert Rutland et al. (Chicago and Charlottesville: University of Chicago Press and University Press of Virginia, 1962–), 10: 354–356.

8. Louis Hartz got it exactly wrong when he argued, "A hero is missing from the revolutionary literature of America. He is the legislator, the classical giant who almost invariably turns up at revolutionary moments to be given authority to lay the foundations of the free society. He is not missing because the Americans were unfamiliar with the images of ancient history, or because they had not read the Harringtons or the Machiavellis and Rousseaus of the modern period. Harrington, as a matter of fact, was one of their favorite writers. The legislator is missing because, in truth, the Americans had no need for his services. Much as they liked Harrington's republicanism, they did not require a Cromwell, as Harrington thought he did, to erect the foundations for it. Those foundations had already been laid by history." Louis Hartz, *The Liberal Tradition in America* (New York: Harcourt, Brace, 1955), 46–47.

9. Thomas Paine captured the ultimate meaning of venerating the Constitution as fundamental law when he wrote in his "Rights of Man" that in America constitutions had been transformed into "political bible[s]" that sat upon every household and legislative table. In America, he continued, it was not uncommon "when any debate arose on the principle of a bill, or on the extent of any species of authority" for "the members to take the printed constitution out of their pocket, and read the chapter with which such matter in debate was connected." Thomas Paine, "Rights of Man, Part Two," in *Collected Writings,* ed. Eric Foner (New York: Library of America, 1995), 574.

Contributors

Colin Bonwick is Professor Emeritus of American History at Keele University. His previous publications include *English Radicals and the American Revolution* (1977) and numerous articles on both the English and American sides of the Revolution.

Robert Faulkner is Professor of Political Science at Boston College and has also taught at Princeton University and Wellesley and Dartmouth Colleges. His books include *Francis Bacon and the Project of Progress* (1993), *Richard Hooker and the Politics of a Christian England* (1981), and *The Jurisprudence of John Marshall* (1968). He has coedited Marshall's one volume *Life of George Washington* (2000, with Paul Carrese) and Alexandras Shtromas's *Totalitarianism and the Prospect of World Order* (2003, with Daniel J. Mahoney). Faulkner has written many articles and chapters on topics in political philosophy and American thought, the most recent being on the essay as a political-literary form, on the general philosophy of the Enlightenment, and on Locke's *Second Treatise*. He is completing a book on grand ambition. Faulkner is a past Chair of his Department and a past President of the New England Political Science Association.

Martin Loughlin is Professor of Public Law at the London School of Economics and Political Science. His publications include *Public Law and Political Theory* (1992), *Legality and Locality: The Role of Law in Central-Local Government Relations* (1996), *Sword and Scales: An Examination of the Relationship between Law & Politics* (2000), and *The Idea of Public Law* (2003). He is General Editor of *The Modern Law Review*.

Gary L. McDowell is the Tyler Haynes Interdisciplinary Professor of Leadership Studies, Political Science, and Law in the Jepson School of Leadership Studies in the University of Richmond. From 1992 to 2003 he was the Director of the Institute of United States Studies and Professor of American Studies in the University of London. He has taught at Dickinson College, Tulane University, Harvard University, and the University of London. Among his publications are *Equity and the Constitution: The Supreme Court, Equitable Relief, and Public Policy* (1982), *Reason and Republicanism: Thomas Jefferson's Legacy of Liberty* (coeditor with Sharon Noble, 1997), and *Friends of the Constitution: Writings of the "Other" Federalists, 1787–1788* (coeditor with Colleen Sheehan, 1998).

Johnathan O'Neill is Assistant Professor of History at Georgia Southern University. His previous publications include *Originalism in American Law and Politics: A Constitutional History* (2005) and articles in *The Review of Politics, Northwestern University Law Review,* and *The Modern Law Review.*

J. R. Pole retired in 1989 as Rhodes Professor of American History and Institutions at Oxford University where he remains as an Emeritus Fellow of St. Catherine's College. He is a Fellow of the British Academy and of the Royal Historical Society and an Honorary Foreign Member of the American Historical Association. His most recent work is an annotated edition of *The Federalist* (2004). *The Pursuit of Equality in American History* is scheduled to appear in a Chinese translation.

Paul A. Rahe is Jay P. Walker Professor of History at the University of Tulsa, author of *Republics Ancient and Modern: Classical Republicanism and the American Revolution* (1992), Coeditor of *Montesquieu's Science of Politics: Essays on the Spirit of Laws* (2001), and Editor of *Machiavelli's Liberal Republican Legacy* (2006). He holds a BA from Yale University, an MA in Litterae Humaniores from the University of Oxford, where he was a Rhodes Scholar, and a PhD in ancient history from Yale University. He has published chapters in a host of edited works and articles in a great variety of scholarly journals, including *The American Journal of Philology, Historia, The American Journal of Archaeology, The American Historical Review, The Review of Politics, History of Political Thought,* and *Social Philosophy and Policy.* He has received a number of research fellowships and was most recently a visiting fellow at All Souls College, Oxford, and Daimler/Chrysler Fellow at the American Academy in Berlin.

Jack N. Rakove is the William Robertson Coe Professor of History and American Studies, and Professor of Political Science and (by courtesy) of Law at Stanford University, where he has taught since 1980. His book *Original Meanings: Politics and Ideas in the Making of the Constitution* (1996) was the recipient of the Pulitzer Prize in History.

Frederick Rosen is Professor Emeritus of the History of Political Thought, University College London and was Director of the Bentham Project and General Editor of the Collected Works of Jeremy Bentham, 1983–2003. He is the author of numerous books and articles, and his latest book is *Classical Utilitarianism from Hume to Mill* (2003).

Steven D. Smith is Warren Distinguished Professor of Law at the University of San Diego and Codirector of the Institute for Law and Philosophy. A graduate of Brigham Young University and Yale Law School, Professor Smith works mainly in the fields of religious freedom and jurisprudence. His publications include *Law's Quandary* (2004), *The Constitution and the Pride of Reason* (1998), and *Foreordained Failure: The Quest for a Constitutional Principle of Religious Freedom* (1995).

C. Bradley Thompson is the BB&T Research Professor at Clemson University. He is the author of *John Adams and the Spirit of Liberty* (1998) and the Editor of *The Revolutionary Writings of John Adams* (2000) and *Antislavery Political Writings, 1833–1860: A Reader* (2004).

Gordon S. Wood is Alva O. Way University Professor and Professor of History at Brown University. He received his BA degree from Tufts University and his PhD from Harvard University. He taught at Harvard University and the University of Michigan before joining the faculty at Brown in 1969. He is the author of many works, including *The Creation of the American Republic, 1776–1787* (1969), which won the Bancroft Prize and the John H. Dunning Prize in 1970, and *The Radicalism of the American Revolution* (1992), which won the Pulitzer Prize for History and the Ralph Waldo Emerson Prize in 1993. He is currently working on a volume in the Oxford History of the United States dealing with the period of the early republic from 1789 to 1815. His book *Revolutionary Characters: What Made the Founders Different* was published in 2006. Professor Wood is a Fellow of the American Academy of Arts and Sciences and the American Philosophical Society.

Index

CPSIA information can be obtained at www.ICGtesting.com
Printed in the USA
LVOW07*2309300815

452153LV00004B/22/P